The Heritage of Christian Education

James Riley Estep, Jr. (Ed.) • Jonathan Hyungsoo Kim
Alvin Wallace Kuest • Mark Amos Maddix
with Michael Douglas Barton

COLLEGE PRESS PUBLISHING COMPANY
Joplin, Missouri

Cover Design by Mark A. Cole

Library of Congress Cataloging-in-Publication Data

C.E.: the heritage of Christian education / by James Riley Estep, Jr. . . . [et al.].
    p.   cm.
Includes bibliographical references.
  ISBN 0-89900-904-2
  1. Christian education—History.   I. Estep, James Riley, 1963–   II. Title.
  BV1465.C23 2003
  268'.09—dc21

                                   2003010809

Dedicated to

Linda M. Cannell

Professor, Scholar, Mentor, Encourager, and Friend

Table of Contents

Introduction
Answering Your Questions

What is Christian education?

We can respond to this question in a variety of ways. We can appeal to theories of education, pastoral theology, personal experience in our home congregations, professions in the field of Christian education, or even institutions providing biblical instruction. However, all these sources provide only snapshots of Christian education, limited to our experience and our own times. To fully understand the nature of Christian education, we must have a perspective beyond the experiences of our life and time. One way of responding to the question "What is Christian education?" is to appeal to the history of education within the community of faith. History provides a lens on Christian education broader than our experience and deeper than our life span. What was education like in previous centuries? What factors have influenced education in the community of faith, and continue to impact us today? How has education been conducted in previous eras and cultures, and how does it compare to our experience? Who were the instructors in ancient Israel, the Church, and western culture? This is the value of the history of Christian education. It broadens and deepens our perspective beyond ourselves and forms a heritage of faith and instruction.

"Why bother studying the history of Christian education?"

I have taught the history of Christian education at three different institutions every year over the past eleven years, and inevitably this question is one of the first raised by students. The general perception is that history has to do with dates, events, time lines, endless minuscule details that lack relevance to what is happening in my ministry, congregation, or classroom. No one has the time, desire, or interest for such trivial pursuits. *I wholeheartedly agree!* That is why I sponsored the writing of this book!

> **Contributors**
>
> James Riley Estep, Jr., Ph.D.
> Lincoln Christian Seminary
> Jonathan H. Kim, Ph.D.
> Talbot Theological Seminary
> Alvin W. Kuest, Ph.D.
> Great Lakes Christian College
> Mark A. Maddix, Ph.D.
> Northwest Nazarene University
> Michael D. Barton, College Senior
> Kentucky Christian College

History has rhyme and reason—and relevance. Historical periods are not arbitrarily divided and sectioned. The same reasons that cause historians to note a shift from the ancient to the Medieval to the Renaissance to the Enlightenment periods in Western history likewise denote *fundamental shifts* in educational theory and practice. The problem is that many textbooks on the history of education become snowed under in the details of history rather than its rhyme and reason. In short, what we need is an *analysis of the history* of Christian education that is based on the details. This book endeavors to provide just that.

C.E.: The History of Christian Education is the culminating work of five contributors over a two-year period. I personally know all the contributors as friends and colleagues. Jonathan Kim, Mark Maddix, and I attended Trinity Evangelical Divinity School (Deerfield, Illinois) together and now all serve at our respective seminaries. (In fact, Jonathan and I graduated together from T.E.D.S. in 1999). Alvin Kuest and I have served on the same faculty at Great Lakes Christian College (Lansing, Michigan) for several years and have previously co-authored a chapter on Christian education. The CD-Rom was assembled by a friend and former student of mine, Michael Barton, a senior at Kentucky Christian College (Grayson, Kentucky).

The book's purpose is to deliver to the reader a concise survey of the history of education that is analytical and relevant to you as students, educators, and ministers. In so doing, I hope it prepares you not simply to pass a test or converse intelligently about the past, but to prepare you for the future that you are entering. To prepare you as a Christian educator to fulfill God's calling of service on your life for His Kingdom.

How is the book analytical?

The book must be analytical if students are to understand the history of Christian education. Each chapter, which is divided by historical period and/or geographical region, views education through six lenses. While every chapter utilizes the same six lenses, on occasion two lenses may be combined for clarity, or an excursus will be provided to address an issue that did not readily fall into the pattern of analysis. The six lenses are as follows:

- *Overview of the Period* – What factors shaped education during this period?
- *Purpose of Education* – Why did the Church or society bother to educate?
- *Contexts of Education* – What are the institutions of instruction?
- *Content of Education* – What was taught? What was to be learned?
- *Process of Education* – How was instruction provided? Who were the teachers?
- *Voices* – Who were the major voices that contributed to education theory?

In so doing, you the reader will begin the process of *understanding* the history of education, not simply memorizing the trivia of it. To aid you in this process of better understanding the history of education, each chapter concludes with four additional items: "What can we learn from . . .?" itemizes practical lessons we can learn from the history of Christian education, a glossary of key terminology for clarification, personal reflective questions to aid the process of internalizing the information, and a recommended bibliography of suggested materials (books, articles, and Internet resources) for further study.

How is it relevant?

When I teach the course "History and Philosophy of Education," or under whatever title it may appear, I start by telling my students, "This is the most practical course I teach." Typically, this comment receives strange stares, quick glances between students, or even eyes rolled into the back of student's heads. *How can the history of education be practical? How can this textbook achieve a practical objective?* First, the text focuses on Christian education, not exclusively public education. Granted, these two subjects are sometimes inseparable, but greater attention is given to Christian education. For example, in regard to education in ancient Rome (Chapter 5), while we do address their public education system and educational theorists such as Cicero and Quintilian, the chapter explains how the New Testament and early Christian community was influenced by or reacted to the Roman's system of education. In short, the book demonstrates the relevance of education's history to the ministry and formation of education in the Church.

Second, the contributors endeavored to sift through the historical materials and determine what information was actually relevant to the understanding of Christian education. Far too often, history texts endeavor to simply compile the most information possible in order to provide as comprehensive an account as possible of the subject at hand. *This text is different.* It endeavors to provide relevant information. For example, the biographical information presented in the book focuses on those facts that shaped the theorist's educational theory, and not simply present a comprehensive sequential list of life events.

Third, the analytical approach allows the reader to understand the history of Christian education, not simply memorize the facts of its history. How has education in the community of faith changed over the millennia? What factors impacted the theory and practice of Christian education? Who were the major proponents of education's theory and practice? These are the critical questions that should be addressed clearly and concisely by the text if it is to provide the reader with an understanding of Christian education's history.

Finally, and perhaps most personally, I'd like to pose a question. How did what you did *yesterday* impact what you have to do today, or even tomorrow? How about what you did a week ago, a month ago, or even last semester or year? For example, how did putting off course reading impact how you performed on a test or quiz? How did choosing to delay starting a term paper cause grief later in the semester? Or, how did your lack of academic performance last semester impact this semester? I seriously doubt anyone is saying, "The past has absolutely no influence on my present or future . . . it's irrelevant!" *We never escape the grasp of history.* The decisions, theories, institutions, movements, and ministry of the past provide the foundation upon which contemporary Christian education ministry is built. We are the inheritors of our predecessors' work; what they accomplished or failed to do influences us daily.

What's in the book?

This text is readily divided into three general time periods. Christian education in ancient cultures receives four chapters, Chapters 2–5. Education in the Old Testament and among the Jewish culture following the close of the Old Testament is treated in Chapters 2–3. Attention is given to the neighboring cultures in the ancient Near East, but also how Jewish education influenced Jesus, Paul, and the early Christian community into which it was born. Chapters 4–5 address the Greek and Roman educational roots of Christian education. They provide a sketch of the immediate historical backdrop for early Christianity, with which the early Christian missionaries and communities engaged. *Why didn't you provide a separate chapter on Jesus, Paul, and the New Testament models of education?* It was a difficult choice, but it seemed wiser to include these subjects in the chapters which provided the most relevant historical background, and not attempt to understand the earliest Christian educators outside of their cultural surroundings. Hence, these chapters provide an integrated biblical-historical understanding of the earliest age of education in God's faith community.

The central section of the text (Chapters 6–9) presents the history of Christian education from the early Church (5th century A.D.) through the Reformation of Luther, Calvin, and the Jesuits (16th century A.D.). It traces the advent and development of a distinctively Christian education, covering some 1100 years of theory and practice in Christian education. In them, we trace the rise of early Christian education to the height of Papal authority in the Medieval Church, with Christian education being the exclusive education in Western culture, and then to the Renaissance and Reformation period, marking the dawn of greater and more significant diversity in Christian education.

The final section (Chapters 10–15) covers the advent of modern Christian education from the Enlightenment in Western Europe and America (colonial and early Republic) to the 20th-century Christian education in the United States. Two chapters are devoted to the rise of the Enlightenment (Chapters 10–11) since the philo-sophical and cultural transitions that occurred during this period were the most significant experienced in previous centuries and influenced Christian education for the next five centuries. The next two chapters explain the impact of the Enlightenment on Christian education in Europe (Chapter 12) and America (Chapter 13), high-lighting the rise of the Sunday school as a result of Enlightenment thinking on education. The final two chapters of this section analyze Christian education in 20th-century United States. Chapter 14 pres-ents the two dominant forms of Christian education in the first half of the 20th century (Classical Liberalism and Neo-Orthodoxy), leav-ing Chapter 15 to present Evangelical Christian education and other forms of church-based education that arose during the latter half of the 20th century.

What about Chapters 1 and 16? They serve as "bookends." Chapter 1 attempts to explain the dynamics of Christian education. What factors influence the formation of a Christian approach to edu-cation? What issues or themes are influential throughout history, and remain so today? It will introduce the reader to the idea of an analytical history of Christian education, and hopefully provide you with a new appreciation of the challenge of formulating a relevant theory of Christian education for today's world.

Chapter 16 is not the typical conclusion, with summary and reflection. Rather, it provides a portrait of the influential factors of the 21st century, and how they have already impacted Christian edu-cation. It is a picture of the educational realities that the communi-ty of faith must face as it enters its third millennium.

How do I use the CD-Rom?

The CD-Rom contains supplemental information that provide images, documents, charts or diagrams, as well as web-links to sig-nificant resources on the Internet (hence, for some of them you'll have to be on-line to connect). Throughout the chapters you will see this symbol ● to denote a CD-Rom item. The items are denoted by chapter and number. For example, ● 1.1 means this is Chapter 1, Item 1. Hence, click onto the main page, then to Chapter 1, and the "Figures" will be listed on the right side of the screen. Just click on the appropriate Item number and you're there! *The CD-Rom is not absolutely essential to read the book.* However, it does provide some excellent information and resources that may help you as you read. It is highly recommended to gain the full benefit of the book. See the CD-Rom label for instructions on how to access these files.

On a personal note . . .

I want to personally thank you for reading this book. History is sacred to me because in it I see God's hand moving to fulfill His will in His world. Just as God is at work in each of our lives, He has also worked in the lives of those men and women who came before us. Through them, He has delivered the ministry of Christian education into our care. We are all the product of faithful men and women who have passed their faith to the next generation through the centuries. Hence, neither our faith nor our call to Christian education ministry is in a vacuum.

History is *always* being written. What we regard as "the present," with all its relevance, importance, and vitality, is in fact only yesterday's "tomorrow" and tomorrow's "past." History is always dynamic and relevant because we don't live in a historic vacuum. In fact, while writing this book, we had to edit two sections due to the death of two leaders in Christian education (Dr. Warren Benson in February 2002 and Dr. Findley Edge in October 2002). *History is always changing, being made and remade.* I hope this book, and the history contained in it, will lead you not only to a greater appreciation of the past of Christian education, but will equip you to approach your future as Christian educators.

Lincoln, Illinois   *James Riley Estep, Jr., Ph.D.*
January 2003   *Professor of Christian Education*
                                               Lincoln Christian Seminary
                                                             Ezra 7:10

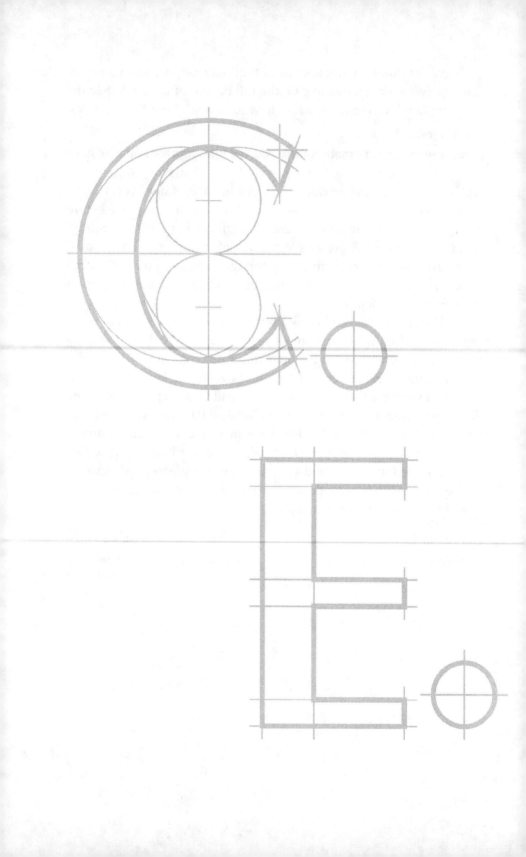

Chapter 1
The Challenge of
Christian Education

James Riley Estep, Jr.

Our experience of Christian education is rather limited. Regardless of who we might be, what position we might hold, or with
which congregations we may be familiar, we all have experiential limitations.
We are limited in several ways, but the
one *black box* we all experience is that of
our life span. For this reason, we typically make judgments and decisions,
form attitudes and dispositions, and
think in pastoral paradigms that are

> **Black box** is the term
> scientists use to describe
> the limits of investigation,
> the point at which the
> data has outreached their
> ability to capture it.

contemporary, but not knowing why they work or from whence they
came. In short, we need a broader perspective in which to understand Christian education. We need a perspective that can expand
our concept of Christian education beyond our own experiential
boundaries. Even if we were to visit other congregations, visit curriculum houses, attend conferences and workshops, these too would
be limited to our contemporary scene. They would expand our concept of Christian education, but only horizontally, along a line within the same life span or era in which we live and minister. *We must
turn to history to provide depth to our concept of Christian education, to
advance the vertical dimension wherein we can understand the dynamics of
Christian education and provide depth beyond our experiential limitations.*

For example, consider the Sunday school. It is the experience
of most people that the current condition of the Sunday school is less
than what might be desired. In fact, the Sunday school is described

as traditional, stagnant, not innovative, and certainly not dynamic. We conclude this based on our limited experiential perspective. Does the Sunday school have a future? Should it be replaced? Can it survive in the 21st century? Will it celebrate its 300th birthday in 2080? Before we make these assessments, perhaps it is important to note that our contemporary experience of the Sunday school is not the Sunday school of 1950, or 1900, or 1820, or 1780. In fact, it is perhaps one of the greatest ironies of Christian education's history that the Sunday school is one of the most versatile and responsive institutions ever formed by the Church! In its inception, the Sunday school was not even part of the church, it was a paracongregational outreach ministry to the impoverished and disenfranchised of Gloucester, England, in 1780. Teachers were paid and space was rented, and the curriculum was not simply Bible content, but literacy, hygiene, and morality. By 1820, however, in its American context, the Sunday school was adopted by denominational bodies as a means of instructing the faithful, and became an internal ministry of the church, shifting from its original outreach intent. In the late 19th century Sunday school even included special services and midweek Bible studies for adults and children. Following this, in the 20th century, it moved from a content-oriented, equipping ministry institution to one focusing on life application. So, now I ask you, is the Sunday school outdated? Or, is the current form of the Sunday school outdated? Just as it has adapted itself in the past, could it not likewise make yet another intentional innovation and reassert itself as a means of instruction? You see, the Sunday school is not as stagnant, traditional, or noninnovative as you perhaps first perceived it. It is in fact very adaptable and pliable to the needs of the Church and society.

I like dominoes. (I mean the blocks, not the pizza.) I don't know really how to play the game, but I do like to set dominoes up in a line and with one flick of a finger watch the chain reaction unfold. A greater number of dominoes yields a larger chain reaction. Contemporary Christian education is simply the last domino to fall in a long line of dominoes that extends far into the past, and will continue from us into the future. We need to ask questions like, "Why did Robert Raikes in 1780 invent the Sunday school?" "Why in 1780?" "Why didn't someone previously conceive of the notion of the Sunday school?" By understanding the roots of the Sunday school, or any Christian education program for that matter, we enter the thought processes of our predecessors and begin to learn from their thoughts on education. As a matter of fact, the Sunday school is an outgrowth of Enlightenment education, which assumed that children could be molded through instruction and that society could address the worst of its faults through providing instruction to everyone—even the impoverished children of Gloucester, England. Digging even further back we'd see that Enlightenment thinking was a result of the intellectual conditions produced by the Renaissance and Reformation, which were a reaction to the Medieval Church control on society and education, which grew out of the Early Church period which was based on the traditions practiced in ancient education (Hebrew-Jewish, Greek, and Roman). *That's a domino line about 4000 years old.*

A Model for the Dynamics of Christian Education

The Christian educator does not exist in a void, and Christian education does not take place in a vacuum. Christian educators are influenced through a variety of elements and the dynamics between them, as they theorize or practice instruction in the community of faith. Without oversimplifying, Christian educators conceive of education as the combination of vital factors (1.1):

- Theology: The beliefs of the theological community, i.e., the Church
- Social Science: The theories and practices of the education community
- Culture: The influence of politics, technology, music and literature, etc.

What makes education Christian? The influence of theology extends beyond the content of Christian education. It impacts our understanding of every facet of education. For example, it informs us of the nature of

> One of the great debates in Christian education is exactly how does one integrate these three dynamics? To what degree does one influence the other, or which one is taken into consideration first? Different answers provide a different kind of Christian education.

the student. Do students have free will or are they totally depraved, which in turn influences how we instruct them? How do we define revelation, God's self revealing acts to humanity (God to us) or humanity's conceptions of God (us to God)? This will impact not only how we teach, but what we teach. In short, theology is a major factor in theorizing and developing a concept of Christian education.

But what makes Christian education . . . education? Just as theology influences the Christian educator, we are also influenced by the educational community. The theories of social science allow us to understand human development. For example, human nature is more than simply what St. Paul wrote. Humans are also like Piaget's theory of cognitive development describes. We need the educational community to provide insight into learning theory, aiding us in the task of designing effective instructional venues. Christian educators are active in both circles, the theological and the educational. *We're a hybrid!*

However, one final element in the dynamic must be addressed, *culture*. Culture influences and even shapes the life and work of the Christian educator. Also, without considering culture in the dynamic, Christian education becomes simply a theory, with no relevance to the society and times in which it exists. In short, the events and developments that shape culture impact the formation of Christian education as well. Theologies and theories are not born in a vacuum, but as they engage the culture from their own communities (Church or Education).

Historical Factors Influencing the Development of Christian Education

As a student of the history of education, and specifically the educational theories and practices of the community of faith, several factors seem to be present throughout the history of education's development. These factors provide insight into the macroenvironment of Christian education. They are themes that are the most influential in shaping Christian education through the centuries.

Theology/Philosophy: As previously noted, theology is influential in the formation of Christian education. When theology changes, and it does indeed change throughout the centuries and even within our own generation, new educational implications

> Protestants placed emphasis on the "priesthood of *all* believers," standing in opposition to the authoritarian role of the clergy in the Roman Catholic Church.

become part of the ripple effect of the new direction. Shifts in theology even impact the society in which the church exists. As theology shifts, the church must adapt and change in response, and in turn its relation to and influence on the society is changed. For example, the educational agendas of the Roman Catholic Church and the Protestant reformers of the 16th century were quite different because of their divergent views of the nature of the Scriptures, role of the Church in society, and place of the laity. Their theological differences produced distinct differences in their approach to education, such as the Protestant's endeavor to translate the Bible into the common language of the people and provide vernacular schools to increase literacy among the populace. The Roman Catholic Church was rather content with using a Latin translation of the Bible, discernible only by the clergy, and providing no agenda for expanding public education or training the populace to read Latin. Hence, one of the macrothemes impacting the formation of Christian education is the content, role, and nature of theology in relation to Christian education theory and practice.

Technological Advances: I remember how my family and I entered A.D. 2000. We were driving home to Lansing, Michigan, on December 31, 1999. While still on the road, we huddled around a handheld portable color television at 5:00 a.m. EST as the Togo Islands were the first place on earth to usher in A.D. 2000. When we arrived home, we spent the day watching worldwide coverage of the new millennium, delivered by satellites which only fifty years before did not exist. While watching the cable coverage of the event, I received numerous e-mails on my laptop, as well as visited several web sites on the Internet, based on a technology that only twenty years ago was considered science fiction, something residing in the reality of Star Trek. No one today would question that technology has influenced every facet of our society, including education.

However, technology is not limited to the electronic or digital revolution of the last decades of the 20th century and beyond. Technological advancement has always met with either rejection or

FYI: Realize that when the original Star Trek series first aired in 1966, the notion of handheld global communications devices, like our modern cell phones, worldwide information networks, and desk-based computers (not to mention laptops) using square colored plastic disks for information storage were thought to be *23rd century innovations*.

acceptance by educators. Socrates, the famous Greek philosopher, rejected the most innovative technology of his era, regarding the *alphabet* to be a threat to education, since it threatened the long-standing tradition of memorization as the basis of learning. The printing press did indeed provide Western culture with the first information explosion, allowing for the rapid and mass production of books and journals at a comparably inexpensive cost, and hence led to the expansion of libraries, availability of textbooks, and publication of scholarly theories in periodicals, not to mention the production and distribution of more Bibles than had ever been previously produced.

Societal Context: Wars, plagues, poverty, famine . . . peace, plenty, economic expansion, and immigration . . . the societal context impacts education in obvious ways. Christian educators seek to provide educational initiatives to address societal problems, with each society and era having its own set of issues to address. Also, these events in history shape the thinking and disposition of the Christian educator. No better illustration can be given than that of John Dewey, the most influential American educator of the 20th century. Dewey departed from the traditional philosophies and approaches to education, advocating a radical shift toward pragma-

Some may debate labeling John Dewey a *Christian* educator, but he was indeed influential on Christian education and a founding member of the Religious Education Association.

tism, which holds that *change is the only absolute*. Why would he do this? What caused him to invest his life and career into forming a pragmatic approach to education? Dewey lived in a period of the most monumental changes in American history. He grew up following the Civil War, during the Reconstruction of the southern states. He was heavily influenced by the newly published writing of an obscure British scientist, Charles Darwin's *Origin of the Species*. He witnessed the Industrial Revolution, periods of mass immigration, the economic prosperity of the 1920s, and the Great Depression of the 1930s following the collapse of the stock market in 1929. *Change was his life experience, derived from societal context.* This is likewise why turn-of-the-century America was so willing to accept Dewey's progressive form of education. How could the traditional approaches to education hope to address the ever-changing culture of this era? How could traditional methods of instruction hope to instill the ability to think in such a complex society? Hence, the society in which Dewey lived indeed did influence his approach to education.

Concept of Human Learning and Development: The social sciences are regarded as a relatively new field of endeavor. The scientific study of psychology and sociology in the areas of human development and learning theories become more evident in education during the 20th century. However, educators throughout the centuries have contrived developmental theories and theories of learning, though using less than scientific means. For example, the Roman educator Quintilian (one of my personal favorites) presents a rather extensive view of the cognitive development of his students, from childhood to early adulthood. While his observations are somewhat questionable, and certainly not based on contemporary methods of scientific inquiry, his understanding of cognitive development did indeed influence his educational theory. Similarly, the progressive theorist Jean Rousseau's notion that learning was natural to the child, and hence should not be coerced did present a unique approach to instruction in his fictitious book *Emile*. His writings not only contradicted the prevalent concept that learning was resisted by the totally depraved minds of children, but fostered new approaches to education and instruction still alive today in the work of Friedrich Froebel's *garden of children* or, in his native German, *kindergarten*.

Relationship of the Church to the Culture: Richard Niebuhr wrote *Christ and Culture* in 1951. In it, he describes five ways in which the church has chosen to relate to society, ranging from rejection of culture (i.e., Christ against Culture) to the surrender of the church to the culture (Christ of Culture). With each of the five models of church relation, the educational agenda of the Church takes a startling twist. This lends itself to the whole discussion of the integration of faith and learning. Should a Christian be exposed to pagan learning? Is there any value in studying non-Christian literature? Should we expose ourselves to non-Christian institutions of education? For example, Tertullian, the third-century early church father, advocated that children not attend Roman schools, even forbidding Christian adults from serving in these schools since they were incompatible with the Christian faith. Tertullian's closed view toward the culture produced a closed educational system for the Church, advocating the formation of Christian schools. However, those advocating a more open relationship between the Church and society presented a less exclusive and more tolerant approach to education that was not Christian. Today we still wrestle with the same issues. Should we send our children to a public school rather than a Christian school? What about a Bible college rather than a state university? Or even more simply, should a Christian read *Harry Potter*? These are not new questions, just new versions of ancient questions. Hence, the perceived relationship of the church to the culture is a macrotheme that influences the formation of Christian education throughout the centuries.

Advances in Knowledge: We have all experienced the information explosion produced by the advent of the Internet and digital technologies. It has been so astounding that students frequently are more comfortable and acquainted with the advanced technologies than their instructors (or at least that has been my experience). With information instantaneously available, the knowledge base has expanded beyond what was even plausible 20 years ago. However, this is not the first knowledge explosion. Previously I mentioned the advent of the printing press as another period producing the rapid expansion of knowledge, having a similar impact on the expectation of education. Additionally, exploration opened whole new worlds for study. Aristotle made of his prize pupil, Alexander the Great, one request, to send to him samples for scientific study of the flora, fauna, and geology of the regions he conquered. Rome's contact with the Far East, especially China, opened an avenue not only for trade goods, but for information exchange. The returning Crusaders and collapse of the Byzantine Empire in the East led to the Renaissance in the West, with the infusion of knowledge and information previously lost or forgotten. The discovery of the New World by Europe likewise opened the door for advances of human understanding and knowledge. More recently, in our times, space exploration has proven to be enlightening and an astounding source of knowledge. Education, Christian or otherwise, is indeed impacted by the volume of information, source, and kind of information, as well as the availability of information at its disposal. With each advance in knowledge came an accompanying appraisal and reorientation of education.

Condition of the Family: Every culture from ancient to modern times started its system of education with the family. Even when cultures advanced beyond the capabilities of familial education to provide adequate instruction, the family still maintains an active role in the educational process. Regardless of what educational institutions and initiatives the community of faith may launch, they are only supplemental to the family's influence on childhood education. The Jews formed the synagogue and with it schools for childhood, but still relied on parental instruction. Education in the Greek and Roman cultures began with home instruction, with the family still maintaining responsibility for educating their child. Even later, the founder of the kindergarten, Froebel, designed a series of children's toys to develop cognitive and motor skills, with parental play as a means of instruction. Even in today's public school, the Parent-Teacher Association and in the Church, family life education reflects the historic precedent of family-based education.

Personal Life of Educator: This final megatheme in the history of Christian education is perhaps so obvious that it can actually go unnoticed. In our ❀ 1.1 the Christian educator, *not* Christian education, is placed in the center of the dynamic. All the factors (theological, educational, and cultural) ultimately come to interact in the mind of the Christian educator. Educational theories and practices do not spontaneously generate *ex nihilo* (Latin, *out of nothing*). They are the product of the commitment and intellect of men and women throughout history. *History is biography,* and hence history cannot be separated from the people who make it, nor can the theories and practices be fully understood apart from the individual who formed them. For example, many of the progressive educational theorists of the 18th–19th centuries who advanced a more nurturing, child-centered approach to instruction had rather tragic lives. Many of them had lost parents to death or desertion, were forced to be raised by relatives, or had dire experiences in the educational system of their era. Perhaps their approach to education was a result of these personal experiences. My convictions about the value and potential of Christian education are partially based on my experiences growing up in my home congregation in Lexington, Kentucky, Southern Acres Christian Church. My earliest exposure to Christian education was an experiential one, not an intellectual encounter. Hence, perhaps the most obvious factor in the shaping of Christian education are the lives of the educators themselves.

What Should We Remember from This Chapter?

- Christian education is broader than our experience or our times can understand.
- Christian educators do not have to reinvent the wheel, or work on an educational paradigm in the dark, since history can provide ample insight into the theories and practices of education in the faith community.
- Christian education is *dynamic*. It is not simply concerned with the transmission of God's Word (content), but the practical relevance of God's Word to the world (process).
- Christian education is a hybrid field of inquiry, a product of the integration between the theological and educational communities, both of which are in the context of culture.
- We cannot escape the influence and impact of history on Christian education.

The Challenge ✝ Chapter 1

Study Helps

Reflection Questions

1. What is your definition of Christian education? (After reading this book, return to this question and review your response. What has changed?)

2. What convictions do you have about Christian education? From whence did they come?

3. Given the factors which influence the formation of Christian education, which ones have you experienced? Which ones have perhaps impacted your life or congregation?

4. In regard to the history of Christian education, what questions do you hope this book (or course) will answer?

Technical Terms

Black Box A metaphor denoting the limits of scientific inquiry.

Culture The collective traits of a given society that defines them. For example, norms, beliefs, values, authority structures, music, literature, history, science, and technology.

Social Science The study of human beings, personally and corporately, psychologically, and sociologically.

Theology A human construct of biblical content into a systematic or thematic understanding of God's revelation.

Chapter 2
Education among the Hebrews (2300–586 B.C.)

James Riley Estep, Jr.

Overview of Period

Hebrew education? Don't you mean Jewish education? Actually, no. The history of the Old Testament can be generally divided into two major sections: Pre-Exilic (2300–586 B.C.) and Post-Exilic (586–430B.C.), the Exile being the pivotal event marking the most significant cultural shift within the faith community. For example, prior to the Exile of 586 B.C., God's people were called "Hebrews," but after it they were called "Jews," signifying a fundamental shift in the identity of the people. The Pre-Exilic period may be further divided into the premonarchical and the monarchical. Hence, Hebrew education is historically and culturally distinct from Jewish education.

The Old Testament depicts Israel of the pre-Exilic period as a family (Abraham's), ethnic group (the Hebrews), confederation of tribes (12 tribes of Israel), and a national entity during the monarchy (the united and divided kingdom). See ❈ 2.1 for a survey of Hebrew history in the Old Testament. What were the characteristics of Hebrew culture and, in turn, education? Swift identified several factors that influenced education:

- *Early nomadism*—required a nonpermanent, movable educational system

- *Environment of Palestine*—lent itself to an agricultural education

- *Contact with foreign nations*—education for the formation of a distinctly Hebrew culture, separate from the neighboring cultures.

- *Political weakness*—no central or national schooling movement could develop until the establishment of a monarchy
- *Prolonged subjection*—education was often for the purpose of preserving faith traditions during times of oppression
- *Place of religion in culture*—God is central to *all* of Hebrew life, even education
- *Character of their religious convictions*—faith is a central element of Hebrew culture, and hence faith dominates every aspect of Hebrew culture, including education.[1]

Everything in Hebrew culture was viewed religiously. Hebrew culture was essentially agricultural, which was regarded religiously (cf. Deut. 11:13-17; Lev. 25:23; Isa. 28:24-29; Jer. 5:24; 14:22). Similarly, interaction between individuals and their culture took on an *intentionally* educational purpose. In short, every aspect of Hebrew culture by design aided in the process of forming the belief of the faith community. For example, even the great feasts and festivals, which are often described in terms of religious or historical significance, had agricultural significance as well, e.g., Pentecost as the Feast of First Fruits.

Purpose of Education

Both Hebrew culture and education are dominated by one central figure: *God*. Throughout the Old Testament God's self-revelation, both in terms of His deed and His prophetic words, placed Him in the position of primary teacher of the Hebrew community. As Job posed, "God is exalted in his power. Who is a teacher like him?" (Job 36:22). The aim of education was tied directly to the nature of God, for belief and behavior. Hence, Hebrew education was essentially religious education, but occupational and military training had a religious element.

Education in the Hebrew culture was for the purpose of developing both personal and communal faith. Hebrew education was comprised of socialization, nonformal education, and formal educational opportunities for study and learning. It started with the socialization of children into the Hebrew community life, with a strong emphasis on nonformal education provided through the family. This was particularly true during the Patriarchal period. These approaches to education are consistent through the pre-Exilic period, and continue through the post-Exilic period and beyond. While priests and prophets, following the time of Moses, made nonformal education available, it was not until the establishment of the Hebrew monarchy that there is any indication of formal education, scribal schools, being provided beyond the instructional activities of the priests and prophets. The rise of formal education is indicative of the development in monarchical administrative bureaucracy and the establishment of international relations with other cultures in the Near East.

Educational Contexts

Hebrew education was very diverse, developing multiple educational media. Over the centuries the Hebrew culture developed a rather comprehensive system of education. Where did Hebrew education occur? How was instruction provided? As ❷ 2.2 illustrates, with every developmental period of Hebrew culture came new contexts of education. For example, the cultural and political shifts that occurred with the establishment of the Monarchy yielded new educational initiatives and contexts.

° Cultural Encounter
° Family, Home, & Tribe
° Tabernacle & Temple
° Royal Courts
° Scribal Schools

Cultural Encounter

Israel was a theocracy, a nation ruled by God, and hence its culture reflected its spiritual and religious devotion. In so doing, community life itself became an instrument for instruction. The reasons for feasts and festivals, placement of worship sites, and activities of public assemblies not only had expressed religious and historical significance, but educational importance as well (Deut. 4:14; 6:1; 26:1ff; Josh. 8:30-35; 2 Kgs. 2:3; 4:38; 5:22; 2 Chr. 17:7-19). For example, the Sabbath taught about creation, Passover reminded them of their slavery in Egypt and the Exodus, Feast of Tabernacles recounts the wilderness experience, and God's mercy for His people was demonstrated in *Yom Kippur*, the Day of Atonement. Hence, education was experienced through the cultural encounters of the Hebrew people.

Family, Home, and Tribe

Hebrew education began with Abraham and the family unit that eventually became the nation of Israel. Faith was obviously passed along through informal means, from one generation to the next. The Hebrew family was the primary educational institution for children, through both deliberate instruction and encountering family life (Exod. 12:26-27; 20:4-12; Deut. 4:9-10; 6:1-9; 11:19-20; 29:9; Ps. 78:3-6; Prov. 6:20).

The nomadic life of the Patriarchs would have precluded the possibility of formal education or schools. Even though some Hebrews may have experienced schooling while in Egyptian captivity, once they returned to Canaan after the Exodus the family once again claimed its central position as educational institution. It should be noted that the Hebrews were a tribal culture, and as such the tribe, as an extended family, had a role in the educational process.

Both parents were responsible for the education of children (Prov. 1:8; 6:20), as well as other members of the family, creating an intergenerational context for Hebrew education (Deut. 4:9-11; 11:19-20; Exod. 12:26-27; Ps. 78:3-6). Fathers particularly were given the charge to discipline children (Prov. 22:15; 23:13-14; 29:15-17), whereas mothers provided moral instruction and nurture. As David wrote:

> O my people, hear my teaching; listen to the words of my mouth. I will open my mouth in parables, I will utter hidden things, things from of old—what we have heard and known, what our fathers have told us. We will not hide them from their children; we will tell the next generation the praiseworthy deeds of the LORD, his power, and the wonders he has done. He decreed statutes for Jacob and established the law in Israel, which he commanded our forefathers to teach their children, so the next generation would know them, even the children yet to be born, and they in turn would tell their children (*Ps. 78:1-6*).

A Note of Caution: While the family was indeed the foundational educational "institution" in Hebrew education, it was *not* the *sole* provider of childhood education in the Old Testament. Others assisted in the family's instruction, e.g., nurses or Naomi to Ruth's child (Ruth 4:16; cf. Num. 11:12; Isa. 49:33), and members of the priesthood. Second Kings 10:5-6 likewise mentions guardians to Ahab's sons. Additionally, as this section will demonstrate, other members of the Hebrew community of faith were appointed the task of providing instruction.

Tabernacle and Temple as Educational Institutions

The Tabernacle and later the Temple of Solomon were the first "permanent" sites of education in Hebrew culture. Related to the role of the priests in education (which will be discussed later in this chapter) was the building of Solomon's temple, dedicated in 963 B.C. Swift describes this as "an event of great educational as well as of great religious importance."[2] When the question is asked, *where* did the Hebrews go to receive education, the tabernacle and temple provided access to the priests and other learned individuals from which to receive instruction.

Royal Courts

Gangel and Benson note the educational contributions of both David and Solomon as kings of Israel.[3] The education of the princes became an educational initiative during the monarchy. However, the access to this avenue of education was extremely limited to members of the royal family and possibly the court, not for the general populace. Once again, while the royal family played a significant role in the teaching of princes, during the reign of David provision was made for the education and care of his sons (1 Chr. 27:32). Solomon was guided by Nathan the prophet (2 Sam. 12:25; 1 Kings 1), and Joash was influenced by his uncle Jehoiada the high priest (2 Kings 11–12). Hezekiah likewise benefited from the attention Isaiah paid him (Isa. 9:5-6, 11:1ff). Similarly, Neo-Babylonian texts show that Jehoiachin, the exiled king of Judah, had attendants for five of his sons, possibly instructors.[4] In short, education became more formalized in the monarchical period than in any previous time period of pre-Exilic history.

Were there schools in Hebrew culture?

The Old Testament may contain some reflections of schooling in the monarchical period. The advancement of education in ancient Israel may have risen when formal diplomatic relations with Egypt were established during the time of David and Solomon, requiring a parallel bureaucratic system of government (2 Sam. 8:16-18; 20:23-25; 1 Kgs. 4:1-6). Second Kings 6:1 refers to "the *place* where we sit before you [a teacher] is too small for us" seeming to indicate a place or structure wherein instruction occurred. Proverbs 4:7 may refer to a fee paid for instruction. The reference to pupils (Heb. *limmûd*) in Isaiah 8:14,16, and "students" (Heb. *talmîd*) in 1 Chronicles 25:8, Proverbs 22:29, and Proverbs 25–27 may suggest that officers of the state received schooling. Also, the reference in Proverbs 5:13 to "Those who taught me . . . Those who instructed me," is probably not limited to parents since it would be more reasonable to assume the author would use *father* or *mother* instead.

Archaeological evidence likewise reflects the presence of schools among the Hebrews. Discoveries of *ostraca* that appear to be schoolboy practice drills, such as a line of repeated letters, letters with the same general appearance, the same word written repeatedly, childlike drawings, number groupings (either the same number repeated or sequentially written), and even translation texts.[5]

> **Ostraca:** Pieces of broken pottery upon which messages were written.

While the Hebrew language uses a simpler script than other cultures of the ancient Near East and would not necessarily require schools in order to learn reading and writing, it is likely that schools would be employed due to the cultural influences of Egypt and Mesopotamia, both of which had scribal schools, as well as the quality of writing evident during the monarchical period. Some pieces of evidence are more explainable with schools rather than familial instruction. For example, schools rather than individual families would better accomplish the need for bilingual scribal education.

Hence, the presence of scribal schools during the monarchical period seems to be a logical conclusion. However, the problem that remains is the extent and nature of the schools. Nonetheless, schools seem to have had their start during the late pre-Exilic period. Once again, these scribal schools would have provided education, but were not open to the populace in general. However, it was indeed perhaps the first measure toward the provision of universal education for God's people.

Educational Content

The content of Hebrew education changed with each shift within its culture. It is critical to remember that just as the means of providing instruction evolved along with Hebrew culture, the curriculum expanded with it. *Why?* It is not always possible to make blanket statements about the content of Hebrew instruction. For example, "Hebrew education made use of the Torah." True or False? Yes, it did make use of the Torah, but prior to Moses, during the Patriarchal period and period of enslavement, the Torah did not exist! Hence, the Torah was not always present in Hebrew education.

The curriculum of the Hebrews was indeed always centered on God, but the source of this information and the source of godly wisdom for living differed throughout the period. As previously asserted, Hebrew education was essentially religious education. Perhaps the most basic elements of the Hebrew curriculum were the *Shema*, *Torah*, and wisdom literature.

Shema was the essential confession of faith and is central to the educational mandate given by Moses to the Hebrew community.

> Hear, O Israel: The LORD our God, the LORD is one. Love the LORD your God with all your heart and with all your soul and with all your strength. These commandments that I give you today are to be upon your hearts. Impress them on your children. Talk about them when you sit at home and when you walk along the road, when you lie down and when you get up. Tie them as symbols on your hands and bind them on your foreheads. Write them on the doorframes of your houses and on your gates (Deut. 6:4-9).

Torah, typically translated "Law," is more precisely rendered "instructions." The "instructions" given by Moses begin in the book of Exodus. Three types of materials comprised Exodus's instructions: The Decalogue (Exod. 20:1-26), Codes of Social Behavior (Exod. 21:1–24:11), and Religious Obligations (Exod. 24:12–31:18). For the Hebrews, the Torah was more than regulations, rules, and codes; it was their means of living a righteous life pleasing to God and securing His blessing upon their person, tribe, and nation.

Later, with the arrival of the Hebrew Monarchy and the rise of sages or wise men within their culture, came the advent of *wisdom literature*. As Daryl Eldridge observes:

Education in the monarchy cannot be totally understood until the vast instructional capability of King Solomon is taken into consideration. The educational

> **Wisdom Literature** was practical, daily-living advice. Proverbs and Ecclesiastes are examples of wisdom literature in the Bible.

value of the book of Proverbs alone will never be surpassed for its elevation and distribution of wisdom. Education began to take on a more personal dimension in the writings of Solomon and the wise men.[6]

However, while pre-Exilic education was essentially religious, *all* of life was essentially religious in a Hebrew context. Hence other subjects in Hebrew education were indeed seen as being done out of religious duty.

While Greek and Roman education emphasized gymnastics or physical education, Hebrew education did not. However, several passages in the Bible note the presence of physical education such as dance (Ps. 149:3; 190:4; Exod. 15:19-20; 32:19; 1 Sam. 18:6; 21:11), archery (1 Sam. 20:20; Lam. 3:12; 1 Chr. 12:2), the use of slings (Judg. 20:1g; 1 Sam. 17:40; 1 Sam. 17:50), hunting, or even the mention of playing childhood games with balls (Isa. 22:18).[7]

Education for Literacy

The formation of an alphabet, rather than a symbolic or pictographic language, facilitated the possibility of a literate society. Numerous individuals and groups (e.g., parents, priests, prophets, military personnel) in the Hebrew period are described as being able to write and/or read, some passages even dating prior to the monarchical period.[8] Five frequently cited passages of Scripture regarding literacy in the pre-Exilic period are Judges 8:14; Deuteronomy 6:9; and Isaiah 8:2; 10:19; 29:12; all of which indicate that children and/or common individuals could generally read and write. Hebrew literacy may be illustrated by several early texts from the period, such as the Gezer Calendar (● 2.3), a 10th-century B.C. school copying exercise, and the Inscription over the Pool of Siloam at Jerusalem during Hezekiah's reign, c. 700 B.C. (● 2.4).

Many societies had a literate element, and hence writing on monuments or official state-related documents were common, but in Israel an abundance of common texts is evident, e.g., ostraca (writing on broken pottery) or graffiti (writing on structures). The common populace of the nation produced these common writings. Allen Millard concluded correctly, "Ancient Hebrew written documents, recovered by archaeology, demonstrate both that there were readers and writers in ancient Israel, and that they were by no means rare.

Few places will have been without someone who could write, and few Israelites will have been unaware of writing."[9]

Perhaps the best example of this is found in Lachish Letter 3 (❧ 2.5). Letter 3 is a military correspondence written from Hoshaiah to Yoash, in which the literacy expectations of 6th-century Judah are implied. Part of the letter reads, "And now let be opened prayer, the ear of your servant concerning the letter which you sent to your servant yesterday evening; for the heart of your servant has been despondent since you sent [it] to your servant, and that my lord said . . ." The section closes with the sarcastic assertion translated, "Don't you know how to read a letter?" or more succinctly, "Are you illiterate!"[10] Hence, it would seem that literacy was an expectation in 6th-century B.C. Judah.

Educational Process

But, *how* did the Hebrews and Israelites educate their children? What was the process of instruction? Crenshaw identifies "three ways of acquiring knowledge" in Hebrew thought: (1) Observation of nature and human behavior, (2) Analogy: Creed and Reality, and (3) Encounter with the Transcendent One.[11] In short, engagement with the community and family, study of the Scriptures, and personal devotion and experience with God. Similarly, Sherrill identifies the uniqueness of familial education in Hebrew culture in three ways: Vocational, Behavioral, and Oral Traditions (later containing the interpretations of Torah and the rest of Scripture).[12] Similarly, the learning of religious rites and ceremonies were part of the process of education, since they symbolically conveyed information and signif-icance.

Methods of memorization and repetition also seem to have been used in the process of instruction. Isaiah 28:9-10 may reflect on such instructional methods: "Who is it he is trying to teach? To whom is he explaining his message? To children weaned from their milk, to those just taken from the breast? For it is: Do and do, do and do, rule on rule, rule on rule; a little here, a little there." Hence, the traditional methods of education in the Hebrew system of education could be characterized by copying the example of parents and their community, reading and memorizing of materials, as well as partic-ipation in religious rituals.

Voices

Who were the Hebrew educators? Who were the contributors to the Hebrew system of education? Who was responsible for providing instruction? As previously mentioned, God was the primary Teacher of the Hebrew people, and the family was the primary educational institution in Hebrew culture. However, who shaped the educational system? Who else contributed to the education of the Hebrew people?

> ° God
> ° Priests
> ° Moses & the Prophets
> ° Sages & Wisdom Literature

Priests

Priests were the first organized group designated as instructors *outside* the family. We oftentimes regard the priests as fulfilling a solely religious or ceremonial function. However, they were one of Israel's earliest groups of educators. Throughout the early part of the pre-Exilic period the priests were Israel's instructors. They both received formal instruction to assume the priestly role and provided instruction to the people. When Moses addresses the tribe of Levi, from which the priests come, he noted as part of their duties, "He [Levi] teaches your precepts to Jacob and your law to Israel."[13] Similarly, Deuteronomy 31:9-13 describes the priests reading the law to the assembly of Hebrews (adults, children, and resident aliens included). The educational practice of the priests would continue for over two millennia (Deut. 33:10; Jer. 2:8; 18:18; 2 Chr. 15:3; 17:7-9; 35:3; Mal. 2:7).

Perhaps the best compliment given to the priests was in Nehemiah 8:7-8: "The Levites . . . instructed the people in the Law while the people were standing there. They read from the Book of the Law of God, making it clear and giving the meaning so that the people could understand what was being read." Reading the law to the people on a regular basis, making it accessible to both the community of faith and "aliens" living within Israel's borders was the educational task of the priesthood. For example, the public reading of the Law was reinstated by King Jehoshaphat of Judah to restore the faithfulness of the people (2 Chr. 34:29-31). King Jehoshaphat is reported to have sent Levites to the cities of Judah where "they taught throughout Judah, taking with them the Book of the Law of the LORD; they went around to all the towns of Judah and taught the people" (2 Chronicles 17:9).

Reed and Prevost comment that "the priests remained the primary public educators of the nation until the exile," noting that the "educational role of the priests was expressed in two ways": (1) theological education, the training of other priests, and (2) religious education, the training of the people in observance of the Law.[14]

Moses and the Prophets as Educators

Among the many tasks of the prophets of the Old Testament was the instruction of God's people. Often the message of the prophets was directed toward both the religious and social dimensions. While priests provided a more stable, located body of educators, clustered near the tabernacle or temple, prophets journeyed throughout the nation's landscape as God's messengers.

Moses was a paradigm for the prophetic ministry (Exod. 18:20; 24:12; Deut. 4:14; 6:1; 31:19). Not only did he deliver the Torah to the Hebrew community, but within it outlined the educational roles of the family, priesthood, and community. Acts 7:22 asserts that "Moses was educated in all the wisdom of the Egyptians and was powerful in speech and action."

Several passages make reference to the "school of the prophets" (2 Kgs. 2:3-5; 4:28; 6:1; 1 Sam. 10:10; 19:20). This "school" is mentioned only in connection with Elijah and Elisha in the 8th century B.C., within the vicinity of Beth-El, Jericho, Gilgal, and the region of the Jordan (2 Kgs. 2:3-5; 4:38; 6:1) and similarly in 1 Samuel 10:10; 19:20. However, this is actually a mistranslation of the Hebrew *ben* meaning "*son* of the prophets," and denotes the followers who received instruction from the prophets or those partnering with the ministry of the prophets. It was common in ancient Near Eastern cultures, especially in Mesopotamia, to use familial language to describe educational relationships. However, it was indeed noting an instructional relationship shared between the prophet and his pupils.

Sages/Wise Men and Wisdom Literature

Proverbs 1:2-7 conveys the function and aim of the sages' educational endeavors; serving as an outlet of applied, life-relevant truth. The passage states:

for attaining wisdom and discipline; for understanding words of insight; for acquiring a disciplined and prudent life, doing what is right and just and fair; for giving prudence to the simple, knowledge and discretion to the young—let the wise listen and add to their learning, and let the discerning get guidance—for understanding proverbs and parables, the sayings and riddles of the wise. The fear of the LORD is the beginning of knowledge, but fools despise wisdom and discipline.

The presence of sages in Hebrew culture is attested to in the Job narrative, set in the Patriarchal period, and in the riddles of Samson (Judg. 14:12-18). Not to be confused with the *magi* of ancient Persia, who are mentioned in the birth narratives of Jesus, the sages of Israel were an informal group of men able to instruct others in the Torah.

"The teaching of the wise is a fountain of life, turning a man from the snares of death" (Proverbs 13:14). Ecclesiastes opens with "The words of the Teacher . . . I, the Teacher, was king over Israel in Jerusalem. I devoted myself to study and to explore by wisdom all that is done under heaven. What a heavy burden God has laid on men!" (Eccl. 1:1,12-13). Solomon concludes Ecclesiastes with the affirmation, "Not only was the Teacher wise, but also he imparted knowledge to the people. He pondered and searched out and set in order many proverbs. The Teacher searched to find just the right words, and what he wrote was upright and true. The words of the wise are like goads, their collected sayings like firmly embedded nails—given by one Shepherd" (Eccl. 12:9-11). Hence, the sages provided what could be described as "higher education" in the Hebrew culture, particularly during the monarchical period.

Influence of Ancient Near Eastern Cultures

To what degree did the ancient Near East cultures influence Hebrew education? Did the Egyptians, Mesopotamian nations (Sumer, Assyria, Babylon), or the Canaanite tribes exert any influence on the formation of Hebrew education? If so, how much of Hebrew education was unique and how much copied? Opinions differ in this matter. For example, R.J. Williams argues for scribal schools in Hebrew culture based on cultural inferences, namely the rise of the Hebrew culture during the monarchical period, beginning with David or Solomon, the presence of schools in Syria-Palestine prior to the Hebrew occupation under Joshua, and the use of Egyptian words typically referring to scribal activity (e.g., Jer. 36:18).[15]

The most significant educational achievement of the Phoenicians at Byblos was the invention of the alphabet. Their twenty-two letter alphabet represents the earliest alphabetic script in the world, and was even used by the Hebrews, e.g., the Gezer Calendar (❧ 2.3). In fact, the earliest alphabet from the ancient Near East was in Ugaritic, discovered in 1948, dating to the middle of the second millennium B.C. Thought to be an instructional device for scribal students, it contains a sequence of letters, similar to providing a list of the ABCs to students (❧ 2.6).

> Phoenicians at Byblos? The Phoenicians were a Canaanite culture located on the shores of the Mediterranean Sea. They were known for their navigational skills and merchandising. Their capital city was Byblos, from which we get the word Bible!

However, Jamieson-Drake comments that crosscultural comparisons between Israel and its neighbors are of little value since the cultures differ so drastically as do the Hebrew alphabetic script and the relatively difficult Egyptian hieroglyphics and Mesopotamian cuneiform.[16] Yet, as previously noted the rise of the Hebrew monarchy and its bureaucratic structure may have been facilitated by formal contact with foreign powers, and hence schooling for scribes and other governmental officials would have been necessitated due to these newly formed international relationships. Hence, the educational influence of the neighboring cultures may have been present, but more indirect.

Conclusion

Hebrew education was the precursor to Jewish education. It was a primitive form of education for a primitive culture. However, as the Hebrew's developed from a family into a monarchical nation, the educational system changed with it, adapting to service the needs of the faith community. It serves as an example of how dynamic Christian education must be if it is to remain relevant to its people and a change-agent for our culture.

What Can We Learn from Hebrew Education?

- Christian education is centered on Scripture, leading to a confession of faith; *Torah* and *Shema*.

- Christian education must be dynamic, developing in response to the changes within the faith community.

- Christian education must provide education for every age group within the faith community, particularly children, e.g., intergenerational education.

- Christian education must not rely solely on *one* educational context or provider.

- Christian education must facilitate education within the family unit if it is to be successful, since familial education is the basis for the Hebrew system of education.

- Christian education must not only be concerned with the spiritual formation of the individual, but of the community as a whole as well.

- Christian education must be holistic and heterogeneous, i.e., addressing the whole person and community of faith by using a variety of methods and means of delivering education.

- Christian education must concern itself with the transmission of faith not only through the study of Scripture, but through relationship and experience within the faith community.

- Christian education is not in a vacuum. It must respond and adapt to the changes outside the faith-community as well to maintain a relevance to the culture.

Study Helps

Reflection Questions

1. How did your family influence your faith? How is Christian education still a family matter?

2. Think of your own community of faith. What does someone learn by encountering its culture? What impressions are left after experiencing your congregation?

3. What is the "Wisdom Literature" of Christian education? Where is contemporary Christian wisdom to be found?

4. Does culture lead educational innovation, or does educational innovation lead culture? Which comes first? What is the relationship of culture and education?

5. How does literacy, the simple ability to read and/or write, affect your understanding of Christian education? What if you were dealing with an illiterate society, how would it change what you do in a class or group?

Technical Terms

Cuneiform Form of writing in ancient Mesopotamia using various configurations of small lines to symbolize entire words.

Exilic Period of Old Testament history beginning in 586 B.C., following the destruction of Jerusalem by the Babylonians.

Hieroglyphics Form of writing in ancient Egypt using pictures to denote a given sound, not word, i.e., pictures for letters.

Ostraca Pieces of broken pottery upon which messages were written.

Pre-Exilic Period of Old Testament history preceding 586 B.C., prior to the destruction of Jerusalem by the Babylonians, beginning with the Patriarchs.

Shema Hebrew for "hear," it is the confession of faith referenced in Deuteronomy 6:4.

Torah Hebrew for "instructions," it is the Hebrew name for the first five books of the Old Testament, written by Moses.

Recommended Bibliography

Barclay, William. *Educational Ideals in the Ancient World*. Grand Rapids: Baker, 1959.

Crenshaw, James L. *Education in Ancient Israel: Across the Deadening Silence*. New York: Doubleday, 1998.

Heaton, E.W. *The School Tradition for the Old Testament*. Oxford: Oxford University Press, 1994.

Schoeman, S. "Early Hebrew Education and Its Significance for Present-Day Educational Theory and Practice." *Hervormde teologiese studies* 53 (1997): 407-427.

Smith, William A. *Ancient Education*. New York: Philosophical Library, 1955.

Swift, H. Fletcher. *Education in Ancient Israel from Earliest Time to A.D. 70*. Chicago: Open Court, 1919.

Notes

[1] H. Fletcher Swift, *Education in Ancient Israel from Earliest Time to A.D. 70* (Chicago: Open Court, 1919), 11-16.

[2] Ibid., 31.

[3] Kenneth Gangel and Warren Benson, *Christian Education: Its History and Philosophy* (Chicago: Moody Press, 1983), 27.

[4] William W. Brickman, "Education," *Encyclopaedia Judaica*, vol. 6 (Jerusalem: Encyclopaedia Judaica, 1971), 390.

[5] Andre Lemaire, *Les ecoles et la formation de la Bible das l'ancien Israel* (Göttingen: Vandenhoeck and Ruprecht, 1981), 9-32. See also G.I. Davies, "Were There Schools in Ancient Israel?" *Wisdom in Ancient Israel* (New York: Cambridge University Press, 1995), 199-211; James L. Crenshaw, *Education in Ancient Israel* (New York: Doubleday, 1998), 111.

[6] Daryl Eldridge, *The Teaching Ministry of the Church* (Nashville: Broadman Holman, 1995), 15.

[7] Cf. Debold B. Van Dalen, Elmer D. Mitchell, and Bruce L. Bennett, *A World History of Physical Education* (Englewood Cliffs, NJ: Prentice-Hall, 1953).

[8] Exod. 17:14; 24:7; 34:1; Num. 5:23; Deut. 6:9; 11:20; 17:18-19; 24:1-3; 31:11; Josh. 8:14,32,34; 18:4; 1 Sam. 10:25; 2 Sam. 11:14; 1 Chr. 24:6; 2 Chr. 21:12; 34:24; 35:4; 1 Kgs. 21:8; 2 Kgs. 5:7; 10:1; 19:14; 22:8-10; 23:2; Neh. 8:3-8; 9:3; Esth. 8:8-9; Prov. 3:3; 7:3; Isa. 8:1; 10:1,19; 38:9; Jer. 8:8; 22:30; 29:29; 36:2-6; 51:61; Ezek. 4:18,23; 24:2; Dan. 5:17; 7:1; Hab. 2:2.

[9] Alan R. Millard, "An Assessment of the Evidence for Writing in Ancient Israel," *Biblical Archaeology Today* (Jerusalem: Israel Exploration Society/Israel Academy of Science and Humanities, 1985): 308.

[10] Ian M. Young, "Israelite Literacy: Interpreting the Evidence, Part 2," *Vetus Testamentum* 48.2 (1998): 410, 412.

[11] Cf. James L. Crenshaw, *Education in Ancient Israel: Across the Deadening Silence* (New York: Doubleday, 1998), 120-130.

[12] Lewis Joseph Sherrill, *The Rise of Christian Education* (New York: Macmillan Company, 1944), 18-21.

[13] Deuteronomy 33:10a. Note: The mention of "Jacob" is metaphorical for Israel.

[14] James E. Reed and Ronnie Prevost, *A History of Christian Education* (Nashville: Broadman and Holman, 1993), 47.

[15] R.J. Williams, "A People Come Out of Egypt: An Egyptologist Looks at the Old Testament," *Vetus Testamentum Supplements* 28 (1975): 238-239.

[16] D.W. Jamieson-Drake, *Scribes and Schools in Monarchic Israel* (Sheffield, England: University of Sheffield, 1991), 152-154.

Chapter 3
Education in Ancient Judaism (586 B.C.–A.D. 400)

James Riley Estep, Jr.

Overview of Period

The beginning of Jewish education begins with the close of the Hebrew period of Old Testament history. What was the pivotal event? What changed God's people from Hebrews to Jews? In 586 B.C. the Babylonians, under Nebuchadnezzar, destroyed Jerusalem, the capital of Judea. Following this event, the inhabitants of Judea were deported throughout the Babylonian Empire. With the rise and fall of empires (Persian, Greek, and Roman) and their successive conquests of Palestine, the people of God, *now* known as Jews (from Judea), were dispersed throughout the Mediterranean world. This dispersal pattern of Jewish communities was later called the Diaspora. Hence, the socio-political climate of the Jewish period of history was drastically distinct from that of the Hebrew period. (See ❷ 3.1 for a survey of Jewish history.)

> The *Diaspora*, as a geographic region, is mentioned in James 1:1!

Hebrew to Judaism: Cultural Transitions

The culture of the Hebrews and that of the Jews were quite distinct. The Hebrews lived in Palestine (Israel and Judah); Jews were present throughout the Mediterranean world, as indicated by location of synagogues mentioned throughout the book of Acts in the New Testament. This meant that Jews had to address social circumstances never before encountered by their Hebrew predecessors. The dominant language of the Jews was not Hebrew, but Greek. In fact, one educational accommodation was to tolerate the use of Greek translations of the Old Testament (such as the Septuagint), and on occasion even Latin (during the Roman Empire). Even the *Shema* (Heb.) and other traditional prayers were recited in Greek rather than Hebrew, although some practices required that only Hebrew be used, such as priestly blessings.[1] Whereas the priests and prophets had been the principle leaders and educators of the Hebrew community, during the Jewish period new educational leaders emerged—the rabbis. As Aaron Demsky observes, "A new intellectual model had emerged: the biblical *hakham*, or wise man, gave way to the rabbinic *talmid hakham*, or scholar."[2] With the advent of the rabbis came the development of sectarianism, and hence denominations within Judaism developed, the two most significant being the Pharisees and Sadducees. The Sadducees served in Jerusalem, primarily in the Temple; whereas the Pharisees were leaders within a new institution, the synagogue. *What's the point?* The culture of Judaism differed from that of the Hebrews in location, language, centers of worship, religious leaders; in short, the educational system had to adapt to an entirely new set of cultural factors and challenges.

> **FYI:** The term "rabbi" comes from the Hebrew word for "great."

Developmental Periods of Jewish Education

Education in Judaism is an expansion of Hebrew education, with adaptation and additional instructional initiatives to respond to the cultural transitions within the community of faith. The Jewish educational system developed in three distinct phases. The first phase immediately coincides with the return of the Jews to Jerusalem following their exile in Babylon. The *Sopherim* period (515–200 B.C.) extends through the first half of the intertestamental period, including such Old Testament events as the end of the Babylonian exile, the Jews' return to Judah, and the rebuilding of Jerusalem's walls and the temple. During this period, the scribes (Heb. *sopherim*) were the principle educational leaders (cf. Ezra 7:6-10; Neh. 8:2,8,13).

The second developmental period of Jewish education was the Zugot (200 B.C.–A.D. 10). *Zugot*, Hebrew (derived from Greek) for *pairs*, designates a period where the Sanhedrin was ruled by a pair of leaders. During this period five such pairs of leaders ruled, the last pair being the most recognized, Hillel and Shammai. The practice of dual-rule ended prior to Jesus' entering his ministry.

The final period of educational development in ancient Judaism was the Tannaitic Period (AD 10–220). This period was dominated by the leadership of the rabbis. It was the time of Jesus' life, during which he frequently engaged the rabbinical community. The rabbis became even more influential following the destruction of Jerusalem, and its Temple by the Romans in A.D. 70. To replace the temple services, which were impossible following its destruction, education in the Torah was elevated as the spiritual center of Jewish life, with the rabbis being the providers of instruction.[3]

Purpose of Education

Unlike the educational approaches used by their contemporaries (Greeks and Romans), Jewish education continued to be essentially religious education. (See ❸ 3.2 for a fictitious conversation between a Greek educator and a Jewish rabbi on educational theory.) In fact, Torah study was considered an act of worship. For this reason, education did not stop at childhood, but intentionally continued into adulthood. The Jews became pioneers of lifelong education. However, in light of their cultural and religious turmoil caused by centuries of transition, the focus of Jewish education became the *preservation* of faith. It answered questions such as: What does it mean to be Jewish? How can I maintain my Jewish faith and heritage while living in a non-Jewish context? What constitutes Jewishness? Education had to respond to new questions raised by the Jewish community as it encountered its non-Jewish context.

> "The Jewish educational ideal has left its mark deeply upon the world, because in the last analysis it aims to educate the child in order to fit him to be the servant of God; it is education of children for God."
> – William Barclay, *Educational Ideals in the Ancient World*

Educational Contexts

Jewish education maintained most of the institutions of education developed during the Hebrew period, but with some significant alterations. For example, the family retained its function as primary educational institution, *but* the Jewish rabbis surpassed the teaching ministry of priests and prophets, which was prevalent during the Hebrew period. Hence new institutions of instruction formed around the rabbis. What were the Jewish contexts of instruction? Chronologically, four educational institutions germinated within Judaism: the synagogue, secondary schools, elementary schools, and rabbinical academies or colleges.

Synagogue

The synagogue has been known by a variety of descriptive names. It is most typically called the *Beth ha Kenesset* or "House of Assembly." Philo, a first century Jewish scholar in Alexandria (Egypt), called it the "House of Instruction."[4] The New Testament most frequently describes the synagogue with the word *didaskein* (Gk.), "to teach" (Matt. 4:23; Mark 1:21; Luke 4:15).

According to Nathan Drazin, the mission of the synagogue was threefold: (1) nationalism, (2) religion, through worship and instruction, and (3) universalization of educational opportunity, for both adults and children.[5] However, it ultimately led to the "popularizing [of the] Torah and democratizing Jewish life."[6] While the function of the synagogue in the Jewish community was multidimensional, it was essentially an educational assembly for adults. However, boys began attending synagogue with their fathers around age three. In fact, the synagogue typically conducted two separate services: a morning service for preaching and worship and an afternoon service dedicated to teaching. The teaching service provided for the reading and interpreting of Scripture, as well as group and individual studies.

The synagogue is not formally mentioned by name in the Old Testament. While Josephus and Philo attribute the synagogue to Moses,[7] this is more likely a propaganda statement for its acceptance by the post-Exilic Jewish community. It was most likely a post-Exilic institution started by the Jewish communities in Babylonia (e.g., Ezekiel) and Egypt (e.g., Jeremiah), but not formalized until the Hellenistic period (4th century). Many modern scholars attribute the origins of the synagogue to Ezra, per-

> "Jewish education proved to be the salvation of the Jewish people"
> —Drazin, *History of Jewish Education*, 32

haps the most recognized post-Exilic leader in Judah. By the third century B.C. the synagogue had become the educational center of the Jewish people. The synagogue grew throughout the Jewish Diaspora for community, identification, and worship away from Jerusalem and its Temple. "The synagogues became centers of social and religious life, but their chief function was to act as popular universities, a kind of extra-mural department of the main university, which was the newly built [Herod's] Temple at Jerusalem."[8] Eisenberg comments that "the synagogue was never regarded as a competitor to the Temple, but rather as a sort of extension of it," noting that even the Temple had rooms designated for use as synagogues.[9]

The synagogue did not necessarily denote a building or formal structure, but rather the assembly of Jews comprised the synagogue. The archaeology of the synagogue demonstrates the evolution of the synagogue from gathering in a house to an attached structure on a house to an independent facility designated for use by the assembly. The earliest free-standing structures designated as synagogues are located at Galma, Masada, and Herodium. All are first-century A.D. synagogues dating prior to the Roman destruction of Jerusalem in A.D. 70, with an additional one possibly in Qumran, an Essene settlement located southeast of Jerusalem near the Dead Sea (origin of the Dead Sea Scrolls) which is an even more formal structure (● 3.3).

Schools in Ancient Judaism

What happened to the long tradition of parental instruction in Hebrew education? Why the advent of schools? During the Jewish period, parents were not able to adequately prepare children for secondary education. Parents could no longer teach such basic skills as reading and writing to their children. The cultures encountered by the Jews living in the Diaspora served as examples of schooling as a means of providing childhood education. Also, the expansion of Jewish literature and knowledge made the task of instruction too demanding on a family-based educational system. Hence, the Jewish community established elementary educational institu-

> "Above all we pride ourselves on the education of our children, and regard as the most essential task in life the observation of laws and of the pious practices, based thereupon, which we have inherited."
> Josephus *Against Apion* 1.60

tions to provide basic instruction, preparing children for more advanced studies in secondary institutions and later higher education. It is important to note that formal schooling was restricted to boys, while girls received instruction in the home from their parents. Three levels of Jewish formal education were established: Mikra (elementary), Mishnah (secondary), and Gemara/Talmud (higher education).[10] See ❋ 3.4 for a summary of Jewish schools.

During the Hellenistic era (4th century B.C.) schools began to appear in the Jewish community. Ben Sira (3rd century B.C.) advanced this cause with tuition-free education and Simeon ben Shetah (2nd century B.C.), brother of Queen Salome, started the first full system of secondary education supported financially by the community.[11] The final educational advancement in formal education came from Joshua ben Gamala (1st century AD) who planned how each community could provide a school for its children's elementary education.[12] Gamala, who was High Priest (A.D. 63–65) during last days of the Temple, made education compulsory in A.D. 64. (See ❋ 3.5 for an edited text of Baba Bathra 21 describing these educational initiatives.) One reason for the rise in distinctly Jewish schools was the disdain for Greek and Roman academies. In fact, Jason, a high-priest of ill report, had earlier attempted to introduce these academies into Jewish culture, but to no avail.[13]

Why were Jewish schools so successful? Several reasons can be given: (1) Jewish schools followed the example of Greek and Roman schools, which heavily influenced the design of the Jewish school system (e.g., three levels); (2) formal education through schooling addressed the complexity of integrating the oral traditions with interpretation of Torah, with application to the cultural context; and (3) the rise and influence of the Pharisees in the synagogues, especially after destruction of Herod's Temple in A.D. 70, caused the synagogue to become the center of Jewish community life.[14]

Beth Hassepher

The *Beth Hassepher* ("House of the Book") was for 5-9-year-old boys, corresponding to an elementary education. It was originally a gathering in any room in the house, but later it became part of the synagogue. While the scribes (Heb. *sofer*) and rabbis provided instruction in the synagogue, in smaller towns instruction was given by the "ruler of the synagogue" (Gk. *archisynagogus*) or a *chazzan*, the minister or attendant of the synagogue (cf. Luke 4:20). Jerusalem is reported to have had 400 synagogues, each with a school, though some hold it is an exaggeration.[15]

Elementary schools in ancient Judah started after 100 B.C. Reading was the basic objective since the ability to read was essential for the study of Scripture. Hence the study of the alphabet and grammar was essential, as well as the memorizing of texts. *Schools were to be very accessible.* For example, larger towns may have had two schools, or if a river divided the town it would have one on either side. Also, it was to be placed in less crowded areas. During the summer months they only convened for four hours, and not between 10:00 a.m. and 3:00 p.m.. The teacher-student relationship was critical, and hence a ratio of 25:1 was maintained, and when a classroom reached 40 students an assistant was added to the classroom.

Beth ha-Midrash

The *Beth ha-Midrash* ("House of Study"), also called *Beth ha-Talmud*, was for 10-14-year-old boys, corresponding to secondary education. Started before 100 B.C., it was the first school among the Jewish people. One of the earliest references to such a school is found in the Apocrypha's Sirach 51.23, "Draw near to me, you who are untaught, and lodge in my school." Originally it was preceded by parental instruction in reading and writing, but later by the elementary school (*Beth Hassepher*). It was less structured than the *Beth Hassepher*, since it was designed for academic study and discourse, rather than the sheer memorization of alphabet, grammar, and vocabulary. At this level of Jewish education, students were given a systematic presentation of the Jewish faith, both oral and written.

Rabbinical Academies or Colleges

Higher education was provided through rabbinical instruction, beginning at age 15. These academies were *also* called *Beth ha-Midrash* or *Beth ha-Talmud*, but were distinct in that entrance usually required completion of the secondary curriculum.[16] A possible reference to the first "faculty" of rabbinical schools is from the Apocrypha. The "assembly of scribes" in Maccabees 7.12 may refer to a permanent group of teachers.[17] The rabbinical schools were the place of debates between learned men, rabbi, and headed by a rabbi. Rabbinical schools became centers of authority for Jewish faith after the fall of Jerusalem in A.D. 70; for example, gathering of the rabbis in Jamnia (Jabne) in northern Galilee. (See ❧ 3.6 for Sukkah 28a, an ancient passage regarding rabbinical instruction.) However, these were not permanent schools, but rather established on occasion or whenever opportunity arose, such as several rabbis being present in a city for an extended period of time.

Other Educational Opportunities

As previously mentioned, the forms of education present in the Hebrew period continued to be active within the Jewish community. Instruction at the Jerusalem Temple, public reading of Scripture, participation in feasts and festivals, as well as parental instruction continued to contribute to the education of God's people. In addition, Jewish literature began to contribute to the educational process. Literature such as Hallakkah (formulations of oral law) and Aggadah (legends) added to the collective knowledge of the Jewish community.

Educational Content

As in Hebrew education, Jewish education was essentially religious. "There was no text-book except the Scriptures; all primary education was preparation for reading the Law; and all higher education was the reading and studying of it."[18] However, this by no means implies a narrow focus of subject matter. Rather religion was at the core of the Jewish curriculum, not the extent of instruction. For example, basic math was taught as a necessary practical skill *as it applied to biblical studies*, but advanced mathematics was not since it had no religious or practical value. Similarly, Jewish students were prohibited from studying many of the pieces of literature from their non-Jewish surroundings. Hence, the study of literature, philosophy, and geography *independent* of the Scriptures was inconceivable. For example, a Jewish student would become acquainted with zoology through his study of clean and unclean animals.

> "To the pious Jew . . . the knowledge of God was everything; and to prepare for or impart that knowledge was the sum total, the sole object of his education." Alfred Edersheim, *Sketches of Jewish Social Life*, 124

Age-Graded Instruction in School

Selected passages of Scripture, the teachings of the sages, and prayers were impressed upon the child from an early age, even infancy.[19] *The Sayings of the Fathers* states an agenda for lifelong personal achievement, beginning with a rigorous plan for study and instruction: "At five years old, Scripture; at ten years, Mishnah; at thirteen, the Commandments; at fifteen, Talmud . . ."[20] This adequately outlines the basic content of instruction within the ancient Jewish educational system. The curriculum's content was as follows:

Age 5:   TaNaK (Torah, Nebhim, and the Kethubim), however, the study of the Torah began not with Genesis, but with Leviticus.

Age 10: Mishnah (oral law, probably including the supplementary information called Gemara). *Mishnah* means both instruction and repetition.

Age 15: Talmud and literature of the nation. For example, the Gemara was commentary on the Mishnah. (See ❷ 3.7 for a summary of rabbinical literature.)

In regard to the instruction of children, elementary school students were to know several basic pieces of information upon completing their education: The *Shema* (Heb.), the Hallel (Psalms 113–118), the creation story, and the essence of the Levitical Law (Leviticus 1–8). Students were typically given a scroll with these passages inscribed upon it. Also, during their course of study, students selected a personal text to memorize and study. The personal text usually began with the first letter of the student's name and ended with the last letter of the student's name.

Educational Process

> The Jewish teacher "was the servant of God and of the community, held in honour . . ."
> —William Barclay, *Educational Ideals in the Ancient World*, 46

The teacher was a moral and intellectual exemplar, and was expected to instill the same in his students. In fact, the most important qualification for a teacher was not his scholastic ability, but his moral fiber. Education was for Torah (intellectual) and Mitzvot (right conduct). They taught without pay, and hence they avoided a purely academic life since their financial means of support came from other sources. The only exception to this was teachers in the *beth hassepher*, elementary school.[21] Jewish tradition provides a distinctive insight into the role of the instructor:[22]

- His aim must be to keep children from all intercourse with that which is vicious.

- To suppress all feelings of bitterness, even bitterness at wrong done to the child's own parents.

- To punish all real wrongdoing.

- Never to prefer one child to another.

- He must rather show sin in its essential repulsiveness than try to threaten a child out of it by speaking of its consequences in this world, or in the world to come.

- He must never discourage the child.

- He must never promise and not perform, lest the child's mind become familiar with falsehood and the broken word.

- He must never lose patience but explain the matter over and over again, in order to make it plain.

- He must treat the child like a young heifer, whose burden is daily increased.

- In every case he must first try kindness, and only when kindness fails must he physically punish. Such punishment must never be oversevere; a teacher could be dismissed for too much severity.

- When punishment was given, it must be given with the strap, and not the rod.

- Teacher must be married and must be male.

- The teacher must have an even temperament.

- The teacher must not compromise his dignity, never joking or dining with students.

William Barclay comments, "Two basic facts must always be borne in mind about Jewish teaching. First, it was based entirely on *oral teaching*; and therefore it was conducted entirely by repetition. The word *mishnah* itself means both repetition and instruction, for they were one and the same thing."[23] Students literally sat at the feet of the instructor as a show of respect to him, e.g., Paul and Gamaliel (Acts 22:3). Instruction was provided through a variety of methods, all emphasizing the mastery of content and practice of the Law. For example, teachers provided instruction through oral discourse, repetition and memorization, reciting materials aloud, mnemonic aids, and mutual respect between teacher and student.

Eliezer Ebner identified four educational principles, primarily based on the Jewish adherence to Scripture:

- Unchanging nature and content of the curriculum
- Early indoctrination
- Torah studies as a lifelong pursuit
- Popular scope of education.[24]

Josephus emphasizes that instruction in the Jewish tradition was twofold, but highly integrated: Knowledge of the Law and Practice of the Law.[25] See ❧ 3.8 for text of Josephus *Against Apion* 2.18. The basic premise of instruction was that knowledge yields conviction which in turn yields action.

In Jewish education, memorization was crucial. Childhood was viewed as the most opportune time for students to commit to memory large bodies of information. The ideal Jewish student was often compared to a cistern that does not lose a single drop, and hence Josephus boasts of his ability to memorize materials as a boy.[26] Perhaps an exaggeration, but it was held that twelve learned rabbis could restore the Talmud verbatim.[27]

Voices

Two voices dominate the formation of Jewish education. The voice of the scribes in early Judaism and the voice of the rabbis in later Judaism shaped Jewish education at its inception.

Scribes

Scribes emerge near the close of the Old Testament, dominating the educational scene (Neh. 8:1-9; Jer. 8:8). Ezra is the paradigmatic scribe. "For Ezra had devoted himself to the study and observance of the Law of the LORD, and to teaching its decrees and laws in Israel" (Ezra 7:10). Ezra is portrayed as reading the Law to the assembly of God's people, providing commentary and further instruction to the text. However, this paradigm of instructor was advanced during the fourth century B.C. into a new group of instructors, the rabbis. The scribes were a transitional group, maintaining the traditions of Hebrew education while beginning to address a formative Jewish culture.

Pharisees/Rabbis

Jewish sects tended to be of either a political or religious nature, spanning the spectrum of social and cultural opinions. For example, in the political realm the Zealots and Sicarii were Jewish fanatics bent on the destruction of Rome, while the Herodians favored the Roman-established dynasty of Herod. However, among the religious sects the Pharisees exercised the most significant educational influence. How? The rabbis were Pharisees! Ben Sira, Simen ben Shetah, Joshua ben Gamala were all rabbis. The rabbinical teachers and literature previously mentioned were in fact products of the Pharisees.

FYI: The Pharisees are the only ancient Jewish sect still in existence today! Who are they? Rabbis.

The origins of the Pharisees can be traced to the *Hassadim*. Their name means "Pious ones," indicating the Pharisees' commitment to a strictly Jewish life, separate from the non-Jewish context in which many Jews lived throughout the Diaspora. They began as a social reform movement with religious motives during the 4th and 3rd centuries B.C., but were formally organized shortly after the Maccabean revolt, around 165–160 B.C. In the Apocrypha, 1 Maccabees 2:42 describes them as "mighty men in Israel . . . such as were devoted to the Law." They were instrumental in the struggle to free Israel from the Seleucids, a dominating foreign power committed to supplanting Greek culture into Israel, which resulted in the Maccabean revolt, which eventually expelled the Greeks from Palestine.

Women's Education

Did women have a voice in education? As previously mentioned, girls were excluded from formal education in the ancient Jewish community. For women, the educational opportunities afforded them during the Hebrew period were still available, but the educational advancements made in Judaism were not accessible.

Women were generally regarded as not deserving nor being capable of equal learning as men. Women were considered fit for domestic work but not academic life, and hence did not require formal education but rather parental education at home. The education of a girl was predominately provided through her mother, focusing on her future role as woman-wife-mother.

A woman was to support her husband in his study of the Torah. This was by no means a menial task, nor one that went unacknowledged. Rabbi Akiba told disciples, "All that I am, and all that you are, is owing to her . . ."[28] However, women were never a part of the formal Jewish educational system, though they indirectly could be instructed through cultural encounter and familial education. For example, perhaps the most well-known educated Jewish woman was Benuriah, the wife and daughter of rabbis. Her learning was so extensive that once she even had a scholarly point upheld by rabbis even though it opposed another scholar![29]

Excursus:

The Education of Jesus, Paul, and in the Early Christian Community

Education within Judaism provides the immediate backdrop for understanding education in the church of the first century A.D. It is easily forgotten that Jesus, his disciples, and the earliest Christian communities were in fact Jewish. We observe several points of intersection between the education within Judaism and the development of Christi-

> "Jesus . . . did not establish a school with a philosophical doctrine or special method of interpreting the law. His followers learned by observing what he said and did in different situations"
> —Pheme Perkins, *Jesus as Teacher*, 1

anity within the first century A.D. While this section will not provide a study of the New Testament foundations of education,[30] it will provide insights into how the earliest Christian education was influenced by and even benefited from its Jewish predecessor.

Jesus as Jewish Student and Teacher

Jesus was born, lived, and died a Jew. It may be difficult to conceive, but at one point the Son of God was a schoolboy. Education was so accessible within the Jewish community, even one as small as Galilee, that even the son of a Galilean carpenter could read and write. Jesus would have participated in the synagogue, as well as perhaps the *Beth Hassepher*. Jesus would have also been acculturated into Jewish society through socialization as he participated in the rituals and feasts of the Jewish community (Luke 2:21-30,46).

Jesus was primarily a teacher, as he is most frequently called in the Gospels.[31] Mark 10:1 best illustrates this when it states, "as it was his custom, he taught them." Jesus is portrayed in the Gospels as being an active participant in the synagogue (Matt. 4:23; 5:35; Mark 1:21; 6:2; Luke 4:15; 6:6; 13:10; John 6:59). However, while Jesus functioned as a teacher and was even referred to as "rabbi," Jesus did not conform to the teachers of his day. "When Jesus had finished saying these things, the crowds were amazed at his teaching, because he taught as one who had authority, *and not as their teachers of the law*" (Matt. 7:28-29). Jesus was different from the rabbinical traditions and teachers of his day. Several distinct differences are as follows.[32]

Rabbis of Ancient Judaism	Jesus in the Gospels
• Cited other rabbis as sources of authority	• Was His own authority
• Disciples chose rabbi as teachers	• Jesus chose His disciples
• Disciples were adherents to the rabbi's tradition	• Disciples were adherents to Jesus, not just a "tradition"
• Used repetition, recitation, and memorization as teaching tools	• Jesus did not teach in this way; He used parables, object lessons, etc.
• Taught in a fixed, usually indoor, locale	• Taught on various occasions in a variety of locales
• Disciples were servants of the rabbi	• Jesus served His disciples, calling them friends (John 15:14)
• Taught the details of ceremonies and rituals, and moral living	• Jesus taught on moral living, but in the absence of ceremonial or ritualistic observances
• Isolated from socially marginalized, e.g., women, prostitutes, tax collectors	• Jesus frequently associated with such people.

Rabbis	Jesus
• Disciples became rabbis upon completion of their studies	• Jesus told His disciples not to call themselves rabbi (Matt. 23:8)
• Traditions went beyond the demands of Scripture	• Jesus opposed many of these traditions, identifying them as hypocritical (Matt. 15:7, Mark 7:6)

Hence, Jesus was both the recipient and provider of instruction within the context of Judaism. However, he took instruction in a direction different from his contemporary rabbis.

Paul as Rabbi and Apostle

Just as with Jesus, Paul began his life as a Jew. But Paul was "more" than a Jew; he was a Pharisee. As he expressed, "I was advancing in Judaism beyond many Jews of my own age and was extremely zealous for the traditions of my fathers" (Gal. 1:14). He would have received education on all levels of Judaism, including higher education in the rabbinical academies. "I am a Jew, born in Tarsus of Cilicia, but brought up in this city. Under Gamaliel I was thoroughly trained in the law of our fathers and was just as zealous for God as any of you are today" (Acts 22:3). The intellect of Paul was partially the product of the Jewish educational system.

Paul likewise utilized the presence of the synagogue as a means of teaching others about the Christian faith. Acts 13:14-52 contains the discourse of Paul to a Jewish congregation wherein he identifies himself with the Jews (13:16,26) and continued synagogue participation (13:44). However, Paul provided instruction within the early Christian community not only through his teaching in the synagogues, which seems to have been customary for him (Acts 17:1-4), but also through his writings to the churches and public addresses. Paul, in essence, became a Christian-rabbi, providing instruction for the faith-community and contributing the most material to the New Testament.

Teachers in the Early Christian Community

As with Jesus and Paul, the early church was essentially Jewish, being comprised of converted Jews. Education in the early Christian community was far less formal than the schools of Judaism. It would have borne more similarity to the instructional practices of the synagogues. The early church had both an oral and written tradition. It utilized the Old Testament as Scripture for both Jew and Gentile alike, but it also was dependent for most of the first century on the oral traditions of the Apostles.

Teaching was considered part of the primary mission of the church and a task not to be taken lightly. "Not many of you should presume to be teachers, my brothers, because you know that we who teach will be judged more strictly" (Jas. 3:1). The ability to teach was not simply seen as an essential for pastoral leadership in the early church (1 Tim. 3:2, Titus 1:9), but as an essential for the preservation of the faith (2 Tim. 2:1-2). The context of instruction was informal during the first century A.D., and the content more practically oriented toward Christian living, centered on the life and teachings of Jesus and his apostles.

Conclusion

Judaism is still present over two millennia after its beginning. *How? Why?* The Jewish community through the centuries has made a significant investment in the establishment of educational systems to maintain the distinctiveness of its faith and life. The addition of the synagogue and formal schools to the traditions and practices of Hebrew education formed a very resilient system of instruction. When you drive by a synagogue in your community, or see one in the media, realize you are looking at an institution of worship and instruction that began at the close of the Old Testament, over 2400 years ago.

What Can We Learn from Ancient Jewish Education?

- It provides the immediate background of New Testament education.

- It allows us to postulate the early years of Jesus' life, those not covered in the Gospels, at least in regard to his education.

- Jewish education emphasized and reminds us of the value of memorization.

- It provides us an example of faith-learning integration, with a curriculum that is Bible-centered but with subjects taught in relation to it.

- Jewish education emphasizes the value of higher education in theological studies, such as was the case with rabbis and Paul.
- It reminds us of the necessity of multiple levels of formal education for sequential instruction.
- It demonstrates a Bible-centered model of instruction with emphasis on the teacher's relationship with the student.
- Jewish education highlighted the paramount importance of the teacher's knowledge and moral character.

Study Helps

Reflection Questions

1. How did your educational experience compare to that of a Jewish child?

2. Does formal education mean parents are unnecessary in the educational process?

3. How much of the Bible have you memorized? Is this adequate? What would be the value in memorizing more?

4. How has your experience in higher education prepared you for ministry? How does it compare to what Paul experienced in rabbinical academy?

5. As you look at your life, how would you evaluate your knowledge and moral character on a scale from 1-5? What are some steps to growth and improvement?

6. If the Jews had not developed such a comprehensive system of education, how might the history of the New Testament have been changed? Just speculate!

Technical Terms

Aggadah   A collection of Jewish legends.

Apocrypha   Extracanonical Jewish writings produced between 200 B.C.–A.D.250, not produced by the rabbis nor acknowledged as canonical.

Beth ha-Midrash   Jewish secondary school, but the term also denoted advanced rabbinical studies.

Beth Hassepher   Jewish elementary school, typically for ages 5-9.

Chazzan   Synagogue attendant, usually the elementary teacher in a small town.

Diaspora   A term denoting the location of all Jews living outside of Palestine. In ancient times it generally referred to the Mediterranean world and Persia.

Gemara   Heb. for *completion*, commentary on Mishnah.

Hallakkah   Jewish summations and applications of the oral law, which was commentary on Torah.

Hassadim   Heb. for *pious ones*, term thought to refer to a group that evolved into the Pharisees

Judaizers   Jewish-Christian legalists. They advocated the continued adherence to Jewish tradition even after converting to Christianity. They were Paul's adversaries at Galatia.

Maccabean Revolt   Jewish revolt against Seleucid (Greek) rule in Palestine between 167–160 B.C. Its name is derived from the Maccabeus family which began the revolt.

Mishnah   Heb. for *repetition* or *instruction*, it was also a collection of legal commentary on the Torah.

Mitzvot   Term denoting moral conduct, expected of elementary school teachers.

Pharisees   Sect of the Jews originating in the 2nd century B.C. It was comprised of rabbis who advocated strict adherence to the Torah *and* oral law, a collection of interpretations and applications of the Torah.

Sadducees   Sect of the Jews comprised of aristocratic members of the Jerusalem community. They held to only the Torah, regarding the rest of the Old Testament as being less authoritative. They served almost entirely in the Temple.

Sanhedrin   Ruling religious body in Judah/Judea. It oversaw the formation of the Jewish educational system, particularly during the second formative period.

Septuagint   Greek translation of the Hebrew Bible completed in Alexandria, Egypt, around 250 B.C. Most popular translation of the Hebrew Bible.

Sopharim   Heb. for *scribe,* leading educators at the beginning of the Jewish period.

Synagogue   "House of Assembly," primary location for worship and instruction beginning in the 3rd century B.C. It was responsible for adult education as well as usually housing the *Beth Hassepher.*

Talmud   Major body of Jewish literature codifying the oral traditions of the rabbis, contains the *Mishnah* and *Gemara.*

Tannaitic   Third formative period of ancient Jewish education, A.D. 10–220.

Zugot   Heb. for *pairs,* second formative period of ancient Jewish education, 200 B.C.–A.D. 10.

Recommended Bibliography

Barclay, William. *Educational Ideals in the Ancient World*. Grand Rapids: Baker, 1959.

Drazin, Nathan. *History of Jewish Education from 515 BCE to 220 CE*. Baltimore: Johns Hopkins, 1940.

Ebner, Eliezer. *Elementary Education in Ancient Israel during the Tannaitic Period (10–220 CE)*. New York: Bloch, 1956.

Perkins, Pheme. *Jesus as Teacher*. New York: Cambridge University Press, 1990.

Zuck, Roy B. *Teaching as Jesus Taught*. Grand Rapids: Baker, 1995.

_____. *Teaching as Paul Taught*. Grand Rapids: Baker, 1998.

Notes

[1] Alfred Edersheim, *Sketches of Jewish Social Life* (Grand Rapids: Eerdmans, 1950), 125–126.

[2] Aaron Demsky, "Education (Jewish)," *Jewish Encyclopedia*, 385.

[3] Ernest Simon, "Hebrew Education in Palestine," *Journal of Educational Psychology* 22.3 (1948): 190.

[4] Philo *Life of Moses* 3.27.

[5] Nathan Drazin, *History of Jewish Education from 515 BCE to 220 CE* (Baltimore: Johns Hopkins, 1940), 15–23.

[6] Eliezer Ebner, *Elementary Education in Ancient Israel during the Tannaitic Periods (10–220 CE)* (New York: Bloch, 1956), 17.

[7] Josephus *Against Apion* 2.17-18; Philo *Life of Moses* 3.27.

[8] E.B. Castle, *Ancient Education and Today* (Baltimore: Penguin Books, 1961), 166.

[9] Azriel Eisberg, *The Synagogue through the Ages* (New York: Bloch, 1974), 41.

[10] Drazin, *History*, 32.

[11] *Kethubot* 8; *Ecclesiasticus* 39.1-3, 51.28-30.

[12] *Baba Bathra* 121a.

[13] *2 Maccabees* 4.12-13.

[14] Ebner, *Elementary*, 43.

[15] *Jes. Meg.* 73b.

[16] S. Schoeman, "Early Hebrew Education and Its Significance for Present-Day Educational Theory and Practice," *Hervormde teologiese studies* 53 (1997): 419.

[17] Donald E. Gowan, *Bridge between the Testaments* (Allison Park, PA: Pickwick Publications, 1986), 235.

[18] William Barclay, *Educational Ideals in the Ancient World* (Grand Rapids: Baker, 1959), 13.

[19] Josephus *Against Apion* 1.8, 12; 2.18, 25, 26.

[20] Barclay, *Educational Ideals*, 34.

[21] Ebner, *Elementary*, 54.

[22] Barclay, *Educational Ideals*, 43-44; Edersheim, *Sketches*, 135-136.

[23] Barclay, *Educational Ideals*, 39.

[24] Ebner, *Elementary*, 20.

[25] Josephus *Against Apion* 2.18.

[26] Josephus *Life* 2.

[27] Barclay, *Educational Ideals*, 40.

[28] Linda Cannell, *Summary of Historical Periods for DES936* (Deerfield, IL: Trinity Evangelical Divinity School, Spring 2000).

[29] Gowan, *Bridge*, 236.

[30] See James Estep, "Biblical-Theological Foundations of Christian Education," *Foundations for Christian Education*, ed. by Eleanor A. Daniel and John W. Wade (Joplin, MO: College Press, 1999), 13-33; and, "Biblical Foundations of Christian Education," *Evangelical Dictionary of Christian Education* (Grand Rapids: Baker, 2001), 82-85, for a survey of the biblical foundations of Christian education.

[31] Five Greek terms *didaskalos* (4x), *rabbi* (14x), *epistates* (7x), *rabboni* (2x), and *kathegetes* (1x). See Roy Zuck, *Teaching as Jesus Taught* (Grand Rapids: Baker, 1990), 25, for the most extensive treatment of the terms describing Jesus as teacher.

[32] Adapted from Zuck, *Teaching*, 40-41.

Chapter 4

It's All Greek to Me!
Education in Greek Culture

James Riley Estep, Jr.

Of all the cultures that have contributed to the formation of Western culture, it is the Greek civilization that has had the most evident influence. The reason for this is not only due to their contributions to philosophy, science, architecture, or literature, but for their *schools*. The formation of the first Western educational system provided for the preservation and advancement of the Greek culture, even into the 21st century. As with other cultures, the educational system of the Greeks developed with each successive stage of cultural complexity, from familial instruction to the formation of a multitiered system of education; but this pattern is strikingly similar to what is experienced throughout the world today. *What was Greek education like? How did it impact Christian education, both in its formative years and now?*

Overview of Period

Paidia, Greek for *education*, was a concern of Greek culture throughout its long history. Education was directly tied to the social structures of each period of Greek history. Stated simply, a *good* man was a *good* citizen requiring a *good* education to acculturate individuals to the Greek way of life. For example, the city-state was the center of culture, each one with its own definition of a *good* citizen, and each with its own "safeguards of conduct" through law, customs, con-

> **FYI:** *City-state* refers to a period in ancient Greece when cities, and their surrounding regions, had their own culture, laws, and education. It was a time when cities functioned like countries.

cepts of patriotism, family honor, literature, and ideologies.[1] All of these required education as a means of acculturating individuals to the ideals of the city-state.

This chapter will look at three periods of development in the history of Greek education:

Early Greek, corresponding to the rise of the city-states during the Homeric period (8th–6th century B.C.)

Classical, corresponding to the Golden age of Greece in Athens, with attention also given to Athens' rival, Sparta (6th–4th centuries B.C.)

Hellenistic, corresponding to the time of Alexander the Great through the advent of the Roman Empire, where the cultures of Greece and Rome are fused into a Greco-Roman education (4th–1st centuries B.C.)

One note of caution must be raised at the outset. We are accustomed to a very unified, structured system of education. For most of us schooling was a very standard, sequential series of grades, courses, levels, and institutions. By default, we typically want to impose these assumptions upon the educational systems of both Greece and Rome. However, as convenient or as desirable as this may be, we *cannot* readily do this. The Greek system of education was not as structured, and hence it is difficult to make blanket statements respecting its practices.

One general comment should be made regarding the presence of formal education in ancient Greece, and that is it was almost entirely aristocratic, designed for the elite of the culture. With little exception, education was not accessible to the city's populace. Hence, the educational agenda was highly influenced by the cultural elite. The only exception to this was in Sparta, where education was state-sponsored for every child, but as you will see, the education in Sparta was quite different from what was experienced in Athens.

Early Greek Education

Purpose of Education

The Homeric era in Greek culture was dominated by one central figure: Heroes. The *Iliad* and the *Odyssey* contain portraits of heroic men who assume the role of leader within the city-state. Heroes had *areté* (Gk.), literally meaning *virtue*, but more substantially honor or character. Education in early Greece sought to develop men of character and virtue for a life of service to the city-state. This required training in military, character, the arts, and religion were all designed to develop the knight-hero image. In short, education was to foster heroic ambition and character.

Context of Education

Two classes existed in early Greek culture, peasants and noblemen, each with their own system of education. For both classes, instruction was provided in the home with no books or schools, and generally taught by both parents. The children of peasants were instructed through the home, father's job and farming, and household duties. Aristocratic education, while taught in the home, had a different curriculum, since they were to embrace the hero-image, e.g., Odysseus or Achilles. Hence, the young nobleman was trained to be a warrior and speaker, athlete, musician, and huntsman.

Content of Education

Homeric education was very practical, totally tied to the social needs of the city-state. The literature of Homer (*Iliad* and *Odyssey*) became the student's textbook for grammar, literature, and history. (Homer's writings eventually became the basis of later Athenian literature in the 5th century B.C.)

> Greek heroes "never spent a day in school. Their mathematical knowledge probably stopped short at counting; it is unlikely that they could understand any language but their own; they could not read or write." —Robin Barrow, *Greek and Roman Education*, 14

Through Homer, boys were introduced to the Greek heroes (e.g., Achilles, Agamemnon, Odysseus) and taught to emulate their lifestyle. The tradition of Homeric literature continued throughout the entire history of Greek education. For example, Alexander the Great, 400 years after the Homeric era, carried a copy of the *Iliad* and *Odyssey* with him on his campaigns against Persia. Similarly, Nicoratus said, "My father, wishing me to become an accomplished man made me learn the whole of Homer, so that even today I can still recite the *Iliad* and the *Odyssey* by heart."[2] Such devotion was reflective of the early Greek's commitment to Homer.

Process of Education

During this period, learning was not formalized. Instruction was given in the home, through parents, relatives, or the *paidagogos*. Instruction was provided by the imitation of characters in heroic literature, e.g., *Iliad* and the *Odyssey* (c. 850 B.C.). Symposiums in poetry, as well as festivals and instructions in the law, also provided a means of instruction.[3]

Voices

Plato called Homer "the educator of Greece."[4] As previously noted, Homer (8th century B.C.) was *the* author of heroic literature for early Greece (🕐 4.1). However, Homer was *not* an educator in the technical sense of the word. He presented no new approach to education, nor did he even provide an outline of a curriculum of study. "In what way, then, is Homer the teacher of Greece? The answer is simple: He is a poet; and the Greeks believed that poets were the primary teachers of mankind" and he provided "a mirror" of past, present, and "what they aspire to be."[5] Homer is a voice for education in that he was *the* dominant figure in the history of early Greece.

Classical Greek Education

Purpose of Education

Education during the classical period was an outgrowth of themes in early Greek culture and education. The two themes, militaristic and what might be called liberal arts education, are represented in the two dominant city-states of the period, Sparta and Athens (respectively).

Education in Sparta "The most evident characteristic of Spartan education is the complete submergence of individuality in a system where the state possessed the child, body and soul."[6] For the Spartans, a good warrior was a good citizen. (🕐 4.2). Barrow comments that "there is a striking similarity between Sparta and modern totalitarian states."[7] Education was militaristic, designed to produce the perfect warrior. In fact, Aristotle, the Athenian philosopher, maintained that Spartan education made boys into *thēriodēs* (Gk.), wild beasts.[8]

> "Come back with your shield, or on it."
> —Spartan Proverb

Education was designed to advance the *city*, and hence was not concerned with instruction for the benefit of the *individual*, but instruction to benefit the *polis* (Greek *city*, for example Indiana*polis*). The two basic attributes to be instilled in a child were obedience and physical prowess.

Education in Athens While the Athenians did provide for military training, their primary educational aim was to produce *kaloskagatos* (Gk. *good* or *fine*), meaning a gentleman or cultured citizen. Hence, education was for the benefit of the individual, which would in turn benefit the city-state.

Education was based on the "democratization" of culture, rather than Spartan totalitarianism, and hence was born the notion of liberal education, available to anyone who could afford it. This system gave rise to elitist education, wherein only the aristocracy could financially provide for an education, and hence perpetuated its place in the life of the city. Athens is the first city-state in Greece to establish permanent philosophical and rhetorical schools, areas that were of no concern for neighboring Sparta.

Context of Education

Education in Sparta The education of Spartan children was an outgrowth of the militaristic theme in Early Greek education.[9] The education one received was determined by caste. The Spartan caste system had three levels: Military, Civilian or Commercial class, and Slave. Education was primarily designed for the military caste. Caste level was determined at infancy, with physical perfection as the criteria. The newborn was bathed in strong wine, and if weak, it would die. The child was later examined by the father and city leaders for deformity or weakness. If any were found, the child was thrown to its death into *Kaiada*, a chasm on Mount Taygetos.

> "The education of a Spartan child began before he was born."
> —William Barclay,
> *Educational Ideals of the Ancient World*, 60

For most Spartan children, education was a childhood *boot camp*. From ages 7-18 he would receive extensive military training, with active service beginning around the age of 20-30. At 30 he would take a wife for the purpose of bearing new children for the city-state.

Education in Athens The contexts of education in Athens were comprised of (1) preschool tutoring, (2) elementary education provided by three different schools (music, grammar, and physical education), and (3) higher education, consisting of rhetorical or philosophical studies. Since education was primarily aristocratic and not intended for the masses, large public facilities and educational systems were not necessary. However, during the Hellenistic era the contexts were more formalized, and a secondary education was introduced between elementary and higher education (❋ 4.3 for Summary of Educational Contexts). During the classical period, educational opportunities for boys advanced, but for girls it remained stagnant with no advances in educational opportunity. *Preschool instruction* was provided not only by the parents, but by a trusted and somewhat educated household slave, a *paidagogos*. The use of a *paidagogos* was probably an educational practice retained from private individual tutors in earlier history.[10] Boys prior to age seven were tutored by a *paidagogos*, but after age seven the *paidagogos* was responsible for guiding the boy between home and school and other schools. The presence of the *paidagogos* is the one consistent feature in ancient Greek education, and even adopted by the Romans.

Elementary Education began during the sixth–fifth centuries B.C. Three different types of elementary schools developed in ancient Athens, each with its own teacher and location:

- *Grammatist*—reading, writing, and letters
- *Kitharistes*—music, poetry, and literature
- *Paedeotribe*—physical education, gymnastics, and athletics

Later, the former two merged into one type of school, leading to a curriculum of liberal arts studies. Students would travel between the teachers and schools through the day, with the aid of their *paidagogos*. The school day generally began at sunrise and continued to late afternoon. Students attended school year round, except for festivals and some other appointed times of the year.

Elementary education, particularly physical education, occurred at the *palestra* (from Greek *pale* for "wrestle") and music schools. Some music schools may have been located in the gymnasium, the site of higher education. The *palaestra* was usually a privately funded institution for elementary physical education, taught by the *paideotribe*, a general trainer. The gymnasium (⊛ 4.4) continued their physical training, for older boys and adults, but was taught by a *gymnastes*, special trainer, and typically state-funded and controlled. Schools were generally clustered around these facilities to aid in the travel between them and to assemble the instructors in one area of the city, forming an informal campus arrangement.

Higher Education, during the early classical period, was most commonly available through the *Ephebeia*, a compulsory military and general higher education for 18-20-year-old members of the aristocracy. It was designed to pre-

> Students in the *Ephebeia* spent one year in the army and one year on the frontier.

pare men for civic and military duties. The more academic pursuits in higher education, such as philosophy and rhetoric, became more desirable later. Academic higher education was provided by Sophists and by teachers of philosophy or rhetoric.

The Sophists, named from the Greek *sophos* meaning *wise*, were the "first teachers of advanced education" in Greece.[11] The Sophists became popular between 470–370 B.C., paralleling a time of economic and commercial expansion. They were not philosophers or scientists, but professional teachers of rhetoric. They specialized in grammar, logic, and rhetoric as a means of achieving political and economic power within the city and frequently argued against the notion of character development. They tended to promote personal and political advancement over the corporate interests of the city, an approach contrary to the very notion of education in Homeric times and even within the *Ephebeia*.

"Not all the sophists were truly as wise as their collective name implies; some were charlatans who were convincing salesmen of shallow ideas."[12] Indeed, the Sophists were professional educa-

> "The permanent schools of Plato and Isocrates mark the beginning of continuous secondary education in Athens."
> —Cole, *Studies in the History of Education*, 41

tors, and as professionals, they were indeed for hire. Fees for instruction ranged from 300–10,000 drachmas, with the most noted Sophist, Protagoras, having been the most expensive.

What was the alternative to the Sophists? While they did indeed have a virtual monopoly on education in ancient

Athens and all of Greece, another class of educator arose: Philosophers. Socrates opposed the Sophists, even to the point of his death in 399 B.C. Plato established his *Academy* (c. 390 B.C.) and Aristotle his *Lyceum* (c. 335 B.C.) as alternatives in philosophical inquiry and rigorous study. (❧ See 4.5 for the selections from Raphael's painting, "The School of Athens" depicting Plato and Aristotle in discourse, surrounded by other philosophers). Isocrates established his rhetorical school in Athens in 390 B.C., but he did not associate his teaching with the Sophists because he considered the Sophists undependable and opportunistic.

The main problem with education in classical Athens was that state-funded, public education was never achieved due to the aristocratic nature of the Greek city-state. Even during the Hellenistic period, when it was ideologically more acceptable, an administrative structure was never developed to provide public education. A city "had neither the resources nor the administrative apparatus that would have enabled it to take direct charge of public education."[13] Hence, education was not city-sponsored for the populace of the city; *it was privatized*, and hence it was economically restricted for the less affluent.

Content of Education

The content of education differed sharply between Sparta and Athens, with the latter having a more comprehensive scope. For example, Paul Monroe speaks of the historical, philosophical, and scientific view of the curriculum in ancient Greece, each with proponents.[14] The education of Athens impacted the content of the world's educational system even today. For the most part, we still study what the Athenian students did over 2300 years ago.

FYI: When a dorm room is barren of any kind of comforts and is fit only for basic living arrangements, it is frequently called a *Spartan* environment!

Education in Sparta As should be assumed, the content of education in Sparta differed significantly from that of Athens. Spartan education focused on the training and equipping of an army. Physical fitness, weaponry, fighting tactics, and survival skills training were all routine. While Spartan educators generally disapproved of reading, writing, and music in the curriculum, it was studied as an essential for leadership and the installation of patriotism. For example, the Laws of Lycurgus (9th century B.C.) were studied to advance loyalty to the state, and the writings of Homer were chanted in Doric measure to recount the heroic character of its warriors. Girls were taught to wrestle, run, throw the javelin, dance naked, and perform a processional walk (❸ 4.6). This was not only for their personal benefit, but to insure that babies would be born healthy and raised accordingly.

Education in Athens Each of the three schools of elementary education had its own curriculum. (See ❸ 4.7 Content of Classical and Hellenistic Education.) The *paideotribes* (physical education) taught sports, running, long jump, discus, javelin, wrestling, boxing, gymnastics, *pancratium* (combination of boxing and wrestling), hygiene, and care. The *kitharistes* (music) taught drawing and music, typically the seven-string lyre, singing, and dance. The *grammatistes* or *grammatodidaskalos* (Gk. literally "teacher of writing") taught reading, alphabet, syllables, words, texts (anthologies), recitation, writing, counting. Since literacy was in elementary education, "the test of education was therefore not literacy, which was taken for granted, but ability to play the lyre."[15]

Higher Education in Athens differed sharply between the Sophists and their opponents. Sophists, as previously noted, were "fundamental utilitarians," providing instruction only for practical application and political advancement, nothing more.[16] Sophists taught the art of rhetoric and dialectics simply as skills for personal, political, and economic gain; for example, oratory skills could win an argument or influence a judge in a legal case.

Opposing the Sophists, the philosophers (e.g., Plato and Aristotle) focused on less "practical" exercises and taught philosophy and some of the liberal arts, e.g., math.[17] Additionally, Isocrates, while a rhetorician, did not teach as the Sophists. Rather he valued a combined education between the academic emphasis of the philosophers and the study of rhetoric for the public, not personal, welfare. Hence, he provided an alternative school of rhetorical training.

Process of Education

Education in Sparta Students in Sparta were divided into three groups: "little boys" (ages 7-11), "adolescents" (ages 12-15), and "adults" (16-20). With each of these stages instruction was provided differently (● 4.8: Spartan Male Educational Process). Opposite the attitude of Athens, Spartans could not conceive of consigning the responsibility of education to a slave or placing it upon the parents, the father particularly. Prior to age seven, parents were assigned instructional duties. At age seven, when the child officially became property of the city-state, the *paidomonos* was the principal of education, responsible for managing disciplinarians to supply discipline to children. However, he was not the boy's sole instructor. The *paidomonos* had two aides. The *bouagor* was a troop leader, someone from the boy's own class, an advancing or promising student of 7-11 years old. Also,

> Of the 81 Olympic victories achieved between 220 and 576 B.C., 46 of them were by Spartans (over 56%) and in the stadium race, 21 of the 36 victors were Spartan.
> —William Barclay, *Educational Ideals of the Ancient World*, 68.

the *eirenes* (19-20-year-old senior student) aided the *paidomonos* with the adolescent children (12-15 years old).

The process of education could best be described as a boot camp, since that is exactly what it was. It was characterized by a barracks life, with rigid discipline and treatment. For example, students were trained to survive in the wilderness. They were given no shoes, one garment, were expected to sleep in the open (even in inclement weather or winter), and work bare-handed, without the aid of tools.

Education in Athens From the simplicity and rigor of Spartan education, the Athenian system of instruction was indeed more complex and sophisticated. As previously noted the primary instructor of children, in addition to the parents, was the *paidagogos*, the household slave who tutored the child before age seven and then escorted the child to school. It should be noted that eventually the *paidagogos* system failed due to poor selection.

Following the instruction of the *paidagogos*, the child became part of an elaborate set of instructors, one for each of the institutions and curricula previously mentioned. The most basic term for teacher was *didaskalos*, however, each instructor bore a title relative to his subject, such as the *paidotribes* (physical education teacher), the *kitharistes* (music or lyre teacher, see ● 4.9 and ● 4.10), or the *grammatistes* or *grammatodidaskalos* (the elementary teacher, school-master, literally "one who teaches letters" see ❀ 4.11, note the chart). The primary model of instruction used by the elementary teacher was memorization and recitation, as well as simple writing exercises to improve skills, similar to any elementary school today. Plato viewed the use of games as beneficial with children, but abandoned them for advanced studies.[18]

The most significant instructional method introduced by the Greeks was the *Socratic Method*, so named from its originator, Socrates. Rather than lecture, he advocated a dialectical method of discourse using questions to bring focus and direction. A topic was raised, student opinion was sought (as a means of assessing the students' current understanding of the subject), and then questions were posed to further shape and define their concepts. Socrates used two types of questions:

- *Ironic*, intended to loosen or destroy the student's present conception of topic. Learning is seen as a constructive confusion.
- *Maieutic* (Greek lit. "to give birth"), intended to facilitate the synthesis of a new, more comprehensive or complete thought.

This method of instruction, which was regarded as radical for its time, is now a common assumption in education, particularly higher education. In regard to rhetorical training, Isocrates advanced the methodologies of the Sophists. He trained students through rhetorical exercises, analysis of speeches, practice delivery of speeches (some scheduled and others improvisation), and delivering public orations with review.

Voices

Education in Sparta: Xenophon (428–354 B.C.) was a friend and student of Socrates (❀ 4.12). He authored *The Lacedeamonian Constitution*, outlining much of what we know of Spartan education. He had primary knowledge of the Spartan system of education since he not only had lived among them, but had two sons educated by the Spartans. He also authored *Cyropaeda* on the education of Persian king Cyrus. A work of historical fiction, it was in fact a rebuttal of Athenian education and affirmation of the militaristic Spartan model of education.

Education in Athens: The educational voices of Athens were many and diverse, including Sophists, philosophers, and more serious orators.

The Sophists are primarily known through Plato's critique of them, which was designed to avenge the death of his mentor Socrates in 399 B.C. The leading Sophists were Protagoras of Abdera (c. 490–420 B.C.), Prodicus of Ceos, Gorgias of Leontini (483–375 B.C.), and Hippias of Elis. While the Sophists deserve historical recognition as the first providers of higher education in classical Athens, "Their ideas were too heterogeneous, too vague and fleeting for them to belong to any school, in the philosophical sense," with the profession of teaching being their only common link.[19] Hence, their influence on education is limited to those who reacted to them.

Socrates (469–399 B.C.) was eccentric in behavior, dress, and thought (● 4.13). He had been a soldier in the Peloponnesian War between Athens and Sparta in 431 B.C. He was a teacher who dared to ask "Why?" of everything and everyone, including religious, political, academic, and military authorities, who were not used to being questioned. "Socrates was the first great teacher in history because he sought truth for the improvement of moral character by his questioning of all sides of an argument and refusal to accept easy answers and traditional slogans."[20]

> "The trial started almost 2380 years ago and continues to engulf Western civilization to the present hour. . . . in over two millennia educators have still not been able to resolve the issues grappled with at the trial of Socrates."
> —Gangel and Benson, *Christian Education: Its History and Philosophy,* 33

His intellectual pursuits put him in opposition to the Sophists, the established educational order of his day. As Hibler concluded, "Sophists bragged about their wisdom, while Socrates claimed ignorance on every subject."[21] His main message: *gnosthi seauton* (Gk. "Know thyself"). Others have likewise provided insights into his wit and commitment to education by recording the words of Socrates on education:

- "It is better late than never with learning."[22]

- "There is only one good and that is knowledge; there is only one evil and that is ignorance."[23]

- When asked if the King of Persia was happy, Socrates replied, "That is an impossible question to answer unless we know what kind of an education he has received."[24]

- "Bad education and bad friends." "Uneducated people are like strangers in a town, they lose their way in the streets." Also, "A person without education has no shape to his character."[25]

We know nothing of Socrates from his own hand, since, ironically, Socrates was against the written alphabet. He held that the ability to write would oppose the age old tradition of memorization. Hence, he was against the educational technology of his day. We do know of him from his student Plato, who wrote three discourses on the trial and death of Socrates: *Apology*, *Crito*, and *Phaedo*.

Plato's (427–347 B.C.) real name was Aristocles, but he assumed the name Plato (Gk. *the broad*), probably because of the comprehensive nature of his philosophy[26] (❧ 4.14). He was a student of Socrates, and hence opposed the Sophists. He was not only the father of idealism, but the author of two volumes containing his educational theory: *Laws* and *The Republic*. In these volumes he outlines the educational foundation of a Utopian society (❧ 4.15 for a sample of his educational writings).

Plato considered the ideal society to have three classes: intellectual elite or "Philosopher-Kings," military defenders, and providers-workers. One's class was determined by one's education. He advocated a state-sponsored educational system for all children (parallel for boys and girls, but not co-ed). His educational agenda was as follows:

- Prior to age 6, state-sponsored nurseries
- Ages 6-18—formal education and gymnasium
- Ages 18-20—physical education and military training
- Age 20—students showing intellectual promise, the future philosopher-kings, are chosen
- Age 30—The group of "philosopher-kings" is divided into two subclasses: *less* capable, for civil service, and *more* capable return for further study in metaphysics and dialectics
- Age 35—The philosopher-kings begin their rule
- Age 50—The philosopher-kings "retire" to the role of elder-statesmen

The state-sponsored educational system he envisioned never did become a reality, but the thought of it did indeed foster ideas throughout the subsequent centuries.

Aristotle (384–322 B.C.) was the student of Plato, father of realism (which is the philosophic basis of science), and the tutor of Alexander the Great (❦ 4.16). Rather than knowledge being gained through philosophical speculation and contemplation, as Plato advocated, Aristotle argued that knowledge is *outside* the person, rather than just inside the mind, and hence is knowable through the senses. For Aristotle, the study of nature is the source of knowledge, and a philosophical rationale for science as the study of nature is provided.

Aristotle presents his educational theory in his *Politics* and *Ethics* (❦ 4.17 for a sample of his educational writings), wherein he outlines four stages of educational endeavor:

- *Infant*—play, stories, and physical activity
- *Ages 7-14*—moral and physical education, music, reading, writing, develop good study habits
- *Ages 15-21*—intellectual development (math, grammar, literature, poetry, rhetoric, ethics, and politics)
- *Age 21 +*—physics, cosmology, ethics, psychology, and philosophy (sciences)

Isocrates (436–338 B.C.) was the most influential Greek theorist on Roman education, since his educational theory was designed to promote rhetoric, which was the goal of the lead Roman educators Cicero and Quintilian (❦ 4.18).[27] Marrou describes Plato and Isocrates as the "two columns of the temple."[28] Isocrates was a contemporary of Plato, but not a rival. Though he found Plato unrealistic, Isocrates still valued the form and substance of education. He was an advocate of secondary education, the advanced study of literature, math, debate/dialogue, and rhetoric.

His rhetorical approach to higher education was similar to the Sophist's, advocating rhetoric and political objectives as the goal of education, but opposing opportunism. He wrote *Against the Sophists* as a means of presenting the formal study of rhetoric in a positive, ethical light. He believed rhetoric was the key to social change and political advancement, hence like Sophists, but that it required higher moral and intellectual training, like Plato. Isocrates believed education was for the aristocracy; however, he did not see it as a means for profit, but for the benefit of the city.

Hellenistic Education

Purpose of Education

Following the conquests of Alexander the Great (❀ 4.19) the process of introducing Greek culture into Asia Minor, Palestine, Egypt, and Persia became the task of Greek education. In effect, it was an *extension* of classical education into broader context, a *global* context. Hence the process of changing the culture of the Mediterranean world into a Greek culture, Hellenization, became the aim of Greek education. This required further development of a more formal system of education, which did in fact reach fruition prior to the Roman occupation of Greece and its eastern territories.

Context of Education

During the Hellenistic era, education became more structured and formalized. It advanced from a two-tiered system (Elementary and Higher Education) to a three-tiered system of Elementary, Secondary, and Higher education (❀ 4.3 for Summary of Educational Contexts). Students started elementary school at age seven and completed it by ages 11-14, they entered secondary education and completed it by age seventeen, and attended higher education between 18-20 years of age. Hence, during the Hellenistic period there developed three levels of grammar instructors: Gramatist (elementary), Grammaticus (secondary), and Rhetor (higher education).

Several changes occurred from education in classical Athens. The elementary schools replaced the gymnasium as the location of education in the Hellenistic period, especially in Ptolemaic Egypt, with the emphasis on education turning from the physical toward the academic. Girls were permitted to enter the *palestra* and gymnasium for elementary and secondary instruction, but this was a rarity. Participation in the *Ephebeia* during the classical period declined due to the emphasis on intellectual development that subordinated physical training to a lesser role. The service requirement was first reduced to one year, but was eventually made optional. The first permanent schools established by Plato, Aristotle, and Isocrates during the 4th century B.C. removed the Sophist's monopoly on education, who were eventually no longer highly regarded as educators in Greece.

Higher education in the Hellenistic period diverged into three directions: (1) Teaching of Liberal Arts (grammar, rhetoric, mathematics, and music), (2) Teaching of Philosophy, and (3) Professional education, e.g., law or medicine.[29] Centers of Greek higher education were established throughout the Mediterranean world. Athens, Pergamum, and Rhodes were recognized for their philosophical schools. Cos, Pergamum, and Ephesus were known for medicine, and Smyrna for law. However, Alexandria (Egypt) was the educational crown of the ancient world. "Athens was superseded in importance by Alexandria."[30] The Ptolemys, the ruling family of Egypt during the Hellenistic period, established centers of Greek culture, museums, and the great library of Alexandria (4.20). In fact, the library of Alexandria was famous throughout the Mediterranean world for its scientific studies. It served as a forerunner to the concept of a university and included not only a 120,000 volume library, but botanical and zoological facilities.

Content of Education

Hellenistic education experienced an expansion of knowledge unparalleled in the ancient world. As previously noted, this expansion called for an entirely new tier of study, secondary education. While elementary education and higher education remained relatively the same, secondary education focused on literature, philology, reading and reciting, explanation, moral implications, grammar and composition, math, arithmetic, and geometry, music as applied mathematics, science (astronomy, but science declined in the curriculum). See 4.7 Content of Classical and Hellenistic Education. With the formalization of the content into a liberal arts curriculum it formed the basis for what the Romans would call *humanitas*, the humanities, and the Medieval educators would call the *trivium* (grammar, rhetoric, dialectic) and the *quadrivium* (geometry, arithmetic, music theory, and science), known to us today as the seven liberal arts.

Influence of Greek Education on the New Testament

Paul seems to have had the greatest degree of encounter with Greek education, particularly as reflected in the Corinthian correspondence. Paul, as a citizen of Tarsus, would have had access to Greek education, and would have been aware of its influence on culture firsthand. Paul's fundamental assumption was that people in the church could read, even the Gentiles who had no access to the schools of Judaism. Also, "The basic significance of education as a cultural boundary-marker is clearly registered by Paul"; for example, his division of Greek and barbarian in Romans 1:14 was typical of the educational division of his day.[31]

The New Testament makes use of Greek educational terms, but without the specific educational definitions. For example, *paidia* (Gk. *education*) in Hebrews 12:5-7 is used in a parental sense, as it also is in Ephesians 6:4, not in a formal educational sense. *Gymnasia* is used in 1 Timothy 4:8 for physical training and in 2 Peter 2:14 for guides, alluding to the discipline of physical education. Most significantly is Paul's use of the familiar image of the *paidagogos* in Galatians 3:24 as an image of the law in relation to Christ, and in 1 Corinthians 4:15 in regard to his own instruction of a new convert, as a father, to other custodians of his instruction.

However, Paul seems uninfluenced by the educational theorists of his day and their focus on childhood development and education; rather Paul focuses on spiritual formation and adult educational concerns. Paul seems to have reacted to Greek higher education as a danger to the Christian mind, with its emphasis on aristocratic social order and attitude of superiority. Paul's rejection of the Greek *paidia* is also hinted at in 1 Corinthians 1:20, wherein he challenges the three basic educated camps of his era: the wise (Greek philosophy), the scribe (Jewish lawyer), and the debater (Roman rhetoric), speaking later of the "persuasiveness of speech" (2:4) and "empty deceit" of "philosophy" (2:8).[32]

Rhetorical education, such as that ascribed by Isocrates, may have influenced several events recorded in the New

Testament. For example, Paul's critics in Corinth critique him as "unprofessional" or "uneducated/trained" (Greek *idiotes*, English etymology for *idiot*) in 2 Corinthians 11:6, meaning that he is not a *rhetor*, as they may well have been. However, Luke's mention of Apollos as being from Alexandria and an effective speaker (Acts 18:24-25) could refer to his having received formal rhetorical training in Alexandria.

Beyond the New Testament era, the early church had to deal with the issues of how can one be learned and faithful? How can one have an educational experience, and yet maintain Christian distinctive? Can there be a fusion of Greek and Christian ideas, even educationally? These matters have not *yet* escaped the Christian education community.

Conclusion

The influence of Greek culture is evident all around us. Not only education, but art, architecture, philosophy, and literature all reflect a Greek presence in our culture and its history. While we do not feel the impact of the Spartans as strongly, the liberal education of the Athenians can still be seen in the college curriculum, with its attention to the humanities. The lasting influence of the Greeks was not primarily through their military endeavors, as the Spartans had wished, but through their commitment to the academic life and educational system.

What Can We Learn from Greek Education?

- Education is for character formation, and the two are virtually inseparable.
- Examples of character foster character development.
- Hellenization is still occurring (although unintentionally) as we continue to study the Greek civilization and draw from it.
- In regard to the Spartan system of education, total indoctrination fails. Liberal education (meaning a more open, intellectual inquiry) seems to succeed far better.
- Higher education seems to require choices and directions for selection, specialization.

- Education is designed to provide service to the culture and community.
- An elective, multitiered system of instruction can work, as it did with the Athenians.
- The Sophists raise a caution against education solely for opportunistic or business-driven purposes.
- Education preserves ideas. Greek philosophy is only with us today because Greek schools preserved it.
- Schools have a lasting influence on history and culture.
- Christian education was not born in a vacuum, but through an interactive process between the community of faith and its culture.

Study Helps

Reflection Questions

1. Think of your college curriculum? How does it reflect the Greek idea of *paidia*? Hint: grammar, composition, speech, philosophy, etc.

2. Think back to your experiences in early childhood programs at church, what did they teach about? How were you introduced to Bible heroes, like the early Greeks were introduced to theirs?

3. In our discussion of the influence of Greek education on the early church, how do we face the same challenges? How does secular education impact the 21st-century faith community?

4. How does your early educational experience relate to that of the Athenian children? Where is it similar? Distinct?

5. For those who have served in the military, how did Spartan education compare with your training?

6. How could we use the Socratic Method of instruction in church? What would be the benefits? What could be the drawbacks?

Technical Terms

Bouagor Spartan, troop leader, typically appointed from within one's troop

Ephebia Athenian higher education, military and civic training, popular in Classical period, waned in Hellenistic period.

Grammatist Athenian, elementary grammar instructor

Gymnasium Athenian, site of physical education instruction as well as higher education

Gymnastes Athenian, secondary education in physical education

Hellenization Process of instilling Greek culture throughout the Mediterranean world and Persia, initiated by Alexander the Great

Idealism Philosophy that maintains truth is found in the mind, and hence is knowable through contemplation. First expressed by Plato.

Kitharistes Athenian, elementary music instructor

Paidagogos Athenian, slave who served as a tutor and model of character for children.

Paideotribe	Athenian, elementary physical education trainer
Paidia	Greek for *education*
Paidomonos	Spartan, instructor of boys age 7+, principle educator in Sparta
Palestra	Athenian, location of elementary education
Quadrivium	Athenian, four fields of study (geometry, arithmetic, music theory, and science), when combined with the Trivium they form what was later called the humanities, or seven liberal arts.
Realism	Philosophy that maintains truth is found in nature, and hence is knowable through the senses. First expressed by Aristotle.
Rhetoric	Athenian, study of oratory, preparation and delivery of speeches. Subject of the Sophists and more importantly of Isocrates.
Socratic Method	Athenian, method of instruction developed by Socrates. Using questions to form concepts in the student's mind rather than lecture.
Trivium	Athenian, three fields of study (grammar, rhetoric, and dialectic), when combined with the Quadrivium they form what was later called the humanities, or seven liberal arts.

Recommended Bibliography

Barrow, Robin. *Greek and Roman Education*. London: Bristol Classical Press, 1976.

Clarke, M.L. *Higher Education in the Ancient World*. London: Rutledge and Kegan, 1971.

Hibler, Richard W. *Life and Learning in Ancient Athens*. New York: University Press of America, 1988.

Marrou, H.I. *A History of Education in Antiquity*. New York: Sheed and Ward, 1956.

Notes

[1] Percival R. Cole, *Studies in the History of Education* (Newtown: Sydney Teacher's College, n.d.), 10.

[2] H.I. Marrou, *A History of Education in Antiquity* (New York: Sheed and Ward, 1956), 9.

[3] Frederick A.G. Beck and Rosalind Thomas, "Education, Greek," *The Oxford Classical Dictionary* (New York: Oxford University Press, 1996), 506.

[4] Marrou, *History*, 9.

[5] E.B. Castle, *Ancient Education and Today* (Baltimore: Penguin Books, 1961), 13.

[6] Ibid., 24.

[7] Robin Barrow, *Greek and Roman Education* (London: Bristol Classical Press, 1976), 30.

[8] Aristotle, *Politics*, 8.3.3.

[9] Barrow, *Greek*, 30.

[10] Beck and Thomas, "Education, Greek," 506.

[11] Marrou, *History*, 49.

[12] Richard W. Hibler, *Life and Learning in Ancient Athens* (New York: University Press of America, 1988), 76.

[13] Marrou, *History*, 112.

[14] Paul Monroe, *Source Book of the History of Education for the Greek and Roman Period* (New York: Macmillan, 1915).

[15] Cole, *Studies*, 37.

[16] Marrou, *History*, 57.

[17] Castle, *Ancient Education*, 59; Marrou, *History*, 103.

[18] Beck and Thomas, "Education, Greek," 507.

[19] Marrou, *History*, 49.

[20] Hibler, *Life*, 99.

[21] Ibid., 87.

[22] Stobaeus, *Extracts*, 3.29.68.

[23] Diogenes Laertius, *Lives*, 2.31.

[24] Theon, *Rhetorical Exercises*, 204.

[25] Stobaeus, *Extracts*, 2.31.79; 3.4.61; 3.4.64.

[26] Kenneth O. Gangel and Warren S. Benson, *Christian Education: Its History and Philosophy* (Chicago: Moody Press, 1982), 37.

[27] Gerald L. Gutek, *Historical and Philosophical Foundations of Education* (Columbus, OH: Prentice Hall, 1991), 46.

[28] Marrou, *History*, 69.

[29] M.L. Clarke, *Higher Education in the Ancient World* (London: Ruetledge and Kegan, 1971).

[30] Lester B. Sands and Richard E. Gross, *The History of Education Chart* (Cleveland, OH: World Publishing, 1967), 4.

[31] E.A. Judge, "The Reaction against Classical Education in the New Testament," *Theological Perspectives on Christian Formation*, ed. by Jeff Astley, Leslie J. Francis, and Colin Crowder (Grand Rapids: Eerdmans, 1996), 82.

[32] Ibid., 84. Cf. Colossians 2:4.

Chapter 5
When in Rome:
Education in the Roman World

James Riley Estep, Jr.

Overview of Period

The history of Rome spreads over a millennium, from its humble peasant beginnings in the 8th century B.C. to its rise as an Empire and ultimately to its collapse in A.D. 476 when Rome fell to Odoacer, a leader of ancient European barbaric tribes. With each successive progression of its development, the Roman educational system likewise adapted, changed, and eventually overcame its rivals.

The history of education in ancient Rome can be traced in four distinct stages. The stages are representative of the most critical factor in the development of Roman education: *the level of influence from Greek educational theory and practice*. The four periods of Roman education are as follows (5.1):

- *Native Roman Education* (8th–4th century B.C.): Roman education is independent from Greek models, little or no Greek influence.

- *Transitional Roman Education* (3rd–2nd century B.C.): beginnings of Greek influence.

- *Greco-Roman Education* (2nd–1st century B.C.): Rome mimics Greek education in virtually every way (context, content, and process).

- *Roman Education* (1st century B.C.–5th century A.D.): Roman education becomes independent from its reliance on Greek education.

How extensive was the Greek influence on Roman education? Why did its influence waiver? This section will address the long-standing relation between Roman education to Greek education in detail.

Native Roman Education: Roman civilization began with meager and peasant origins. Within the social structure two classes developed: Patricians, the aristocratic nobility of the city, and the Plebians, the working class. During this period, Roman education was purely Roman, relatively free from the influence of the Greeks (who were in the process of developing their own educational system). However, Marrou notes that Greece was never *completely* absent. For example, the Greek town of Cumae, founded earlier than Rome (c. 775–750 B.C.) influenced the area with Greek ideas. Similarly, the Etruscans were influenced by the Greeks, and later influenced Rome.[1] Also, the cities of Naples, Salerno, Pompeii, Tarentum, and Herculaneum (all in the southern end of Italy) had a Hellenistic influence early in the 4th century B.C.[2] As will be discussed later, during this period Roman education was not a formal education, but familial-practical instruction for life within the city and emerging culture.

During the *Transitional Period of Roman Education* the influence of the more advanced Greek educational system became plainly obvious. In fact, Greek education became so influential that Paul Monroe actually divides Rome's educational history between pre-Greek and post-Greek influence.[3] The unavoidable reality is that Greek schools and educational theory were far more advanced than their Roman counterparts, and hence the Greek approach to education rapidly gained acceptance and even dominance in Roman culture.[4] "The Hellenistic ideal of a culture based on the study of literature, rhetoric, and philosophy was fully accepted in Rome by the middle of the second century B.C."[5]

How did the Greeks influence Roman education so rapidly and extensively? What contact created a bridge between their cultures? Primarily, it was Rome's propensity for war. Foreign wars, particularly the three named the Punic Wars against Carthage (northern coast of Africa), shaped its culture. During this period of conflict Rome began to encounter Greek culture. For example, in 201 B.C. Rome conquered Macedonia, in 188 B.C. the Hellenistic kingdom of the Seleucids fell to the Roman legions,

The Punic Wars

Punic War 1 (264–241 B.C.)
Sicily to Rome
Punic War 2 (218–201 B.C.)
Hannibal
Punic War 3 (149–146 B.C.)
Destruction of Carthage

and finally in 146 B.C. Rome gained complete control of Greece, with the conquest of Sparta at Corinth.

Rome was no longer just a city, or an Italian nation, it was becoming an international empire. A Mediterranean world that was previously Greek, following the conquest by Alexander the Great, was now Roman politically and militarily, but Greek culturally and educationally. The Greeks began to influence Roman education through a variety of means: commerce between Rome and conquered Greek territories; the translation of Greek literature into Latin, sparking a process of cultural adaptation (for example, Livius Andronicus translated Homer's *Odyssey* into Latin in 250 B.C., the first piece of Greek literature to enter the Roman education system); and perhaps ultimately, Greek slaves, *paidagogos* (Greek), who would now be called *pedagogue* (Latin).

Greco-Roman education is represented by a fusion of the Greek educational theory in a Roman context. No longer was the transition from Roman to Greek education occurring, but now a combined Greek and Roman education existed. "It is clear, then, that there were certain important differences between Greek education and the Greco-Roman education that developed in the Roman world after 146 B.C."[6] So influential was Greek culture that Stoic philosophy actually began to replace the ancient Roman religions.[7] As with earlier Greek education, minimal emphasis was placed on the education of youth. Rather the focus was on higher education. During this time, Rome began to produce some of its greatest teachers, but the educational theory was still distinctly and virtually wholly Greek. The Roman education system adopted the three-tiered education system of the Greeks (elementary, secondary, and higher), and began the process of developing it throughout the Empire.

However, just as education had transitioned from Roman to Greco-Roman, in the first century B.C. the transition began to reverse itself and a distinctively *Roman Education* began to reemerge. Eventually, Greek educational theory and practice were Latinized, becoming *innately* Roman, losing their Greek distinctiveness. The Roman educational system proceeded to reduce the emphasis on athletics (the idea of the gymnasium was almost absent from the Roman education ideal), further development of the three-tiered system of schools (but now *without* Homer and Greek literature, favoring Latin authors such as Virgil or Horace), and focusing exclusively on Roman orators rather than Greek philosophers and rhetoricians, the first Latin rhetorical school having been established in 93 B.C.

Tracing the study of language in Roman schools demonstrates the transition from a purely Roman education to one with a significant Greek influence. Instruction in Rome began with Latin exclusively. Romans then studied Greek and moved to a *bilingual* higher education (Greek and Latin). However, once education in Rome was no longer dependent upon Greek education, they returned to strictly Latin instruction (since the Roman educational system had advanced to the point of self-sufficiency, no longer reliant on Greek literature and philosophy). Why study Greek for oratory when Cicero and Quintilian advanced Latin oratory to an equal or greater level of practice?

It would be inaccurate to say that Roman education was simply a Latin mirror of their Greek neighbors across the Adriatic Sea. Rather, the development of Roman education is an example of cultural adaptation. The Romans adapted the Greek model to such an extent that the end result actually surpassed the original model of education. For a short time, Greece had educationally and culturally conquered Rome, but in the end, Rome's education advanced beyond their Greek predecessors.

Purpose of Education

The objective of education in Rome was the *Vir bonus* (Lat. *good man*). Throughout the history of the Roman culture, the definition of this term reflected the educational shifts of the era. *What did it mean to be a good man?* During the Native Period, the *vir bonus* was a moral man with military and vocational capabilities. A moral man was considered one who adhered to the *mos maiorum* (Lat. *ancestral custom* or *traditions*).

> "You know of course that in the past it was the custom of our ancestors to learn from their elders."
> Pliny, *Letters*, 14.4

However, during the *Transitional Period of Roman Education* the *vir bonus* was redefined. With the beginnings of Greek rhetorical and philosophical training, the *mos maiorum* began to lose its emphasis in light of new customs, Greek ones. Practical education to address the needs of the home, military, and economy was still very strong, but they were beginning to be overshadowed by the new Greek ideals and practice in Rome. This shift was fully displayed in the *Greco-Roman* period, when the *vir bonus* became a trained rhetorician. "The orator was the educated man participating in public affairs."[8] Ultimately, the loss of the *vir bonus* was inevitable, with virtue and piety becoming secondary or even optional, and rhetorical skills favored for gaining political advantage.

Educational Contexts

The family characterized education during the Native Roman period. "Two great characteristics. It was an education which was founded on tradition. . . . [and it] took place within the family."[9] Where was one educated? Through what institutions did one receive instruction? The Roman home was central, with the father as the lead instructor. However, the family was not the sole educator of Roman children. Boys were also trained for an occupation through arranged apprenticeships and for military service through boot camps. Society itself provided for instruction through religious ceremonies and festivals. Very similar to the early educational systems of the Hebrews and Greeks, the home retained the central role and place of instruction.

Near the close of the Native Roman period of education came the *ludus* (Latin *school*, *ludi* is plural), the elementary school, which began in the late fourth century B.C., but was not matured until the third century (5.2). Early schools were primitive settings, usually held in a business establishment, including store fronts and back rooms. "Education was not made compulsory even at the primary stage, and the acquisition of literacy was hap hazard. . . . There was no school building programmes, and most of the instruction was given in premises never designed for teaching purposes."[10] Hence, the center of instruction still remained within the family.

In the *transitional period of Roman education* the home and *ludus* provided instruction. The influence of the Greeks on Roman education generally began with the institutions of higher learning, but soon influenced the whole system of Roman education. "The school supplements the home and the camp and forum, and this early training gives place to the formal instruction of the rhetorical school."[11] However, this Greek adaptation was not readily welcomed by all. The Roman Senator Cicero favored parental instruction over the elementary education provided by schools. He was "too much of a Roman" to advance the notion of Greek schools.[12]

In addition to the advancement of the *ludus* as the principal context of instruction, libraries paralleling those in the Greek educational system began to appear in Roman culture, e.g., Aemilius Paulus founded the first Roman educational library in 167 B.C. While the influence of Greece on Rome is well documented, one distinct omission in Roman education was "the gymnasium and emphasis on competitive physical education."[13]

By the time the transition had reached its completion, the *Greco-Roman educational system* was equivalent to that of the Greeks. Bonner calls the three-tiered education system a "standard pattern" for Roman education.[14] "The single improvement made by Rome over Greece was that Rome formalized education by developing an academic assessment system. The Romans developed a three-rung ladder system: elementary, secondary, and rhetorical . . . schools."[15] In short, the Roman propensity for organization and administration lent itself to the improvement of the Greek system of schooling. What education aspects were included in each tier?

> **Tiers of Roman Education**
> Elementary (*ludus*)
> Secondary (*Schola*)
> Rhetorical Schools

- *Ludus*, elementary school (ages 7-12), for reading, writing, counting. School was year round, with the only days off being for official holidays, market days (Latin *nundinae*), or public spectacles.[16]

- *Schola*, secondary or grammar school (ages 12-16), for grammar and literature instruction, participation was voluntary.

- Rhetorical schools (ages 16-20), first one established by Crates in 167 B.C., but he had to rely on Greek resources, since Latin rhetorical models were not available until the first century B.C. It was for the preparation for professional careers, instruction in the humanities, and oratory.

Higher education was available in a variety of fields, such as medicine, law, architecture, and engineering. Clarke identifies three forms of higher education in the ancient world: liberal arts, philosophy, and professional studies; medicine, law, and architecture receiving more attention from the Romans.[17] Science and philosophy remained the domain of Greek higher education, even in Rome, but the Romans advanced the medical sciences as a discipline of their own.[18] Also paralleling the Greek model of education, the Roman equivalent to the Greek *ephebeia* (military and political training) was the *lusus Troiae* in Rome and the *collegia iuvenum* throughout Italy for political and military leadership.

Educational Content and Process

As previously noted, the family was the center of instruction during the *Native Roman period*, and with this familial emphasis came an instruction in the ways of the ancestors. The content of instruction was the *mos maiorum* (Latin, *ancestral custom* or *traditions*). These ancestral traditions emphasized three values:

- *Virtus*—loyalty, to family, city, and nation
- *Gravitas*—character, discipline, morality, kindness, courtesy; as well as a religious element, service to the gods
- *Pietas*—religious piety, including patriotism

Additionally, the first formal expression of Roman cultural ideals was adopted c. 450 B.C., the *Law of the Twelve Tables* (5.3). These served as the foundational affirmations of Roman youth as they became adult members of society. Familial education likewise contained the basic content of an elementary education (reading, writing, and arithmetic), as evidenced by wooden and ivory writing tablets that date back to the 7th century B.C.[19]

During the period of *native Roman education* the family retained the central role as educator. Familial instruction could be provided by parents and relatives, and even later the family pedagogue. Mothers were the primary instructors of the children as babies, then fathers assumed the role as the child grew. However, the principal of *patria potestas*, the absolute authority of the father over the family, was always in force. This placed an emphasis on the moral conduct of the father as example to the child. "Little is known of early Roman education, but one fact is certain. As in every other department of Roman social life, the centre round which all turned was the family; and in particular that most Roman institution, the *patria potestas*."[20] However, it was not always possible for fathers to provide the necessary instruction, since they were often in military service or tied to the affairs of State or business.[21] For example, Cicero and his younger brother Quintus were instructed by their uncle in Rome, along with their cousins. The child learned what it meant to be a Roman citizen through imitation, memorization of the Twelve Tables, the formation of habits, and strict discipline.

The level of instruction received by a child was signified by the wearing of a particular style of toga. Prior to age 7, the mother was the principle teacher and no particular toga was worn. Between the ages of 7 and 16, when the father assumed the principle teaching role, the child wore the *toga praetexta*, a white robe with a purple stripe along the hem line. Later, from the age of 16 to adulthood, the adolescent wore the *toga virilis*, a white robe with no stripe (5.4). Upon completion of his father's instruction, the boy's name was entered on the citizens role, and he was eligible for military service. Later in the Republic, a boy could receive a one year apprenticeship with a notable citizen for additional training and model of citizenship, known as the *tirocinium fori*, or if the individual was in the military, it was the *tirocinium militiae*.[22]

Later in the Empire, familial education failed to provide the foundation it had given for the previous centuries of Roman civilization. "Under the Empire, conditions of family life were, in general, nothing like so stable as they had been under the Republic," noting concubines, adultery, singleness, and rising divorce rates.[23] With this the principal of *patria potestas* simply failed.

Instruction at Roman Schools

As in Greece, three levels of grammatical instruction and instructor developed in Roman education: *litterator*, like the Greek *grammatistes*; *grammaticus*, like the Greek *kitharistes*, and finally the

> **FYI:** The Roman mathematics instructor was called the *calculator*.

most advanced *rhetor*, equivalent to the Greek sophists. While salaries varied, the Emperor Diocletian established a Price Edict that provided a ratio of payment was 1:4:5 for pay at each level of instructor (5.5 and 5.6).[24]

The advancements in the elementary schools during the *transitional period of Roman education* gave rise to the formal study of reading (letters, syllables, and words), writing, and arithmetic. The *ludus* likewise taught ballads and religious content, for example, using the names of Roman gods to teach the alphabet.

Instruction in the *ludus* was lengthy. Not only did it meet from dawn to the mid-afternoon, but school was year round, with the only days off being official holidays, market days (Latin *nundinae*), or public spectacles (5.7).[25] The teacher was a *litterator* (Latin, *teacher of letters*) or a *ludi magister* (Latin, *school master*). Elementary teachers were regarded with some moderate level of social status, but their financial compensation was irregular.

The classroom setting was somewhat simple. The *litterator* sat in a chair (Lat. *cathedra*) while children resided on wooden stools at best, but typically sat on the floor. Students wrote their exercises on wax tablets with a stylus or on a slate tablet (5.8). Arithmetic was taught by using one's fingers and an abacus (5.9). Reading and writing were taught by a progression through language (letters, syllables, and words), with the oral repetition and memorizing of grammatical formulas. Instruction sometimes included the use of drawing, painting, and modeling.

Pedagogues, the Latin equivalent to Greek *paidagogos*; also called *custos* (Latin *guardian*) early in Roman history was the child's tutor and escort to school (5.10). Influx of pedagogues came after the third Macedonian War. "Prisoners were brought across the Adriatic . . . found employment as 'pedagogues' . . . thereby greatly extending the knowledge of Greek."[26] Their presence helped trigger the transitional period of Roman education. In addition to the pedagogue, who delivered general or elementary instruction, was the *praeceptor* (Lat. *tutor*) who was more specialized in instruction.[27] The highest recorded price paid for a pedagogue was 700,000 sesterces.[28] One of the earliest known pedagogues was Livius Andronicus who won his freedom by intellect and service to a Senator's child.[29]

The *schola*, secondary/grammar schools, taught language, literature, and poetry in both Greek and Latin (5.11). These subjects prepared students for further study in the rhetorical schools. One distinction of the Roman secondary school was the bilingual study. It provided the advantage that "the Greek schools which had preceded them [the Roman schools] taught no other language than Greek, the Roman schools taught both Greek and Latin."[30] Instructors employed reading, composition, music and oratory, and a significant amount of memory work as means of providing instruction.

Rhetorical training was likewise parallel to the Greeks'. The rhetorical schools of Rome taught not only oratory, but the *humanitas*: grammar, literature, rhetoric, dialectic, arithmetic, astronomy, music, and geometry. Hence, the *humanitas* of Roman education was much broader than the Greek idea of *paidia*.[31] The theory and practice of oratory was divided into two forms: *suasoriae*, reflection exercises on historical or simulated situations, and *controversiae*, courtroom strategies. Eventually, the study of Greek literature was replaced with the study of the Roman authors Virgil and Horace in schools. Remmius Palaemon authored the first Roman grammar, signaling the release of the dominance of Greek language in Roman education. Eventually, Cicero and Quintilian authored their agenda for the training of Latin orators, removing the necessity of Roman education's dependence on the educational theories of the Greeks. Declamation and debate, Roman law, speaking (extemporaneous and planned), and ethics were stressed as means of improving oratory skills. With an education that was distinctly Roman came the birth of Roman oratory.

Voices

In reference to the most significant voices in Roman education, Dobson commented, "Their lives [Cicero and Quintilian's] cover some two thirds of the period during which Roman education attained its fullest development."[32] While these men were not the sole voices shaping and contributing to Roman education, they were by far the most significant. This section will look at the contributions of Cicero, Quintilian, Plutarch, and the Emperors as supporters of educational advances.

> In his *History of Pedagogy* (1901), Gabriel Compayré poses, "Why Rome had no great educators . . .", noting the Roman propensity to favor the practical over the philosophical.

Cicero (106–43 B.C.). Aristocrat and rhetor, he was the first of two (5.12).[33] He was schooled by his uncle in philosophy and rhetoric in Rome, and later studied philosophy in Athens and Rhodes. Hence, he was "schooled" in the traditional Roman manner, with an emphasis on familial instruction. Beginning in 72 B.C., he became a successful lawyer in Rome, primarily through advanced oratory skills. He likewise served Rome as a politician in a variety of capacities, ultimately as a Roman senator. He used Latin to popularize Greek philosophy.

His *De Oratore* (55 B.C.) was his major work of rhetorical education, but he also penned *Brutus* and *Orator* (❧ 5.13). Cicero advocated education beyond the familial model; he favored formal instruction in Latin and then Greek. He believed *educatio*—the raising of a child—should be the family's responsibility, and the student's *institutio*—instruction in letters— should be provided by the formal education system in Rome. "The orator was to Cicero what the philosopher-king was to Plato."[34] Cicero advocated studies in law, rhetoric, philosophy,

> "Cicero would have the orator be a philosopher."
> —Castle, *Ancient Education and Today*, 135.

psychology, military science, as well as politics, medicine, geography, astronomy, and history. "Cicero presents both sides of the question: the philosopher as viewed by the orator, and the orator as viewed by the philosopher."[35] He argued that philosophy without rhetoric or rhetoric without philosophy was incomplete. Cicero, as a political figure, also published *De Republica*, wherein the chief character, Scipio, contrasts Greek and Roman educational principles.

Quintilian (A.D. 35–95?), whose full name was Marcus Fabius Quintilianus, was a truly *Roman* educator. He was not simply another Roman adaptation of Greek thought, but a genuinely *Roman* educational theoretician. He was born at Calagurris in northern Spain. He began his rhetorical studies in Rome c. A.D. 58. After completing his studies in Rome, he returned to Spain until called by the Emperor Galba in A.D. 68 to Rome, never to leave the City again. He served as an educator under the reign of five Roman emperors (Galba to Domitian), and for twenty years he was regarded as the primary teacher of rhetoric in Rome. Vespasian favored Quintilian and made him the first public professor of Latin, with the exorbitant salary of 100,000 sesterces per year (The Roman sesterces was the basic unit of money, like the United States dollar). "The appointment marks a definite stage in the history of Roman education policy."[36]

His *Institutio Oratoria*, or *The Instruction of Orators* (c. A.D. 91–93) was published by A.D. 95, containing the most comprehensive expression of his theory of Roman rhetoric (✹ 5.13). Quintilian believed that a great orator began training from early

> Quintilian had two additional books published on rhetoric, but without his permission, having been produced from his lecture notes by enthusiastic students.

childhood, almost birth. For example, the family was responsible for providing basic instruction such as the alphabet and memorization of short poetic or oratory passages. He also opposed the use of harsh discipline in education, which was rather common in Roman schools. He articulated a comprehensive, graded system of instruction for the Roman orator:

- *Age 0-7*, learning through immediate need gratification
- *Age 7-14*, sense experiences, formulation of ideas and concepts, development of memory, reading and writing in native language (Latin), games to facilitate learning, minimal use of corporal punishment.
- *Age 14-17*, development of reasoning powers, instruction in the *humanitas*
- *Age 17 +*, instruction in rhetoric and oratory

The most effective instruction would be provided through both individual and group discussion of subjects, individual assessment of student's progress, and plans for independent study. Quintilian's approach to education and instruction was so revolutionary that he remained a prominent figure in education for centuries after his death. Italian humanist Andrea Poggio in A.D. 1410 rediscovered Quintilian's works and reintroduced him to the fledgling Renaissance world.

Plutarch (c. A.D. 50–120) was in fact Greek, but wrote during the Roman period. Born in Chaeronea, he was educated in Athens and Smyrna. Plutarch authored several works that partially addressed education. His *Lives* is a collection of biographical sketches of prominent Greek and Roman figures. These works were used to address the moral decay in the Empire, calling its reader to a more noble standard of conduct. However, in his *Moralia*, a collection of seventy-eight of his works, he addresses "On the education of

Children," outlining how children learn and should be treated, echoing Quintilian's concern over the severe discipline in Roman schools. While he is oftentimes not mentioned as a significant Roman educator, sometimes because of his Greek nationality and other times because of the overwhelming voices of Cicero and Quintilian, Plutarch nevertheless provided another model of education in the Roman world.

Emperors as Educational Leaders: While no emperor of Rome ever served as a school teacher, nor ever wrote an educational treatise, we would be remiss if we did not note their contribution to the Roman educational system. For example:

- Vespasian (A.D. 70–79) endowed Greek rhetors, including Quintilian. He paid 100,000 *sesterces* from the Imperial Treasury annually to endow a chair of Greek and Latin rhetoric. This policy was continued by his successor, the Emperor Hadrian (A.D. 76–138).

- Antonius Pius (A.D. 138–161) financially supported education in the provinces, and exempted teachers from taxes and military service.

- Marcus Aurelius (A.D. 121–180) provided salary for members of the higher education faculty in Athens.

- Serverus (A.D. 222–235) provided scholarships for Roman students to attend higher education.

- Constantine (A.D. 321–333) extended teachers' privileges to other provinces that were previously enjoyed only by teachers in Rome and Italy.

- Gratian (A.D. 378–383) provided subsidies for education by matching contributions for education from individual cities.

- Theodosius and Valentinian (A.D. 425) adopted the policy that only the Emperor could establish schools.

Excursus:
The Beginnings of Christian Education
in the Roman Empire

In previous chapters, we have addressed the Christian adaptation or reaction to education in Judaism and within the Hellenistic cultures of the first century A.D. Even when Paul encountered the Hellenistic educational system in Athens and Corinth, it occurred in the context of a Roman world. It was the Roman culture and educational system that had the most direct influence on the early Christian community. *Rome taught Christianity how to go to school.* Jesus never opened a school, and the word school is only mentioned once in the entire New Testament (Acts 19:9), so where did the notion of Christian schooling originate? The early Christian communities simply copied the educational formats within their culture, including the Roman school system. Chapter 6 will provide insights into the formation and types of Christian schools present in the early centuries of Christianity.

Some early church officials were opposed to the Roman educational system, usually due to the content and methodologies of their instructors, e.g., memorizing the alphabet by reciting the names of Roman deities. Ironically, it was the opinion of such leaders as Tertullian that while children can attend Roman schools, Christians could never consider a teaching career in such a school since it would require them to compromise their faith.[37] However, his opinion was in the minority, with the alternative view held by such authorities as Hippoclytus, Origen, and Clement of Alexandria representing the mainstream of the early Christian community.

Christians adopted the schooling model embodied by the Greeks and Romans. In these early Christian schools the foundations for a Christian civilization were developed: dogma, morals, canonical disciplines, liturgies. Similarly, higher education became an arena for Christian academic endeavor. For example, Anatolius, later bishop of Laodicea, was chair of Aristotelian philosophy in Alexandria in A.D. 264. Similarly, Malchion in Antioch was the administrator of a rhetorical school. In so doing Christianity gained a significant presence in the culture, one that would allow them to convert not only individuals, but the Empire.

Conclusion

Rome used its education system to advance Roman culture and civilization throughout the Mediterranean. It required, or even kidnapped, the sons of noblemen from subjugated lands to be educated in Roman schools.[38] Roman education came to an end with the collapse of the Roman Empire, with the possible exceptions of those Roman cities and outposts in northern Africa and Italy itself. The influence of the Roman civilization is readily apparent throughout the Western world. Roman heritage and education preserved the best of the Greek culture, provided a means of translating it into the Medieval Age, and even contributed to spark the Renaissance (remember the rediscovery of Quintilian's work).

What Can We Learn from Roman Education?

- Literally, it was Roman education that taught Christianity how to go to school.

- Just as the Roman *vir bonus*, we need to define the central goal of Christian education and learn to reapply and define it with each passing generation.

- Family is a continual component of the education of children regardless of the formal system of schooling available.

- There is a need for cultural adaptation of educational models, but an adaptation which becomes thoroughly enculturated.

- Education is for practical service to the culture and civilization.

- Just as the Romans began to theorize educational formats unique to their culture, Christians too must develop educational approaches specialized to our unique purpose and plan.

- The Romans provided a comprehensive plan for education, as broad (general education) as it was deep (grammar and rhetorical studies).

Study Helps

Reflection Questions

1. How would you define the *vir bonus*? What would inform your list of qualities comprising the *good man*?

2. Just as the Greeks heavily influenced the formation of Roman education, what factors do you think have influenced the Church's understanding of Christian education?

3. How has Christian education had to adopt educational theories not its own? How successful do you think we are at adequately adapting them for Christian use?

4. When you think back on your educational experiences (even as a child), where do you see parallels with the experiences of Roman children, adolescents, and adults in their educational experiences?

5. Remember Plutarch's idea of moral biographical models from history. How does this compare with the Christian use of Bible characters for spiritual formation? Can moral examples really facilitate growth?

Technical Terms

Artes liberals	Latin, literally *liberal arts*; term equal to *humanitas*
Educatio	Latin, instruction provided by the family
Grammaticus	Latin, second level of grammar instructor, teacher in the *schola*, secondary/grammar school
Gravitas	Latin, literally *character*; one dimension of the *vir bonus*
Humanitas	Latin, literally *humanities*; term equal to *Artes liberals*
Institutio	Latin, instruction provided by an instructor
Law of the Twelve Tables	Codification of Roman ideals adopted by their society c. 450 B.C. containing judicial procedures, rights of the father (significant to education), property rights, public and sacred laws, and supplemental information updating the previous rulings
Litterator	Latin, *teacher of letters*; teacher in the *ludus*, elementary school
Ludus	Roman elementary school
Ludus magister	Latin, *school master*; teacher in the *ludus*, elementary school
Mos Maiorum	Latin, traditions of the ancestors, the content of native Roman education

Patria potestas	Principle of the father's headship of the family.
Patricians and Plebeians	Two basic social classes in Roman society; aristocracy and working class
Pedagogue	Latin equivalent to the Greek *paidagogos*; household slave responsible for tutoring children and escorting them to school
Pietas	Latin, literally *piety*; one dimension of the *vir bonus*
Praeceptor	Latin, *tutor*; an advanced pedagogue, one with specialized training for instruction
Rhetor	Latin, teacher in the rhetorical school; most advanced instructor of the Roman education system. No direct parallel with Greek education, other than Sophists.
Schola	Roman secondary/grammar school
Vir bonus	The stated goal of Roman education, the *good man*; a concept that changed with each development in Roman education.
Virtus	Latin, literally *virtue*; one dimension of the *vir bonus*

Recommended Bibliography

Barrow, Robin. *Greek and Roman Education*. London: Bristol Classical Press, 1976.

Bonner, Stanley E. *Education in Ancient Rome*. Los Angeles: University of California Press, 1977.

Gwynn, Aubrey. *Roman Education from Cicero to Quintilian*. New York: Russell and Russell, 1964.

Marrou, H.I. *A History of Education in Antiquity*. New York: Sheed and Ward, 1956.

Quintilian. *The Orator's Education*. Volumes 1-5. Loeb Classical Library. Cambridge, MA: Harvard University Press, 2001.

Notes

[1] H.I. Marrou, *A History of Education in Antiquity* (New York: Sheed and Ward, 1956), 242-246.

[2] L. Glenn Smith and Joan K. Smith, *Lives in Education* (New York: St. Martin's Press, 1994), 35.

[3] Paul Monroe, *Sourcebook of the History of Education* (New York: Macmillan, 1915), 327.

[4] Aubrey Gwynn, *Roman Education from Cicero to Quintilian* (New York: Russell and Russell, 1964), 23.

[5] Ibid., 140-141.

[6] Robin Barrow, *Greek and Roman Education* (London: Bristol Classical Press, 1976), 72.

[7] E.B. Castle, *Ancient Education and Today* (Baltimore: Penguin Books, 1961), 120-121; Monroe, *Sourcebook*, 373-374.

[8] Monroe, *Sourcebook*, 425.

[9] William Barclay, *Educational Ideals in the Ancient World* (Grand Rapids: Baker, 1959), 146, 147.

[10] Stanley Bonner, *Education in Ancient Rome* (Los Angeles: University of California Press, 1977), 328.

[11] Monroe, *Sourcebook*, 359.

[12] Gwynn, *Roman Education*, 82.

[13] J.V. Muir, "education, Roman," *The Oxford Classical Dictionary*, ed. by Simon Hornblower and Antony Spawforth (New York: Oxford University Press, 1996), 509.

[14] Bonner, *Education*, 44.

[15] Kenneth O. Gangel and Warren S. Benson, *Christian Education: Its History and Philosophy* (Chicago: Moody Press, 1983), 53.

[16] Barrow, *Greek*, 75.

[17] M.L. Clarke, *Higher Education in the Ancient World* (London: M.L. Clarke, 1971).

[18] Marrou, *History*, 254.

[19] Muir, "education, Roman," 509.

[20] Gwynn, *Roman Education*, 12.

[21] Bonner, *Education*, 12-13.

[22] Castle, *Ancient Education*, 114-115; Barrow, *Greek*, 64-65.

[23] Bonner, *Education*, 98.

[24] Muir, "education, Roman," 510.

[25] Barrow, *Greek*, 75.

[26] Bonner, *Education*, 23.

[27] Ibid., 47.

[28] Gwynn, *Roman Education*, 32.

[29] Bonner, *Education*, 20.

[30] Ibid., 330.

[31] Castle, *Ancient Education*, 135; Gwynn, *Roman Education*, 85.

[32] J.F. Dobson, *Ancient Education and Its Meaning to Us* (New York: Longmans, Green, and Company, 1932), 124.

[33] John Hedley Simon and Dirk Obbink, "Tullius Cicero, Marcus," *The Oxford Classical Dictionary*, 3rd edition, ed. by Simon Hornblower and Antony Spawforth (New York: Oxford University Press, 1996), 1561.

[34] Smith and Smith, *Lives*, 39.

[35] Monroe, *Sourcebook*, 425.

[36] Gwynn, *Roman Education*, 181.

[37] Marrou, *History*, 321.

[38] Ibid., 295.

Chapter 6
The Early Church:
Education of Heart and Mind
(1st–6th Century A.D.)

Jonathan H. Kim

Overview of Period

This chapter focuses on the formative years of the church (from the first to sixth century) when the historical development of Christian education took place. Included in this period are the two fundamental models of education that have shaped the development of the early church ministry—catechumenal and catechetical.[1] Generally speaking, catechumenal education was an informal model of education that trained lay people for Christian life and service whereas the catechetical model was a formal model of education that equipped church leaders for ministry and teaching.

The scope of this chapter is confined to the educational ministry of the early church particularly expressed in the catechesis tradition; it is not meant to be an exhaustive study of the early church ministry. In an attempt to suggest catechesis as an overarching schema of the early church education, its ecclesiastical and institutional (academic) functions will be highlighted. The focus is on examining catechumenal and catechetical educations as integral and constitutive components of early Christian ministry.

Purpose of Education

The legacy of Christian education began with the ministry of the early church. Decades of evangelism following Christ's ascension resulted in countless conversions, yet the church was not prepared to nurture these new believers. Moreover, it was particularly evident during this period that the force of paganism coupled with the culture's hostility and prejudice against Christianity was leading many believers to apostasy.[2] Confronted with the challenge, church leaders sought a way to equip believers, which resulted in the introduction of catechesis (Gk., "instruction")—the instructional system whereby the essentials of Christianity were taught dialogically. Catechesis was used to evangelize, nurture, reform, and initiate seekers and new believers to the Church community, which historians later referred to as catechumenal education.[3] Catechumen is the name applied to a new adult believer going through a course of classes who is to be inducted into the church. On the other hand, institutionally, catechesis was used to equip Christians for ministry, evangelism, and leadership, similar to the role that contemporary models of Christian higher education play (i.e., Christian colleges, graduate schools, and seminaries). Recognizing the strong academic component of the latter catechesis, historians named the movement catechetical education.[4]

To all intents and purposes, education in the early church expressed particularly in the catechesis tradition was for assisting Christians to develop faith integrated with spirituality and intelligibility (❧ 6.1). The education toward spirituality (e.g., catechumenal education) involved the task of inculcating new believers with the rudiments of Christian faith whereas the education toward intelligibility (e.g., catechetical education) involved the task of transmitting the rational, objective content of Christian truth. We will elaborate on the theory and function of both educations throughout the remainder of the chapter, inviting readers to deepen their understanding and appreciation of the early Christian education.

Informal Catechesis: Catechumen Education

Educational Context

For the purpose of securing new Christians, catechumen education—the informal instructional program that surveys the essentials of Christianity—was introduced in the early church. With the intention of nurturing new believers, classes were formed at various locations such as homes and churches. This was the very first form of education instituted in the church; no other systems had existed before.[5] Although the focus of instruction was on the content of faith, its provisional concern was on grounding new Christians in the context of the church community, in deep fellowship with God and with other believers. Perhaps contemporary models of new believers' and membership classes are similar to the catechumen model.

Educational Content and Process

The catechumen curriculum was built on three educative concerns—knowledge (knowing), character (both moral and spiritual beings), and skill (doing). The curriculum centered on moral and spiritual knowledge (knowing) necessary for Christian life (being) and service (doing).[6] Contents were based on the confession of faith (the Apostles' Creed [🔊 6.3] and *Didache*, the teachings of the twelve apostles on moral and spiritual precepts [🔊 6.4]), combined with asceticism and liturgy. The goal was to cultivate spiritual discipline and integrity, which presumably grow out of intelligibility grounded in the Scriptures. In general, new believers were expected to spend three years as students of the word and experience the changes in life (Gk., *tropos*), rather than to merely pass through the three chronological years of education (Gk., *kronos*).[7]

Although forms may vary, the following curriculum existed in various catechumen schools. The students were divided into three grade levels: the first year students were called seekers (i.e., inquirers or hearers, Gk., *akromeni*)—those who were considering Christianity; the second year students were called learners (i.e., kneelers, Gk., *catechumens*)—those who have completed the first stage of instruction; and the third year students were called candidates (i.e., Gk., *photizomenoi*; Lat., *competentes*)—those who were at the final phase of training before being inducted into church as "faithful ones," referring to the devoted members who completed the catechumen training and served to advance the cause of the gospel.[8]

In the first stage, seekers were instructed with elementary yet fundamental matters of Christian doctrines, practices (spiritual discipline), and liturgy—that is, if they wished to become Christians. The purpose of this education (Stage 1) was to secure the seekers' understanding of Christian life and salvation, as they were not yet Christians.[9]

When the church teacher noticed the earnestness and determination in a seeker's character and behavior combined with promising signs that the person could persevere in faith, the seeker was promoted to the second stage as a learner (i.e., kneeler)—meaning that the person is now identified as a Christian. Often some form of ceremonies marked the transition to the second stage; the students were marked with the sign of a cross on their forehead and received intercessory prayer. Advance teachings on Christian doctrine, spiritual discipline, and liturgy were given (❧ 6.2). Also during the worship service, unlike seekers who were dismissed after the sermon, learners were allowed to stay to receive a special prayer, and then were dismissed before the worship of the faithfuls. Commonly, the Stage 2 training would last about a year, but some of the earlier accounts indicate that the training may have lasted up to two years.[10]

After successful completion of the second stage, the learners were promoted to the third level as candidates, the ones who are enlightened. This was the final stage in catechumen training before new believers were formally inducted into the church.[11] Advanced teachings on doctrine (instructional), spiritual discipline (ascetical), and worship (liturgy) were given (❧ 6.2). Since candidates were supposed to be masters of the mysteries of faith, a rigorous ascetical training was given with emphasis on prayer, fasting, confession, and solitude. In addition, seven phase interviews and oral examinations called "scrutinies" were given to the candidates by a council of church leaders.[12] The scrutinies involved the introduction of the candidates to the council, oral examination, confession and affirmation of personal faith, renunciation of Satan, and the study of the gospel and the Creed. Following the final scrutiny was the actual induction ceremony involving baptism, confirmation, and Communion whereby the candidates were declared faithful Christians who could fully participate in the life of the church.

Voices

The ministry involving catechumen training was highlighted by some of the church leaders. Particularly Cyril of Jerusalem and St. Augustine revealed the pedagogical basis with which new believers were trained and introduced to the church. Although catechumen education began back in the first century, explicit examples and perspectives of the movement were not documented until much later. In the subsequent section, we will call your attention to Cyril of Jerusalem and St. Augustine. Let us find out what these leaders had to say about catechumen education.

Cyril of Jerusalem (A.D. 315–387). Cyril, a native of Jerusalem, became a minister (bishop) of the Jerusalem church in A.D. 351. His extensive work of catechesis instruction—twenty-three instructions all together, eighteen of which are for catechumens (stage 2) and five for the newly baptized—represents educational practice of the Jerusalem church during the fourth century (6.5).[13] Although Cyril's work is best known for its doctrinal content based on a systematic exegesis of the Old and New Testaments, a heavy emphasis was on life application with the goal of leading new believers into a transforming relationship with Christ.

To assist new believers in understanding the essentials of Christianity, Cyril organized his 18 catechumen instructions according to the following subject matters: (1) Exhortation, (2) On sin and God's forgiveness, (3) On baptism, (4-5) On the nature of faith, (6) On the Kingdom of God, (7) On the Father, (8) His omnipotence, (9) The Creator, (10) On the Lord Jesus Christ, (11) Christ's eternal Sonship, (12) Jesus' virgin birth, (13) Christ's Passion, (14) Christ's resurrection and ascension, (15) The second coming, (16-17) On the Holy Spirit, and (18) On the renunciation of Satan.[14] The style and structure of Cyril's lectures were clear and logical; the focus was on nurturing new believers with the content of faith. Cyril's detailed catechesis instructions were the valuable remains of the early church and became a primary source for later catechumen educators.[15]

Augustine of Hippo (A.D. 354–430). Perhaps one of the most compelling works of catechumen training comes from Augustine; he was not only a brilliant theologian but also a protagonist for catechumen education whose ideals changed the course of Christian education. With the belief that all believers must know the essentials of Christian theology, Augustine emphasized the systematic and historical study of Christianity.[16] Although he was well aware of the benefits of integrating secular and sacred truths, he opposed the uncritical acceptance of secular knowledge in the church, so he called for theology-driven education. He was convinced that Christian truth had absolute sufficiency to stand on its own, not in need of receiving support from secular sources, therefore he stressed the importance of teaching new believers the issues on the Covenant, Christian community, the life of the apostles, resurrection, and the Trinity.[17]

Recognizing significant shortcomings of the traditional form of education, Augustine wrote several discourses to offer suggestions on teaching new believers. In particular, his discourse on *Instruction for Beginners* (Lat., *De Catechizandis Rudibus*) reveals the importance of teaching integrated knowledge and practice which lead to the development of Christian character and spirituality (✪ 6.6). Augustine believed that learning without integrative application was irrelevant to catechumens, so in suggesting a holistic teaching paradigm, he offered the following recommendations: (1) Teachers need to tailor instruction to the uniqueness of an individual inquirer. (2) Teachers need to vary instructional means based on group size, encouraging a conversational approach (e.g., Socratic method) for teaching a single inquirer but a sermonlike instruction (e.g., Didactic teaching) for teaching a group. (3) Students' educational backgrounds must be considered before teaching. (4) Teaching for comprehension is more important than offering interesting content. (5) The preliminary instruction should employ narratives rather than just propositions of theories. And, (6) teachers need to be in tune with the gospel as they teach.[18]

The catechumenal system reached its mature form as an educational system in the second century, then blossomed into a full catechetical system in the third and fourth centuries.[19] Although the catechetical school became a dominant paradigm in the third through sixth century, the catechumen system maintained its functions in the church until about A.D. 325 to A.D. 450 though it became progressively weaker.[20] The disappearance of the catechumen system was contributed to by two major factors: (1) adult converts (i.e., catechumens) seeking to receive the basic teachings of Christianity declined as Christianity became widely accepted, and (2) with the growing acceptance of infant baptism, the church's educative concern shifted to the nurture of children rather than adult converts.[21]

Having discussed the issues related to catechumen education, we now switch our focus to the institutional form of catechesis known as catechetical education. With the coming of the catechetical model, the educative concern of the early church shifted to an explicit intellectual training of the Christian mind.

Formal Catechesis: Catechetical Education

Historians indicate that scholarly tradition of catechetical school began legitimately for the first time in Alexandria under the direction of Pantaenus in A.D. 179, who was later succeeded by Clement, and then Origen. Little is known of the school until the time of Clement and Origen.[22] There were other schools established in Antioch, Edessa, and Nisibis, which all flourished and functioned as academies for Christian learning until about A.D. 640.[23] Catechetical schools represent the beginning of Christian higher education.[24]

Educational Context

The increased challenge of secular philosophy—literature and Greek and Asian mystery cults of the second-century ethos—set off the church's interest in and need for intellectual training. Although catechumen education provided the rudiments of Christian faith and assisted people in developing religious passion, a rigorous intellectual training was still needed. The solution lay in the development of a robust program called catechetical education. Unlike catechumen education, catechetical education took place in a formal school setting, focusing on the academic study of theology, literature, philosophy, and ethics.[25] This model was primarily designed to equip prospective church leaders who were interested in academic training.

Educational Content and Process

In an effort to suggest an integrative paradigm for education, catechetical schools introduced two following perspectives to the church. First, on the nature of knowing, the schools asserted that there are two levels of knowledge, the lower and higher. The lower knowledge is moral knowledge (*sophia* or wisdom), which facilitates the change in one's life, leading to integrated understanding of practical and abstract principles. However, the higher knowledge, which is referred to as spiritual knowledge, is obtained through knowing divine truth (i.e., the Logos) emanating from God.[26] Higher knowledge brings contemplation and eventually progresses to inner harmony in union with God. This view was an unequivocal affirmation on the value of integrated knowing in which earthly knowledge cultivates inner sensitivity toward the sacred knowledge. Second, on the content and process of knowing, the schools asserted that classical training was a prelude to the development of the Christian mind.[27] Expanding what was believed to be the true model of education, the leaders of the schools developed a crossdisciplinary curriculum in which students were educated in the preparatory studies of classical liberal arts, especially philosophy and literature including theology. Then, in the advanced stage of learning, students would study grammar, logic, comparative philosophy, Christian ethics, and hermeneutics.[28] Also, the schools' interest in integration led them to fashion a hermeneutic principle that used allegorical interpretations of the Scriptures—the concept of seeing the natural revelation (i.e., the universe) as a continuously unfolding doctrine of God which assists learning and becomes "a means of intellectual ascent towards ultimate truth."[29]

As academic institutions, catechetical schools pushed Christianity to the forefront of intellectualism in the second and third centuries.[30] As the catechetical pedagogy was appropriated and gave new meaning to teaching, the concern of Christian education sharply changed toward the pole of intelligibility, embracing a scholastic paradigm of education.

Voices

Among the advocates of catechetical learning were Clement of Alexandria and Origen whose ideals changed the direction of early church education. While some of their contemporaries were adamant about any form of integration, both Clement and Origen called for a critical synthesis of all knowledge particularly theology, philosophy, literature, and science with a high degree of rationality.

Clement of Alexandria (A.D. 150–216). Titus Flavius Clement, following his conversion, came to study under Pantaenus at the Alexandrian catechetical school. Sometime later, he succeeded as leader of the school, and thereafter the school became increasingly scholastic, becoming a forerunner of Christian higher education. Clement's major concern was on fusing secular and sacred knowledge as an overarching schema for Christian education.[31]

Clement's catechetic philosophy is captured in his book, *Paedagogus* (Lat., "Instructor"; ❧ 6.7).[32] This work was a homily on the nature of teaching. Basing on the Greek and the biblical notion of *paedagogus*, which meant the slave-tutor who worked as a moral advisor to his young master, Clement asserted that learning is a collaborative exploration between the teacher and the student whereby mentoring and guiding become chief educative means.[33] For Clement, the quintessential meaning of *Paedagogus* originated from the biblical concept of a servant-teacher. Clement claimed that Jesus is the true *Paedagogus* of humanity whom all teachers should model.[34] In essence, Clement was asserting that the task of teaching is about mentoring and discipling rather than informing students with mere facts. By linking teaching to the very life of the teacher, Clement offered a holistic teaching paradigm to the early church.

Although Clement's catechetic philosophy has explicated and deepened the meaning of Christian education, some of his theological perspectives, on the other hand, were heretical and demand our criticism. The following are the examples of untamed integration gone wild: First, his unequivocal affirmation of Hellenism, especially asserting Greek philosophy as the forerunner of Christianity, must be refuted. In particular, his acceptance of seeing (1) Plato as the Hellenistic Moses, (2) the Greek philosophers as Christians before the coming of Jesus, (3) no antagonism between Christianity and Greek philosophy, and (4) Christianity as the convergence of two streams, Judaism and Hellenism, are prime examples of integration gone out of control.[35] We, the students of the Bible, must wrestle with the irreconcilable difference between the secular and sacred knowledge without compromising biblical truth. Second, drawing heavily on the Platonic tradition, Clement contended that academic training should be limited to a few who desire a deeper knowledge of faith and confined Christian education to the elite class only. While his assertion may seem legitimate in the context of leadership training, nonetheless the evangelistic element of Christian education that invites all people—both Christians and non-Christians—to God must not be forgotten. We should not ignore the evangelistic function of Christian education.

Origen (A.D. 185–254). Following Clement in A.D. 215, Origen was named as head of the Alexandrian school by the bishop Demetrius.[36] The school gained its dynamism under Origen as it upheld the basic tenets of academic catechesis philosophy.[37] The changing function of the catechetical education was timely, relevant, and necessary for this period due to the resurgence of heresies and controversies created by the Jewish and pagan communities.[38]

Origen's contribution to the development of catechetical education was immense. First, principles involving the school of Alexandria offered a revolutionary paradigm for the church educators, emphasizing reason and intelligence as chief means for teaching and learning. It was particularly evident at this point in history that the church lost its old image of being an ecclesiastical school and took on a new image as an academic institution.[39] Second, Origen helped people realize the value of contextualization if the church was going to transform the culture.[40] As had been with Clement, by contextualizing theology, Origen presented Christianity as an intelligent and reasonable paradigm to his secular audience. This in turn resulted in the wide acceptance of Christianity as an intellectually satisfying religion, attracting even secular students to the school. Furthermore, Origen harmonized the classical and sacred knowledge under the truth claim and gave due respect to both traditions in the church.[41] Third, and last, Origen helped educators develop a holistic paradigm for teaching, a paradigm that focused on assisting students into a journey of knowing which challenges and transforms life.

Origen's strong insistence on intellectualism did not mean he overlooked the issue of spirituality; in fact his primary emphasis was on the Scriptures and prayer (6.8), stressing essential doctrines and having a goal to produce holy people who could engage with God and the culture.[42] Some historians contend that Origen's educative philosophy was deeply rooted in the love of God, asserting that learning must lead to faith, faith to hope, and hope to love.[43] Under this claim, Origen desired the church to function as a school for the soul (Lat., *schola animarum*), helping people: (1) obtain the knowledge that provides deep insights to the mysteries of God, (2) experience enlightenment in their souls, and (3) go through the succession of self-realizations to ultimately encounter the supreme teacher (Gk., *Arch-Didaskalos*), Jesus.[44]

The early church educators gave Christianity intellectual respectability and reputation in the ancient society. As a result, catechetical schools eventually became leading centers for intellectualism, drawing even secular students to the schools.[45] Maintaining the catechetical tradition for higher education, the church educators continued to offer rigorous education even into early medieval time.

Conclusion

The early Christian leaders offered relatively simple yet proficient ways of educating students. First, for the purpose of nurturing new Christians to develop spirituality, the catechumen model was introduced; and decades later, for the purpose of training church leaders to develop intelligible minds, the catechetical model was introduced. Basically, both models epitomize the system of early church education, suggesting the importance of having a theology-driven, life-focused, academically solid yet culturally pertinent educational paradigm. The later development of Christian education grew out of these two systems.

The fact that catechumen and catechetical models became essential strategies of the early church, however, is not by any means an indication that contemporary churches should all relinquish their current systems and readopt the old. Rather, the recognition of the two different historical streams should provide deeper insights to further their educative efforts. The early church models implicitly suggest that education ought to be church-based, Scripture-centered, with integrity and spirituality-driven nurture. On the other hand, the early models explicitly suggest that education is about learning the systems of beliefs and principles whereby the foundational systems of knowledge (e.g., doctrines, theology, history, etc.) foster intelligible Christian minds and hearts. Both suggestions should be considered in furthering the contemporary models of Christian education.

What Can We Learn from Education in the Early Church?

- The church needs to function as a school for the soul.
- The ultimate goal of Christian education is the transformation of heart, mind, and soul.
- Christian education must help Christians develop spiritual, moral, and intellectual integrities.
- The church needs to offer theology-driven, life-focused, intellectually solid yet culturally pertinent educational programs.
- Christian education must offer reflective reality, challenging its students to deepen their minds in God.

- Christian education must be doctrinally based.
- Christian education must be concerned with the value of integrated knowing, in which earthly knowledge cultivates inner sensitivity toward sacred knowledge and leads to the development of Christian character and mind.
- Intellectual education should not be separated from Christian education. To educate is to impart knowledge that fosters intelligent Christian minds and hearts.

Study Helps

Reflection Questions

1. To what extent did the first-century church borrow its educational principles from the classical Greeks? What may have motivated the church leaders to integrate secular knowledge with the sacred?
2. What were some of the significant differences between catechumen and catechetical schools?
3. What principles underlie catechetical and catechumen educations?
4. Clement, Origen, and Augustine have had a profound influence on the theoretical development of Christian education. In what ways did these church leaders affect the purpose, content, and practice of Christian education?
5. How are spiritual formation and education related?
6. What integrative concerns or priorities should you have as students and Christian educators?
7. Some Christian educators believed that the content of religious instruction should only come from the Scriptures, not from other secular writings. Do you agree or disagree? Why?
8. What role should faculty members play in the development of students' spirituality beyond their academic performance?
9. How does the practice of academic discipline lead students and faculty members to a deeper experience of intimacy with God?
10. How is the contemporary philosophy and theory of Christian education different from that of the early church?

Technical Terms

The Apostles' Creed (6.3)
The Apostles' Creed is a summary statement of Christian belief developed between the second and ninth centuries. It is widely agreed that the Apostle's creed was initially developed as a baptismal creed for new believers going through catechumen classes. Although some historians prior to the 15th century suggested its apostolic origin, the authorship is not known. With its doctrinal focus on the Trinity, the three sections of the creed focus on each person of the Triune God: God the Father, Jesus the Son, and the Holy Spirit.

Catechesis
Catechesis, which means *instruction* in Greek, was the instructional system of the early church whereby the foundations of Christianity were taught dialogically. The Greek word *catechesis* derives from *catecheo* (Gk.), which means *to sound toward* and *to instruct orally*. As applied in the context of the early church, *catechesis* referred to the instructional system whereby the principles and rudiments of Christian doctrine were taught orally.

Catechetical
Catechetical education was built on the integrative philosophy of secular and sacred educations for the purpose of equipping prospective church leaders with academic training. The curriculum emphasized broad yet integrative study of Greek literature, philosophy, science, and theology.

Catechumen
Catechumen is a modern English expression of *catechumenoi*, the noun form of *catecheo* (Gk., "to instruct"). *Catechumen* was the title applied to a new adult believer going through a course of classes to be inducted into the church. The curriculum for catechumen education was designed to inculcate, nurture, and socialize new believers to the early church community.

Didache (6.4)
Didache (Gk., "teaching"), which is also known as *Teaching of the Twelve Apostles*, is a short treatise on moral precepts, worship, prayer, baptism, communion, fasting, and the ministry. The treatise is believed to have been written in Syria in the first century (ca. A.D. 70–90), discovered by Bryennios, Greek Orthodox metropolitan of Nicomedia, in 1883.

Pedagogy
Pedagogy comes from the Greek word, *paidagogia* (originally from *paidagogos* which refers to the slave-tutor, *Paedagogus* [Lat.], who worked as an advisor and guide to his young master). *Pedagogy* refers to the art of teaching, especially to a theory or principle of teaching children.

Recommended Bibliography

Harmless, William. *Augustine and the Catechumenate.* Collegeville, MN: Liturgical Press, 1995.

Power, Edward J. *A Legacy of Learning: A History of Western Education.* Albany: State University of New York Press, 1991.

Sherrill, Lewis Joseph. *The Rise of Christian Education.* New York: MacMillan, 1944.

Ulich, Robert. *Three Thousand Years of Educational Wisdom: Selections from Great Documents.* Cambridge, MA: Harvard University Press, 1959.

Westerhoff, John H. and O.C. Edwards, eds. *A Faithful Church: Issues in the History of Catechesis.* Wilton, CT: Morehouse-Barlow, 1981.

Woodbridge, John D., ed. *Great Leaders of the Christian Church.* Chicago: Moody Press, 1989.

Notes

[1] Edward J. Power, *A Legacy of Learning: A History of Western Education* (Albany: State University of New York Press, 1991), 96-98; Lewis Joseph Sherrill, *The Rise of Christian Education* (New York: MacMillan, 1944), 186.

[2] Patrick J. McCormick, *History of Education: A Survey of the Development of Educational Theory and Practice in Ancient, Medieval and Modern Times* (Washington, DC: The Catholic Education Press, 1915), 73.

[3] Sherrill, *Rise,* 186.

[4] James E. Reed and Jonnie Prevost, *A History of Christian Education* (Nashville, TN: Broadman and Holman, 1993), 81; Sherrill, *Rise,* 201; Power, *Legacy,* 96-98.

[5] Christopher Lucas, *Our Western Educational Heritage* (New York: Macmillan, 1972), 176.

[6] J.A. Burns, "Catechetical Schools," trans by Douglas J. Potter, in *Catholic Encyclopedia,* XI:1-28, ed. by Kevin Knight, on-line edition, **www.newadvent.org** (New York: Robert Appleton, 1999), 1-2; Sherrill, *Rise,* 186.

[7] Leone L. Mitchell, "The Development of Catechesis in the Third and Fourth Centuries: From Hippolytus to Augustine, in *A Faithful Church: Issues in the History of Catechesis,* ed. by John H. Westerhoff and O.C. Edwards (Wilton, CT: Morehouse-Barlow, 1981), 51.

[8] T.B. Scannell, "Catechumen," trans. by Tom Crossett, in *The Catholic Encyclopedia,* III:1-28, ed. by Kevin Knight, on-line edition, **www.newadvent.org** (New York: Robert Appleton, 1999), 3.

[9] Robert Ulich, *Education in Western Culture* (New York: Harcourt, Brace and World, 1954), 39.

[10] Scannell, "Catechumen, 3.

[11] Mitchell, "Development," 51.

[12] Scannell, "Catechumen, 3.

[13] Mitchell, "Development," 55.

[14] John Chapman, "Cyril of Jerusalem," trans. by Mike Humphrey, in *The Catholic Encyclopedia*, IV:1-28, ed. by Kevin Knight, on-line edition, **www.newadvent.org** (New York: Robert Appleton, 1999), 2.

[15] Ibid., 55 and 59.

[16] Ulich, *Education*, 39.

[17] Lucas, *Western*, 175.

[18] Mitchell, "Development," 75.

[19] Ibid., 49.

[20] H.I. Marrou, *A History of Education in Antiquity* (New York: Sheed and Ward, 1956), 315; and Sherrill, *Rise*, 191 and 196.

[21] Sherrill, *Rise*, 185.

[22] James Bowen, *A History of Western Education*, The Ancient World: Orient and Mediterranean, vol. I (New York: St. Martin's Press, 1972), 240; John L. Elias, *A History of Christian Education: Protestant, Catholic, and Orthodox Perspective* (Malabar, FL: Krieger, 2002), 28; Tim Dowley, ed., *The History of Christianity* (Grand Rapids: Eerdmans, 1977), 77.

[23] Sherrill, *Rise*, 201; Lucas, *Western*, 177; Burns, "Catechetical Schools," 1.

[24] William K. Medlin, *The History of Educational Ideas in the West* (New York: The Center for Applied Research in Education, Inc., 1964), 31; Lucas, *Western*, 158; Sherrill, *Rise*, 202.

[25] Sherrill, *Rise*, 202.

[26] Bowen, *History*, 243.

[27] Ibid., 247.

[28] Lucas, *Western*, 174.

[29] Bowen, *History*, 247.

[30] Dowley, *History*, 77.

[31] Ulich, *Education*, 40.

[32] Bowen, *History*, 241; Mitchell, "Development," 53.

[33] Bowen, *History*, 241.

[34] Elias, *History*, 28; Sherrill, *Rise*, 202.

[35] Lucas, *Western*, 173-174.

[36] Dowley, *History*, 56.

[37] Mitchell, "Development," 52.

[38] Dowley, *History*, 56; Mitchell, "Development," 55.

[39] Mitchell, "Development," 54.

[40] Elias, *History*, 30.

[41] Ibid., 31.

[42] Mitchell, "Development," 55.

[43] Ulich, *Education*, 39.

[44] Bowen, *History*, 248.

[45] Lucas, *Western*, 174.

Chapter 7
Medieval Christian Education: Toward a Theocentric World (5th–14th Centuries)

Jonathan H. Kim

Overview of Period

The medieval period or the Middle Ages generally refers to the period of European history between the Fall of the Roman Empire (A.D. 476) and the rise of the Italian Renaissance (A.D. 1320), though the precise dates for the period are arbitrary depending on the point of view that a person holds. The medieval period is important to those interested in the history of Christian education in that this era witnessed a remarkable development of Christian schools in Western Europe as the dominance of humanistic classics was eradicated by Christianity. As

> The word *medieval* is made up of two Latin words, *medius* (means *middle*) and *aevum* (means *age*). So when people say *medieval ages*, they are literally saying *Middle Ages* Ages.

a result, nearly all medieval scholarships were under the influence of the church and Christian scholars,[1] which in turn resulted in an astonishing development of Christian thoughts and schools. Although the dominance of Christian leadership was weakened as Renaissance humanism entered the historical scene, the legacy of medieval Christian education, perpetuated through Christian scholastics, continued into the Reformation era. The history of medieval education, in my opinion, is well worth our study. Given the significance of the period, this chapter focuses on key issues and people that have contributed to the development of medieval Christian education.

Purpose of Education

Following the Fall of the Roman Empire, the church became the center for educational advancement. There appeared medieval schools such as monastic, episcopal, guild, palace, and universities that were wholly devoted to Christian ideals. The features of the Hellenistic classics, which dominated the early Christian education, were completely eliminated; in their place theology, philosophy, and the Latin classics became the main focus of study. Eventually, the above schools became the leading centers for formal learning in the medieval world.

The aim of education varied from school to school: the goal of monastic education was to train future monks who could live and lead others to the life of contemplation in deep spirituality; the goal of episcopal (or cathedral) education was to train church pastors, and occasionally lay leaders, for ministry and service; the goal of guild education was to equip students in reading and writing (but later adopted the seven liberal arts as the main curriculum); the goal of palace education was to train future scribes, clerks, tax collectors, and magistrates as well as the children of nobility[2]; and the goal of universities was to train students with Scripture, theology, literature, and philosophy. Generally speaking, the overall educational aim of medieval schools was to ground learning in the contexts of Christian mysticism and rationalism. On one hand, the mainstream intellectual motive of the patristic legacy combined with mysticism challenged students to maintain unfaltering spirituality in learning; but on the other hand, the intellectual thirst contributed by scholasticism called for a fuller understanding of Scripture through the lens of rationality.

Educational Context and Process

Monastic Schools

The sociopolitical situation of the fifth century along with the decline of spiritual and moral fervor, and the corruptions of the public and domestic lives of Christians gave impetus for a monastic school movement. Already by the fourth century, many church leaders, who were concerned with the deterioration of Christian influence in society, contended that a new educational movement was necessary to provide the proper religious and moral training of

Christians and their children.[3] Thus, monastic schools were launched. Exclusively, the goal of launching monastic schools was to create a counterculture to resist the encroachment of the Greek classics on Christian education. Although the vows of worldly abandonment, celibacy, and obedience were

> Monasticism comes from the Greek word *monachos* (μοναχός), which means *solitary* or *alone*. Literally the word refers to the *act of dwelling alone secluded from the world.*

expected of all who join the school, people were eager to learn and be part of the new learning community. The exact time of beginning of monastic schools is not known, but many church historians argue that the informal type began with the establishment of monasteries in the third century, the formal by the sixth century.[4] Eventually, monasteries became gateways to Christian higher learning especially to those who desired deep Christian study and devotion. Perhaps next in importance to catechetical schools (see Chapter 6) was the establishment of the monastic schools.

Educational Process

Monasteries became new centers of higher learning. Within various monasteries developed a deep-seated suspicion of all "pagan literature" which resulted in the rejection of all secular knowledge and situated learning in the study of the Scriptures, patristic theology, and asceticism with a particular focus on communal living (7.2). Perhaps the most pervasive issue here was to situate learning in the context of spirituality and Christian community; their main concern was on the transformation of students and their grounding in religious devotion to God. It was also expected that the transformation of the individual would result in community and societal reforms.

Although the quest for the truth was the ultimate goal of monastic education, different traditions controlled the way each school approached teaching. It may be helpful to explore the differences. The monasteries of the East, specifically the regions of the eastern Mediterranean, stressed the contemplative life while the monasteries of the West stressed classical learning. From the early stage of the medieval period, the schools in the East adopted the Desert Fathers' perspective on learning, which emphasized a simple, unlettered, ascetic, and moral learning within the context of mysti-

> Due to the Eastern monks' lack of emphasis on the content of faith, at times they were accused of being *holy illiterate*.

cism.[5] Daily reading and meditation of the Scriptures were called for until the monk comprehended with the heart; each monk was expected to be able to know the Scriptures especially the Psalms and the New Testament by heart, and to practice ascetic discipline. In the case of monks who were illiterate, the monasteries offered literacy training (i.e., grammar school) three hours a day.

The basic method of teaching employed in the Eastern schools was apprenticeship, which suggests perhaps that a fluid and dynamic type of relationship existed between teachers and students. Often an older monk, someone respected for his spirituality and integrity, would function as a mentor (i.e., spiritual father or director) to guide and train young boys entering the monastery. The education in its entirety was about the contemplative study of the Bible and asceticism, challenging students to be passionate about the formation and development of their souls. It is clear that the quest for ascetic reality was a significant goal of education in the East.

The monastic schools in the West, however, employed a rational approach to education, placing an exclusive emphasis on the intellectual learning of the Scriptures and the Latin classics. Consequently there developed a deep appreciation for the written word of God, especially the reading of the Holy Scripture (i.e., the *lectio divina* [Lat.]). However, the same inclination also produced a perspective that equated spirituality with the intellectual attainment of Latin classics and theology.[6]

Two types of schools emerged in the West—the *internal* (Lat., *schola claustri*; resident) and *external* schools (Lat., *schola canonica*; nonresident). It is difficult to pinpoint exactly when these schools were first introduced, but many historians argue for the ninth or tenth century or earlier.[7] The internal school educated novices who had not yet taken final vows to become monks, while the external school educated lay pupils, often the children of the nobility from neighboring communities who voluntarily gave gratuity to the monastery for the instruction they received.[8]

> The principal of the monastic school was called *magister scholarium* (Lat.) or *scholasticus* (Lat.) and his assistant was called *seniores* (Lat.)

The curriculum of the schools in the West was comprised of theology, the seven liberal arts (the *trivium* comprising grammar, rhetoric, logic; and the *quadrivium* comprising arithmetic, geometry, astronomy, and music) (7.2) plus extracurricular activities on agriculture, architecture, transcribing of ancient manuscripts and documents, and the decorative arts. Since books were scarce, the oral teaching (Lat. *legere*, the word signifies the act of oral teaching) became a popular method of teaching.

Episcopal (or Cathedral) Schools

The educational movement initiated by medieval monks became a catalyst for another premier form of Christian education—episcopal (also called cathedral) education.[9] Decades of successful growth and expansion of monastic schools drew many pastoral candidates to monasteries for sacred learning, but soon the students and church leaders realized that monastic training was unsuitable for future pastors. So in order to ensure a regular supply of pastor candidates, the church introduced episcopal education in local cathedrals. The word episcopal comes from a Greek word, *episkopos* (Lat., *episcopus*), which means *an overseer, elder, pastor,* or *bishop* assigned to a church. Literally, the episcopal school means a school for overseers or pastors. In the early stage, episcopal schools mainly attracted ministry candidates; however, when the schools flourished in the 12th century, even secular students came to the schools for higher learning. One of the first recognized episcopal schools dates back to the eighth century founded by Chrodegang (A.D. 742–766), bishop of Metz,[10] though some argue for an earlier school dating back to the fifth century.[11] Although sparsely located, episcopal schools were effective in equipping future pastors and transforming local communities.

Educational Process

The purpose of episcopal education was to prepare future pastors (i.e., priests). As learning centers, what continued to be taught in episcopal schools was theology, canon law, ecclesiastical

> For the purpose of training youngsters for the church worship, music schools were introduced in cathedrals in the ninth century. These music schools evolved into elementary schools two hundred years later.[12]

administration, and rudiments of the seven liberal arts (7.2).[13] Teaching was done by bishops in the early years, but as the schools increased in size, the teaching responsibility was distributed to *canons* (Lat., *scholastici*), priests serving under the leadership of a bishop.

Episcopal schools employed a curriculum with two grade levels—*scholar minor* and *scholar major*. The *scholar minor* offered elementary education in reading, writing, and psalmody; the *scholar major* offered secondary education in the seven liberal arts (7.2), Scripture, and pastoral theology.

Guild Schools

The specific work of medieval education was not restricted to religious schools only. Later in the thirteenth century, nonreligious institutions intended for the general public were introduced in various guilds (also called *collegiate*).[14] Compared to monastic and cathedral schools, guild schools had a relatively later start in the early thirteenth century. To an extent, guild schools can be viewed as the extension of cathedral schools organized in local communities for the purpose of educating the general public although the education was still limited to the rich and the elite class mostly.

The formation and development of guild schools came with the rise of a prosperous middle class (i.e., bourgeoisie) in Western Europe. As trading increased, merchants and craftsmen prospered; consequently a commerce association called a guild—an ancient Roman form of corporate association—would be organized in various cities and towns. A guild is also known as *collegia* (the classical Roman term for religious association), *scholae*, *universitate*, or *sodalitates*.[15] The original purpose of the guild was to regulate business and civil affairs, but when business and civil autonomies were established, the middle class sought a way to provide nonreligious education for their children. This resulted in the establishment of the guild or collegiate schools. Guild schools were first nonreligious schools established under a partnership between church and civic leaders though the general policy concerning cur-

> The original purpose of establishing middle-class guilds was to establish a business network and gain freedom from the jurisdiction of local nobles and church officials.

riculum, admission, teaching, and even the commission to operate was still controlled by church leaders.[16]

Educational Process

History indicates the existence of elementary (i.e., local grammar schools) and secondary guild schools (i.e., Latin grammar schools) in large towns and cities, which flourished in large number in the late thirteenth century. Despite the lack of curricular and educational standards in the beginning, some guild schools became academies for higher learning, even competing with monastic and cathedral schools. Due to a particular context where guild schools were operating, the admission to the schools was mostly limited to the children of wealthy business people (i.e., bankers, merchants, trades people, and artisans) to whom education was an essential ticket to future success.

As for the curriculum, in addition to a prescribed elementary education in reading and writing, secondary education organized around the trivium (i.e., grammar, rhetoric, and logic) was offered. The theory and method employed in guild schools were very similar to that of cathedral schools, but the educative purpose was different: guild schools mainly educated students with secular vocational goals.

The founding of guild schools was important in that they paved the way for public education including the establishment of the medieval university. A greater proportion of the public became literate and was able to improve their lives as a result. Eventually, the growth of guild schools in various cities encouraged liberal arts teachers to form their own collegia which later grew into universities in places like Bologna, Spain (1113); Paris, France (1160); and Oxford, England (1249).

Palace Schools

With the decline of the church's monopoly over education, plus the continual demand and need for general education, palace (or court) schools were launched. Palace schools were the civil counterparts of cathedral schools, established during the educational reform of the eighth century under the leadership of Alcuin, a famous English educator and theologian, and Charlemagne (742–814), the King of the Franks.

Educational Process

Unlike other medieval institutions, the academic authority and control of palace schools were not under the church, but under the king and nobility. Pubic officials therefore were free to choose their own curriculum and to decide on the direction of the schools. The palace teachers offered studies of the seven liberal arts comprising the trivium and the quadrivium, Scripture, the Church Fathers, science, medicine, and philosophy. Although academic aptitude lacked significantly in comparison to episcopal schools, palace schools eventually became patrons for more general, nonreligious education in the medieval society. One of the known palace schools is that of King Henry II of England founded in the late twelfth century.[17]

Universities

The success of medieval schools and the development of scholasticism contributed to the rise and development of the medieval university. In the eleventh century, the term, university (Lat., *universitas*), generally referred to a guild of businessmen of the medieval society. However, when the scope and direction of liberal arts schools became more broad and extensive in the twelfth century, the word *universitas* (i.e., university) was applied to denote academic institutions.[18] Although the precise beginning of the earliest university is debatable, most historians agree that the school of Bologna in Spain (1113), was the first to receive legitimate recognition under the term *university*.

> An academic association of students pursuing scholarly work was commonly referred to as a *stadium* (Lat.) or infrequently a *discipulorum* (Lat.).

As an intellectual community of scholars, the medieval university functioned as the center for higher learning in theology, the liberal arts, law, and medicine. Following the university of Bologna, the university of Paris, France, was instituted in 1160. Soon, seventy-nine other universities were organized between the twelfth and the fourteenth centuries, including universities of Padua (1222), Naples (1224), Pisa (1343), Florence (1349) in Italy; Salamanca in Spain (1243); Oxford (1249) and Cambridge (1284) in England; Prague in the Czech Republic (1347); Vienna in Austria (1365); Deventer in Netherlands (1384); and Heidelberg (1387) and Erfurt (1392) in Germany.[19]

Educational Process

Prior to the later twelfth century, a significant part of the early university curriculum consisted of the traditional seven liberal arts along with the works of Aristotle, law, and medicine. Gratian's *Decretum* and Justinian's *Corpus Juris Civils* were the main texts for law, while the works of Avicenna, Galen, and Hippocrates were the texts for medicine.[20]

Usually three instructional methods were employed in medieval universities: first, formal lecture which involved word-for-word dictation of an instructor's (Lat., *scholastici*) own book or manuscript combined with his side comments. Lectures were highly formal and rigid, involving little or no student interactions. Often, lectures gave teachers an opportunity to display their academic prowess and the pedigree of their scholarly achievements. Second, peer-teaching, a training exercise designed to prepare students for the teaching licensing examination, was used. And, third, debate where students discuss and critically examine the issues presented by the teacher was also employed by the university instructors.

The academic life of university students was not that easy. Although the actual time spent on university study varied from student to student, it was not unusual for students to spend up to twelve years completing a university program. Just the study of the seven liberal arts alone took four to seven years to complete.[21]

> The University of Paris was known as the great center for theological studies, while the University of Bologna, Spain, was known as a center for liberal arts studies.

The rise of the medieval university brought two significant changes to the medieval society. First, the university became an academic center for intellectualism, transmitting knowledge and wisdom to the future generation. Second, with the rise of the university came social reforms, breaking down the barriers that hindered the general public from receiving education. Progressively, the medieval university became Europe's intellectual center for higher learning, ushering the culture to the era of reform.

Scholaticism

Closely tied to the origin and development of the medieval university was the intellectual movement called scholasticism. The word *scholasticism* is a derivative of the Greek word, *scholastikos,* which refers to a philosopher or the headmaster of monastic school (Lat., *scholasticus* or *magister scholae*). As an intellectual movement, scholasticism was more far-reaching than any other movements of the medieval world; it was, as many medieval historians would contend, the premier form of the Christian intellectual system.

The scholastic movement is marked by three distinct stages extending from the early ninth century to the fifteenth century: (1) The formative stage, from the beginning of the ninth century to the middle of the thirteenth century, when John Scotus Erigena (815–877) introduced the Augustinian dialecticism (sees reason as a sole basis for all knowing) to Europe. (2) The expansion stage, from the middle of the thirteenth century to the early fourteenth century, when scholasticism dominated all intellectual movements in Western Europe. During this stage, patristic philosophy reached its climax in the system of Thomas Aquinas (1224–1274) and gave birth to so-called Christian philosophy (also known as scholastic philosophy). (3) The stage of decline, from the early fourteenth century to the end of the fifteenth century, when scholasticism began losing its momentum following the death of Duns Scotus (1308).

> Monasticism embraced patristic theology, asceticism, and Christian mysticism; Scholasticism, on the other hand, embraced the philosophy of Aristotle, and exalted rationalism in Christian studies.

Educational Process

The purpose of scholastic education was to develop a Christian mind leading to faith by the means of logical analysis (reason). The curriculum was comprised of theology, philosophy, especially the Aristotelian logic, the Scriptures, and the seven liberal arts (i.e., trivium and quadrivium).

Scholastics (Lat., *scholastici*) employed dialectics—a method of teaching that systematically arrives at the truth by means of logical arguments—to clarify the religious truth regarding the nature of God, the relation of reason and faith, the authority and nature of Scripture, and theological doctrines. Historically, dialectics as a teaching method refined by scholastics came to be known as Christian rationalism.

Educational Content

The curriculum of early medieval schools was exclusively based on the Scriptures, theology, and asceticism, but later schools adopted the rudiments of the seven liberal arts (i.e., trivium and quadrivium) as the main curriculum (7.2).[22] Elementary education was based on the *trivium* comprised of grammar, rhetoric, and logic—which is better known to the contemporary audience as *language arts studies*. The exclusive emphasis was on the study of the rudiments of *grammar* which included reading, writing, and communication. The *rhetoric* focused on the works of Quintilian and Cicero, the Roman philosophers. The principles of *logic* included the works of Augustine, in particular his syllogisms, disputation, and definition.

Almost all secondary education in the medieval period focused on the *quadrivium* comprising arithmetic, geometry, astronomy, and music. Arithmetic included the study of basic mathematics especially the use of numbers. Geometry included Euclid's principles of geometry on lines, angles, shapes, and figures. Euclid was a fourth-century B.C. Greek mathematician who introduced a thirteen volume treatise on geometry called *Elements* which became the main mathematic text in the medieval world. Astronomy included the study of stars (i.e., astrology) and making the church calendar. Music included the study of church worship consisting of reading, writing, psalmody, memorization of various poems, and the theories and techniques of music. Some historians claim that painting, drawing, architecture, and sculpture were also included with the music education.[23]

Voices

Having explored the educational context, process, and content of medieval education, we now turn our attention to key individuals whose perspectives have shaped the overall theory and practice of medieval Christian education. Although it is difficult to fully grasp the accomplishments of these educators, their unrelenting desire to settle perplexing theological, spiritual, and philosophical issues of education led to the monumental accomplishments seen in medieval schools. They spent much time reexamining the articles of faith and sought after the exact, detailed, and genuine understanding of God and His truth. Such effort not only produced the prodigious achievements in

Christian scholarship, but facilitated intellectual conversation between secular and sacred communities in their pursuit of truth. It will be helpful to study four foundational figures of medieval Christianity in this section: Benedict of Nursia, Alcuin, Anselm, and Aquinas.

Benedict of Nursia (A.D. 480–543) was instrumental in spreading monastic education, and he was also the founder of western monasticism and the author of the outstanding set of European monastic regulations and manuals on asceticism known as the Rule (❀ 7.3). Benedict, a son of a distinguished Roman noble of Nursia, Italy, was born and educated in Rome.[24] In his adult years, Benedict pursued the life of spiritual devotion as a hermit.

In search of a solitary life, St. Benedict began his Order (the term Order refers to an established system of socioreligious organization) in A.D. 529 to educate and lead others to a life of devotion to God. Benedict focused on the deepest and soundest Christian principles in educating his students. For example, he prescribed holistic learning involving ascetic discipline, worship, two hours of daily Scripture reading, copying various manuscripts, and seven hours of daily manual work involving farming, crafts, and woodworking as major means to train young students.

To offer theocentric education, Benedict organized two schools under his leadership: the internal school (Lat., *schola claustri*; resident) to educate future monks, and the external school (Lat., *schola canonica*; nonresident) to educate local community children. Being intolerant of the Greek classics, Benedict emphasized the study of grammar, rhetoric, logic, and religion combined with meditation on the Scriptures and the singing of psalms in his schools. Moreover, Benedict rejected formal learning, which had been the primary medium of church education for centuries, and encouraged active learning, combining theory and practice in Christian education.

Alcuin (735–804), the Master of the Ninth-Century Palace Education, a famous English educator and theologian, is well known for establishing Palace schools and bringing the educational reform of the eighth century (781–790) to France under the leadership of Charlemagne (742–814), the King of the Franks. Alcuin was born and raised in Yorkshire of Northumbria, the Anglo-Saxon kingdom of northern England. He entered the cathedral school of York in his early childhood and was educated under the headmaster Egbert of York, a prominent medieval scholar. Eventually in A.D. 778, Alcuin himself became the headmaster at the school of York.

From A.D. 781 to 790, at the request of Charlemagne, Alcuin took a residence in the royal palace of France and began a school, which initiated the intellectual reform of the eighth century, from which the Carolingian renaissance found much of its inspiration. Alcuin extolled and implemented the monastic and cathedral models of education in his palace schools. His curriculum included the studies of the seven liberal arts, the Scriptures, and patristic writings.

Alcuin's contribution to the development of medieval education was remarkable. First, by eradicating class distinctions and encouraging the education of the general citizen by the church, Alcuin made church schools a major venue for public education. Second, by refuting heretical movements of his day, Alcuin upheld Christian doctrines and practices in his schools. Third, with his passionate disposition toward teaching, he produced

> Alcuin possessed remarkable originality and literary excellence especially in the areas of humanities, grammar, rhetoric, poems, and dialectics.

future church and political leaders who lent their Christian influences to the secular world. His disciples include Arno, archbishop of Salzburg; Theodulph, bishop of Orleans; Eanbald, archbishop of York; Adelhard, abbot of Corbie in Saxony; Aldrich, abbot of Ferrieres; Fridugis, abbot of St. Martin; and Rabanus Maurus, the intellectual successor of Alcuin at Aachen and Tours.[25] Lastly, as a theologian, Alcuin wrote numerous exegetical, moral, and dogmatic books including commentaries on Genesis, Psalms, Song of Solomon, Ecclesiastes, Hebrew names, the Gospel of John, Titus, Philemon, and Hebrews. Alcuin also undertook the revision of the Vulgate, the Latin translation of the Bible, and made the Bible accessible to the general public.

Scholastic Educators

Scholasticism particularly its theory, method, and content opened up a new horizon and enlarged the inclusiveness of Christian theology and philosophy in medieval Christian education. To educate students in spirituality, the early scholastics approached truth from the angle of mysticism and sought to harmonize mysticism and orthodoxy within their reverence for the relationality of faith, whereas the latter scholastics approached truth from the angle of rationalism and rejected all the unreasonable claims of Christian mystics and advocated rationality as the ultimate means to truth. Such attempts to inform and shape the overall direction of Christian teaching were seen in the works of Anselm and Aquinas.

Anselm of Canterbury (1034–1109). One of the early voices of scholasticism was Anselm of Canterbury, a pious philosopher, theologian, and church leader who harmonized philosophy and orthodoxy under mysticism. Anselm was born in 1034 at Aosta, northern Italy. At the age of twenty-five (A.D. 1059), he joined the Benedictine monastery at Bec, Normandy, France—the most prominent school of the eleventh century—where he developed his sound, scholastic mind.

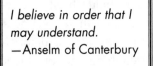

I believe in order that I may understand.
—Anselm of Canterbury

Like Augustine, Anselm believed that people should believe first in order to understand the mysteries of faith (Lat., *fides quaerens intellectum*, which means "I believe in order that I may understand"). This is to say that the love for God must precede the knowledge of Him. Anselm was not rejecting the role of reason in learning; rather he was contending that reason should assist a person in comprehending the truth, and the comprehension must be guided by the affirmation of love and faith in God. Principally, Anselm was approaching the essence of truth from the way in which one's experience functions in the confinement of knowing.

Anselm left numerous projects of faith including the *Monologium* (A.D. 1077), a soliloquy on God's attributes; and the *Proslogium* (A.D. 1078), a discourse on faith (7.4). Anselm's influence was enormous in the medieval world; he even influenced the theology and philosophy of a future scholastic named Thomas Aquinas.

Thomas Aquinas (1224–1274). In the thirteenth century, scholasticism culminated in the systematic union of theology and philosophy, and began dominating the intellectual life of the medieval society. Undeniably, many scholastics' keen and unrelenting searches for the truth have contributed to many splendid outcomes. However, at the pinnacle of the movement, the divergent currents set off by two schools of thought, the Franciscan and the Dominican, weakened its movement. The Dominicans, on one hand, were committed to the systematic and rational study of the Scriptures and therefore endorsed the synthesis of theology and philosophy (i.e., rational theology); but the Franciscans, on the other hand, were committed to the mystical study of faith that exclusively focused on patristic theology and mysticism. Seeing understanding (Lat., *intellectus*) as the precursor of all principles, the Dominicans emphasized the power of dialectics in teaching, while the Franciscans emphasized the will (Lat., *voluntas*) as the chief principle of all knowledge. Eventually, the Dominicans succeeded in refuting the Franciscans and placed rational theology at the forefront of the scholastic movement. The ecclesiastical tradition of mysticism that once restricted the dialectic exploration of the Christian truth was crushed, and students were encouraged to explore knowledge critically and logically.

The leading intellect of the Dominican order was *Thomas Aquinas (1224–1274)*, an Italian monk, philosopher, theologian, prolific writer, and patron of medieval universities whose works appeared at a critical stage in the development of scholasticism. Undoubtedly he was the quintessential thinker among all the movers and shakers of the scholastic movement.

Aquinas was born in Neapolitan (near Rome) Italy as a son of a nobleman. He entered the Benedictine monastery of Monte Cassino at age five (A.D. 1229), and the University of Naples at age twelve (A.D. 1236). In both schools, the young Aquinas was recognized for his brilliant mind, numerous talents, and pure devotion to God. At the

> To know is to become,
> to become the non-I.
> —Thomas Aquinas

University of Naples, Aquinas mastered the seven liberal arts (i.e., Trivium and Quadrivium) and became acquainted with the teachings of the Dominican order.

In 1243, Aquinas decided to desert his Benedictine roots and joined the Dominican Order of St. Dominic. Shortly after, in 1244 or 1245, the Dominicans noticed Aquinas's extraordinary intellect and sent him to Paris to study and teach under Albert the Great (Lat., Albertus Magnus), a renowned German Aristotelian scholar.

Eventually, Aquinas was ordained as a priest (1250) and began teaching at the University of Paris in 1252. In due time, he received the degree of doctor of theology from the University of Paris.

As an educator, Aquinas's contribution to the development of Christian education was remarkable. His dialect grid, which synthesized faith and reason, revolutionized the way Christians approached teaching. Moreover, Aquinas's books on faith became primary sources in church instruction, especially the works on exegesis, homiletics, liturgy, apology, ethics, metaphysics, and epistemology. One of the best known examples of his written work is *Summa Theologica* (1266–1273) (Lat.), the summary treatise of theology (❧ 7.5).

> Aquinas asserted that true theology and philosophy can never disagree in their quest for the truth.

At the summit of its splendid glory, scholasticism witnessed its downfall when *Johannes Duns Scotus (1270–1308)*, a Franciscan scholar, a proponent of Christian mysticism, appeared on the historical scene and mercilessly criticized the authenticity of Thomistic philosophy, especially his premise of the oneness of faith and reason. Unlike Aquinas, Duns Scotus believed that theology is a practical science whose main concern and essence cannot be plausibly proven philosophically (or by reason). Eventually, Duns Scotus succeeded in weakening Thomistic philosophy, and separated philosophy from theology, and knowledge from faith. The effect of the dispute combined with the rise of Renaissance Humanism was detrimental to the scholastic movement; many critics of Christianity began arguing that faith is analogous to mystical, irrational, unreliable perception. Following Duns Scotus, from the fourteenth century onwards, scholasticism began losing its momentum and its splendid glory eventually faded with time.

As an intellectual movement, the influence of scholasticism was felt not only during the medieval period but for centuries to come. The movement brought a deep spirit of intellectualism to the church and marked the beginning of so-called Christian philosophy. Particularly, the integration and application of dialectic to theology helped scholars to situate reason as a primary means of Christian teaching and learning. The influence of scholasticism is still evident in the works of many contemporary Christian scholars.

Conclusion

Far from being a mere religious movement, the medieval Christian schools became the formative force of Christian education, serving as major avenues for intellectual and spiritual formation. The monastic school's attempt to situate learning in the context of spirituality, the cathedral school's effort to integrate the liberal arts studies with theology, guild and palace schools' attempts to provide theocentric education for the general public, and medieval universities' scholarly pursuit of philosophy and theology, all represent the prevailing forces of Christian education in our history.

What Can We Learn from Medieval Christian Education?

- Generally speaking, the purpose of the medieval Christian education was to ground learning in the contexts of spirituality and rationality.

- The ultimate aim of teaching is helping people experience intellectual and spiritual transformations.

- The goal of secular education is preparing men and women for the earthly life, but the goal of Christian education is to prepare men and women for the meaning and significance of life beyond death.

- The content of Christian education must be based on the authoritative body of revealed truth.

- The task of the Christian teacher is to utilize reason in the service of teaching faith and revelation.

- Medieval Christian leaders developed a full system of knowledge under Christian theology and philosophy.

- The university has originated from medieval church schools (e.g., cathedral, monastic, and guild schools), and its development is closely tied to the rise of scholasticism.

Study Helps

Reflection Questions

1. On the basis of your reading of the chapter, what changes took place in the medieval educational system?

2. How did sociocultural and ecclesiastical changes of the middle period impact the establishment of schools?

3. What were the purposes of monastic, episcopal, guild, and palace schools?

4. How did medieval universities come about?

5. How do you explain the fact that the early Eastern monks were illiterate yet holy? How are spirituality and intelligibility related?

6. How did Christian mysticism and rationalism influence the minds of medieval educators?

7. What role did monasticism and scholasticism play in the development of the medieval schools?

8. Can philosophy be Christian? Is the concept of Christian philosophy paradoxical, even nonsensical?

9. What role does Christian philosophy have in Christian education?

10. What is your opinion of the dispute between the Franciscans and the Dominicans on the issue of faith and reason?

11. In your opinion, do you think that medieval schools were successful in establishing a theocentric world?

Technical Terms

Carolingian (or **Carlovingian**)   The name of the Frankish dynasty found by Pepin, which included the regions of France, Italy, middle Europe, and Austria between A.D. 751 and 987. Charlemagne (742–814) is Pepin's son.

Christian mysticism   A belief or the movement originated in the Eastern monastic tradition that attempted to gain a unique knowledge of the mysteries of God through a person's immediate, conscious realization given by the Holy Spirit.

Dialectics   A method of reasoning that systematically arrives at the truth by the means of logic.

Monasticism	The term literally means "the act of dwelling alone secluded from the world" and describes the mode of life chosen by religious people for the ultimate pursuit of spiritual life.
Scholasticism	The premier form of medieval intellectual method and system of reasoning that sought to clarify religious truth and to defend the mysteries of faith.
The Order	An established system of socioreligious organization in the Middle Ages, e.g., monastery.

Recommended Bibliography

Patterson, Glenys. *The University from Ancient Greece to the 20th Century.* Palmerston North, NZ: Dunmore Press, 1997.

Sands, Lester B., and Richard E. Gross. *The History of Education: A Timeline of Scope and Perspective.* Cleveland: The World Publishing Company, 1967.

Smith, L. Glenn, and Joan K. Smith. *Lives in Education: A Narrative of People and Ideas.* New York: St. Martin's Press, 1994.

Notes

[1] William K. Medlin, *The History of Educational Ideas in the West* (New York: The Center for Applied Research in Education, Inc., 1967), 36.

[2] Christopher J. Lucas, *Our Western Educational Heritage* (New York: The Macmillan Company, 1972), 212; Edward J. Power, *A Legacy of Learning: A History of Western Education* (Albany: State University of New York Press, 1991), 148.

[3] J.A. Burns, "Schools," in *The Catholic Encyclopedia*, vol. XI, ed. by Kevin Knight (New York: Robert Appleton, Online edition, 1999), On-line edition: http://www.newadvent.org/cathen, 2.

[4] Levi Seeley, *History of Education* (New York: American Book Company, 1899), 116; Lucas, *Western*, 208-209.

[5] H.I. Marrou, *A History of Education in Antiquity* (New York: Sheed and Ward, 1956), 330.

[6] Ibid., 333.

[7] Burns, "Schools," 2.

[8] Ibid.

[9] Patrick J. McCormick, *History of Education* (Washington, DC: The Catholic Education Press, 1915), 86.

[10] Burns, "Schools," 3.

[11] McCormick, *History*, 86.

[12] Lucas, *Western*, 211.

[13] Medlin, *History*, 37; Power, *Legacy*, 146.

[14] Power, *Legacy*, 147.

[15] L. Glenn Smith and Joan K. Smith, *Lives in Education: A Narrative of People and Ideas* (New York: St. Martin's Press, 1994), 84.

[16] Lucas, *Western*, 215.

[17] Ibid., 213.

[18] McCormick, *History*, 133; and Lucas, *Western*, 227.

[19] Lester B. Sands and Richard E. Gross, *The History of Education: A Timeline of Scope and Perspective* (Cleveland, OH: The World Publishing Company, 1967), 6.

[20] Lucas, *Western*, 236.

[21] Ibid.

[22] Medlin, *History*, 37.

[23] Seeley, *History*, 119.

[24] Hugh E. Ford, "St. Benedict of Nursia," in *The Catholic Encyclopedia*, vol. II, ed. by Kevin Knight (New York: Robert Appleton Company, Online edition, 1999), On-line edition: **http://www.newadvent.org/cathen**, 7.

[25] Burns, "Schools," 3.

Chapter 8
Renaissance Education: Education for Individuality (A.D. 1320–1600)

Jonathan H. Kim

Overview of Period

As the Medieval civilization began to disintegrate, there appeared a cultural renewal movement called the Renaissance, known as a rebirth of classical humanism. The Renaissance refers to the transitional period of European history between the medieval and the modern era, from the early fourteenth century to late sixteenth century. At this time the admiration and emulation of Greco-Roman classics gave rise to a surge of interest in and appreciation of humanistic learning. A heightened interest in theocentric, religious study commenced by medieval scholastics came to a dead end, and a newfound interest in humanities (Lat., *studia humanitas*) now governed the way people approached education.

On the whole, the Renaissance represents the demise of the church's domination and the reinstitution of Greco-Roman antiquity. Historians generally argue that the spirit of the Renaissance arose from the counterforce of the medieval religious culture. The Renaissance was a protest against medievalism, against the church's intellectual and cultural domination, and a return to the classical legacy of Greco-Roman culture.

Although the influence of the medieval church continued through the Renaissance, already by the fourteenth century, the mass of people in both

The word *renaissance* (Fr., *renaistre*; Lat., *renascere*) means *rebirth* or *revival*. The concept *renaissance* was first coined by Giorgio Vasari, an Italian architect, painter, and writer, in his book, *Lives of Artists* (1550).

Italy and Northern Europe were cynical about the medieval church. However, since the church was the primary shaper and interpreter of the medieval culture, people's curiosity toward humanism was suppressed, and they were forced to think within a religious paradigm imposed by the church. The advent of the Renaissance, however, changed everything. The nature and potency of humanity became the principal focus of intellectual exploration. Henceforth, the humanistic philosophy of education began shaping the theory and practice of both public and Christian education.

To develop a composite picture of the Renaissance and its influence on the theory and practice of Christian education, we will first introduce two strands of the Renaissance, the Italian and Northern European.

Italian and Northern European Renaissance

The Renaissance is closely associated with the revival of ancient antiquity and an increased awareness of humanity. Although the Renaissance was a continuous, incessant cultural progress of Western civilization, it is conventionally divided into two different periods: the first during the fourteenth and fifteenth centuries in Italy, and the second in Northern Europe in Germany, Holland, England, and France during the sixteenth and seventeenth centuries. Central to both periods was the consciousness of humanity—the virtues, values, and ideals of the human took root and expanded throughout Europe for nearly two centuries.

The first phase of the Renaissance took place in Florence, Italy, in the early fourteenth century. The Italian Renaissance was characterized by a renewed interest in the novelty of Greco-Roman classicism connected with the increased awareness of individuality. The classical premise which glorifies human virtue and capacity became central to the Italian mind. Scholars during this period sought to re-create the Greco-Roman classicism. As a result, many rediscovered the world of humanity through the lenses of literature, art, science, and religion.

Among various trends and currents of European history, the Italian Renaissance marks the beginning of humanism. Cynicism and suspicion of the medieval traditionalism combined with a new awareness of individuality, nature, and Greco-Roman literature and

> Italian Renaissance humanism emphasized the inherent dignity of the human as the image of the divine.

art enthused the minds of many teachers and students. This was a critical moment in history when the whole of European society started to believe in and acted upon the potentiality, intelligibility, and transcendency of the human. With time, the influence of the Renaissance gradually spread to Northern Europe, bringing the classical form of Humanism to the Northerners. But unlike the modern interpretation of humanism, Renaissance humanism did not reject God although it did reject the stagnant religious past of the medieval church. The Northerners embraced a dynamic vibrancy of human intellect and potency in conjunction with their religious tradition.

While Italians were going through a cultural revolution, many of the Northern European nations were in major turmoil during the thirteenth through fifteenth centuries. The series of conflicts and ecological challenges—including the Hundred Years War (1337–1453) between France and England, the Black Death (1347–1450) which wiped out about one third of Europe's population, peasant uprisings, the schism of the Catholic church, and a series of religious battles in the regions of Austria, the Czech Republic, and Slovakia—weakened the religious, cultural, and political structures of Northern nations. This explains why the Northern Europeans were a step behind Italians.

The Northern Renaissance occurred in Northern Europe in Germany, Holland, England, and France during the sixteenth and seventeenth centuries. A complex mixture of classical and Christian culture influenced the reform. Institutionalism created by the medieval church was rejected, and detailed attention was given to improving education in the context of Christian humanism. Also, various geographic explorations and scientific discoveries during this period made the Northern movement even more dynamic than the Italian. Unlike its southern predecessor, the Northern Renaissance was less classical and more religious in nature. Rather than rejecting the religious ideals of the past, Northern Europeans sought to improve their educational endeavor by translating classical ideals according to their religious beliefs, although the content of humanism still played a major role in teaching. As an educational movement, the Renaissance encouraged the enthusiastic return of Greek and Latin literature, art (e.g., sculpture, painting), and architecture, which were suppressed under Christendom for centuries. What was pivotal to the development of Renaissance education was the emergence of humanism. Such a shift in perspective created an entirely different attitude toward education. First, people attempted to disband the older order of educational institutions, and sought to establish humanist schools under the classical heritage of Greece and Rome. Europeans, especially those of Italy, Germany, England, Holland, and France valued the brilliance and exquisite beauty of the classical antiquities and expanded the cultural and intellectual ideals to surrounding nations. Second, the Renaissance reinstated the study of the Classics as the standard curriculum of education. No longer did people consider scholastic learning as customary to their lives. Perhaps one of the powerful undercurrents of the movement was the public's cynicism toward religious learning, which was fueled by the dismal gloom created by the corruption of the Catholic church. The public favored a return of classical education in Western Europe.

Purpose of Education

The overall aim of Renaissance education was to increase awareness of human value, dignity, and capability. Renaissance educators focused on developing individuality through the lens of humanism; the primary emphasis was on the transformation of beings rather than the transmission of knowledge. Furthermore, Renaissance educators rejected the Christian view of human depravity and began viewing humans as divine. It was within this humanistic paradigm that Renaissance education was established.

> The primary focus of the Renaissance educator was on the dignity of the human rather than God.

Renaissance educators believed that the Greco-Roman period was a perfect age of humanity and that it was their responsibility to reintroduce the classical ideals of education to fourteenth-century Europe. So in an effort to reintroduce a so-called "ideal" version of education, educators recommended teaching Greco-Roman literature, poetry, philosophy, and grammar for the goal of leading students to appreciate the value of humanity and contribute to the common good of the society. Renaissance educators believed that the ultimate outcome of education is producing virtuous individuals who could improve the conditions of the church and society.

Unlike the Italians, the Northerners believed that education provided the impetus for ecclesiastical reform and stressed the importance of translating classical ideals according to their Christian belief; thus they produced the "new" learning based on the synthesis of humanism and religion. This new pedagogy was believed to improve moral and spiritual conditions of people, in turn contributing to social and ecclesiastical reforms.

Educational Contexts

Humanistic ideals introduced in the Renaissance founded three types of schools—the universities, private schools, and public schools.[1] Although many schools were initially founded under scholastic ideals, the revival of classical learning transformed their past image and gave a completely different identity to the schools. These institutions were the schools of humanities, focusing on teaching classical language (e.g., Latin and Greek) and literature.[2]

Universities. An explosion of humanistic ideals founded numerous universities. Early on in the Italian Renaissance, humanistic curriculum called the "new" learning was instituted in the universities of Pavia, Rome, Padua, Milan, and Florence in Italy. As the movement spread to Northern Europe, the universities of Paris, Heidelberg, Erfurt, Leipzig, Oxford, and Cambridge also adopted the new curriculum.[3] However, universities with a long-held tradition of scholasticism were critical of the new humanistic pedagogy. More so than any other institution, the University of Paris, which was the leading center of Christian scholarship in the fourteen century, was very antagonistic toward the movement.[4] Nonetheless, new institutions were founded in Europe including the College of France (*College de France*) (1517) in France and St. John's (1511) in England. Through these new institutions, the "new" learning spread to other European universities.

Private Schools. Despite church schools' (i.e., monastic, cathedral schools) rejection of the "new" learning, many humanistic schools were founded by private individuals. These schools were primarily designed to teach the children of nobility with the newfound curriculum. Although the infrastructure of these private schools was similar to that of the medieval cathedral and palace schools, their core curriculum was replaced by the Classics. The emphasis was on learning the Latin literature and language, and cultivating human virtue and knowledge. Some of the prominent private schools were Vittorino da Feltre's school at Mantua in Italy, Court schools in Italy, Schools for Princes (Ger., *Furstenschulen*) in Germany, and John Sturm's Gymnasium (1537) at Strassbourg in France.[5]

Public Schools. Renaissance humanism also gave birth to so called "public" schools. Unlike church schools, these public schools were founded apart from the jurisdiction of the church. These public schools are similar to the school of liberal arts now. With the commitment to liberal arts education, schools were established in England at Winchester (1387), Eton (1440), and London (St. Paul's school, 1510). St. Paul's school, founded by John Colet, became a leading public school in sixteenth-century England and introduced the new learning into the rest of the English schools.[6]

Educational Content and Process

As the new spirit of education inherited from Scholasticism gained widespread acceptance during the eleventh and twelfth centuries, humanistic principles governed by the ancient classicism were already gaining steady ground among intellectuals.[7] Eventually in the fourteenth century, when the values and general concerns of medieval education dissipated, the demand for a new kind of education increased. Increasingly fewer people showed interest in scholastic education, and more people began preferring the new learning. As a result, the humanistic ideals of self-consciousness, self-fulfillment, and self-satisfaction became the core content of public and religious education. What's more, scholasticism with its natural affinity for Aristotelianism, which emphasized the use of dialectics in education, was removed, and in its place Ciceronianism and Neoplatonism were enthroned. In many respects, Renaissance scholars' open embracing of humanism caused a revolt against the logic-based, medieval curriculum endorsed by scholastic scholars. Rather than focusing on logic and semantic analyses, Renaissance educators emphasized the study of the Classics and the dignity and preeminence of the human along with the rejection of medieval religious authorities. However, such a change of attitude did not amount to apostasy, at least not in the early stage of the Renaissance; nevertheless, there was a definite sense of shift in people's attitudes toward life, religion, and learning. Such a shift of attitude provided the groundwork for the edifice of humanistic education; people began building a new repertoire of teaching techniques.

When all is said and done, the content and process of Renaissance education were the study of humanities (Lat., *studia humanitas*), better known as liberal arts education. The expression *studia humanitas*, originated in the fifteenth century, refers to the study of literature and language (i.e., Greek and Roman), rhetoric, history, poetry, and moral philosophy,

> **FYI:** The term *liberal* in the liberal arts derives from the Latin *libera*, which means freedom.

which was drawn from *the seven liberal arts* (the *trivium* comprising grammar, rhetoric, logic; and the *quadrivium* comprising arithmetic, geometry, astronomy, and music) developed in the Middle Ages (❧ 7.2). The study of humanities (Lat., *studia humanitas*) was interwoven into the "new" learning curriculum. The content and process of the new learning were developed based on classicism which honored human virtue, dignity, and capacities.

Voices

Starting in the thirteenth century, together with the return of Greco-Roman classics, the death of Aristotelian logic, the mystical arrival of Neoplatonism, and the collapse of the medieval church, new perspectives of education were introduced to Western Europe. Europeans in both Italy and Northern Europe became fascinated with the "new" learning which shifted intellectual pursuit away from the pole of Scholasticism to Ciceronianism. Although church leaders (i.e., Catholics) attempted to repress the movement, they were unsuccessful.

Added to this nontraditional education endeavor were the works of the following voices who readjusted the intellectual current of the Renaissance. The end result was the formation of new pedagogy that focused on the cultivation of human virtue, beauty, and potency.

Francisco Petrarch (1304–1374). Francisco Petrarch's ideology contributed to the development of the Renaissance. Historians argue Petrarch, an Italian poet and historian, was the father of

Renaissance humanism whose influence elevated the Latin classics to a new level of academic scholarship during the fourteenth century. As a scholar, Petrarch is best known for his encyclopedic knowledge of classical literature. Although he never taught formally in a university, Petrarch established a reputation as a preeminent scholar of the Latin classics. Opposing the educational ideals of medievalism, Petrarch contended that the human mind should be cultivated with classical literature, the arts, and sciences. He sought to recapture a vivacious image of humanity spoken in ancient literature and spread its ideals and values to the postmedieval society. To Petrarch, literature was the chief luminary to learning.

> Christ is my God; Cicero, on the other hand, is the prince of the language I use.
> —In "Petrarch's Letter to Classical Authors" (Ernest C. Moore, *The Story of Instruction* [New York: MacMillan, 1938], 399.)

During his lifetime Petrarch not only promoted humanistic studies, he also collected the writings of antiquity and made them available to others. In his expedition of recovering the Latin classics (1327–1336), Petrarch traveled back and forth from Italy to Northern Europe collecting numerous literary works of antiquity including those of Cicero and Quintilian.

Vittorino da Feltre (1378–1446). Another scholar who influenced the development of humanist education was Vittorino da Feltre (also known as Vittorino De' Ramboldini). He is known as "the first modern educator" whose influence fashioned the "new theory of learning" in the fourteenth and fifteenth centuries (❀ 8.1). Vittorino studied philosophy, Latin grammar and literature, and theology (i.e., Church law). He eventually earned his doctorate at the University of Padua in 1411. Some historians contend that Vittorino's interest in theology may suggest his consideration of becoming a priest at one time.[8]

Influenced by Petrarch and Quintilian's theories of education, Vittorino desired new education embodying both Christian and classical ideals. He believed that classical literature can be reconciled with Christianity.[9] His theory of teaching was Christian in spirit and principle though the content of his instructions was classical. Students were taught with Latin, Greek, logic, dialectics, ethics, history, astronomy, music, and mathematics combined with physical and moral educations.

Vittorino was a man of conviction. His faith, value, and passion were embodied in his teaching. Along with the teaching of the humanities, he encouraged students to integrate knowledge with the content of faith in developing personal and spiritual integrity. The students were directed to attend daily worship service (i.e., mass) and to study both classical and Christian ideals for the purpose of integrating faith and knowledge. Vittorino also spent much time communicating his own faith and encouraging students to develop their own faith combined with the acquisition of character and knowledge.[10]

As a teacher, Vittorino was deeply involved in the life of each student. He was an exemplary teacher whose love and devotion toward his pupils inspired and enriched everyone who came to study under him. He did not overlook students' personal needs and problems; he spent much time counseling and helping students with their problems. Even while he worked as a private tutor to children of Marquis Gianfrancesco Gonzago of Mantua, he invited and taught many poor students with the same love and devotion he had for the rich and the prominent.

Vittorino's contributions to the development of Christian education were remarkable. Although Vittorino was revered as a distinguished scholar of the Greek and Latin classics, he is better known for his exclusive contribution to teaching. He was an exceptional teacher. He introduced a new paradigm for teaching and learning without compromising scriptural principles and the fundamental beliefs of the church. Vittorino's teaching theory was pivotal to the growth and development of the liberal arts education in the late fourteenth and early fifteenth century. Vittorino was one of the outstanding educators of his time whose ideology has shaped the educational landscape of Western Europe.

Northern Renaissance Figures

The new learning originated in Italy during the fourteenth century brought another awakening in Northern Europe in the fifteenth century. Unlike the southern Renaissance whose primary concern was on humanistic ideologies, the Northern movement focused on religious reforms combined with a renewed interest in biblical and classical studies, which, in my opinion, became the impetus for the Reformation. Underlying the movement was the scholarly leadership of Gerhard Groote, Desiderius Erasmus, and Juan Luis Vives. Inspired by new religious and educational ideals, these educators guided Northern Europeans through the reform. It is this very leadership that inspired early church reformers to begin their religious crusade of the early sixteenth century. Although Northern humanist education is subject to various interpretations, it is safe to conclude that humanism accentuated in Northern Europe was highly religious in theory, content, and practice. We will discuss three exemplary educators of northern Christian humanism here.

Gerhard Groote (1340–1384). One of the most influential educational bodies that influenced the leaders of the Renaissance and Reformation was the Brethren of Common Life.[11] The schools of the Brethren of Common Life were perhaps among the best schools of the Renaissance period. Gerhard Groote (1340–1384) founded the group for the purpose of providing an elementary and devotional education for boys. Groote was born in Deventer, Holland. He was instructed at Aachen, Cologne, and several other schools. At the age of 15 he began his studies at the University of Paris for a Masters degree. As with the later reformers, he valued the Bible, lengthy sermons (2-3 hours), which he often preached twice daily, as well as the use of teaching and education as a means of reforming faith. Following his conversion in 1374, he entered a monastery for three years to study mysticism, which became the principal basis for his mystic ideology known as the Modern Devotion (Lat., *Devitio Moderna*). Groote's spiritual ideology, devotional thoughts, and ministry heavily influenced his followers—most notable was Thomas à Kempis's *Imitation of Christ*. By the mid-1370s Groote's movement assumed the name Brethren of the Common Life and was recognized by the Pope.

After 1450 many of the Brethren taught in schools. Their focus was on elementary-school-age children; they used Scripture study and copying, as well as instruction in Christian devotion. Education for women opened via the Sisters of the Common Life. The basic educational approach for all was simplicity of instruction with rewards for performance. Instruction was provided in the student's vernacular, in a graded program based on one's capabilities and level of achievement (eight levels of instruction), and in community living. The curriculum consisted of surveys of the Old Testament and New Testament, the lives of saints, spiritual disciplines, and practices of Christian principles.

The Brethren published Bibles, devotional literature, textbooks, and copies of à Kempis's *Imitation of Christ*, as well as other miscellaneous publications. By 1490 the Brethern had over 60 printing presses. Their printing endeavors were so intensive that by 1500 they had over 450 books printed by the one press at Deventer.[12] The Brethren's influence far exceeded the scope of their own members, reaching Erasmus, Martin Luther, John Sturm (an influential educator in Strassburg, Germany), John Calvin, and even Pope Adrian VI.

Desiderius Erasmus (1466–1536), a Dutch scholar and theologian, was the principal figure who greatly influenced the intellectual and religious currents of Northern Europe (🌐 8.2). He was instrumental in developing the religious humanism of the sixteenth century which encouraged Europeans to eliminate social and political boundaries to form a culture of inclusivity and partnership that aided the Reformation. Despite various criticisms surrounding Erasmus's liberal theology, he remains as a prominent voice of the Northern Renaissance and forerunner of humanist education. Huldreich Zwingli, a Swedish reformer, called Erasmus Europe's greatest philosopher and theologian.[13] Historians consider Erasmus the "prince of Christian humanism."

> Francisco Petrarch is known as the *father of humanism* whereas Desiderius Erasmus is known as the *prince of humanism.*

Erasmus was born in Rotterdam, Holland (1466), as an illegitimate son of a priest, Gerard of Gouda, and the daughter of a local doctor, Margaretha Rogers.[14] At age four, he started schooling at Gouda. At age nine, Erasmus entered a monastic school at Deventer run by the Brothers of the Common Life where he learned Groote's Modern Devotion. Following his mother's death at age thirteen, which was soon followed by his father's death, Erasmus wandered and experienced gloomy years of life under his guardians. When he was eighteen, Erasmus entered the Augustinian monastery of Emmaus at Steyn, and took a vow to be a monk (1487). But soon he realized his discontentment with monastic life and left the monastery. In 1492, at age 25, Erasmus became an ordained priest. Two years later in 1496, he entered the University of Paris to study Scholastic philosophy, but he realized his deeper passion for classical antiquity, so he spent much time studying classical language and literature instead. Eventually, he earned a doctorate in theology at the University of Turin later in life. Years later, while he was visiting England (1499–1500), Erasmus's friendship with English humanists, Thomas More and John Colet, drew him towards Christian humanism.

Erasmus's view of education was religious in philosophy but humanistic in content. Believing that knowledge contributes to religious and social advancement and could end the corruption of the Church, Erasmus focused on educational reform in Northern Europe. Erasmus contended that knowledge and wisdom of the liberal arts would help people gain a deeper understanding of the Bible, which in turn would help people develop moral consciousness in creating order in the Church and society[15]—this was the view that many church reformers held as well. The content of his teaching, on the other hand, was humanistic. Erasmus believed that classical ideals are valuable to humankind so he encouraged his pupils to study the Classics and learn Latin.

As an educator, Erasmus was influenced by Vittorino and Groote. Like Vittorino, Erasmus contended that learning should be adaptable to the needs and aptitudes of an individual child so that he or she could take ownership of the learning process and would be able eagerly to pursue knowledge.[16] Erasmus also favored creative teaching methods for young children, employing activities and games that promoted interest in learning.[17] Influenced by Groote's Modern Devotion (Lat., *Devotio Moderna*), Erasmus sought to postulate learning on the basis of biblical sources rather than the dogmatic traditions of the Church. Erasmus also relentlessly challenged his students to develop a direct, personal relationship with God.

Erasmus was a respected teacher and a prolific writer of his time. Many still regard him as the greatest mind of the northern Renaissance. Written in stylish Latin, Erasmus's books exhibit reputable scholarship that is still respected and envied by many. In 1516 Erasmus translated the Greek New Testament to Latin along with his side comments. He also wrote numerous books on education—*On the Method of Study* (1511), *On Teaching Children Firmly but Kindly* (1529), *Lily's Grammar* (1540), *The Colloquies* (1518), and *On Copia of Words and Ideas* (1500)—which were widely used by schools in England during the sixteenth and seventeenth centuries. The influence of Erasmus was phenomenal. His masterful mind, combined with freshness and originality of educational ideas, has had a long-lasting influence on both public and Christian education in Western Europe.

Juan Luis Vives (1492–1540). One of the Renaissance educators who fused Christianity and the philosophy of Quintilian was Juan Luis Vives (● 8.3). He was a native of Valencia, Spain. He studied at the University of Paris from 1509 to 1512 and earned his doctorate in law at Corpus Christi College in England (1523).

Vives is best known for his view of progressive education, which is similar to that of John Dewey. In his exposition on the theory and methodology of education, Vives contended that "the mind learns inductively"[18]; thus he argued that teaching should go from simple to complex, concrete to abstract, with the emphasis on reflective experimentation and application. Vives claimed that reflective experience will add personal meaning to learning, and will lead to transformation of heart and mind. Vives's ideology not only provided valuable insight to his contemporaries but had a profound effect on Comenius's modern view of education (1592–1670). Among numerous publications on the subject of education, Vives is best known for the books *On the Transmission of Knowledge* (1531), *On Instruction of a Christian Woman*(1523), *On the Education of Children* (1523), *Concerning the Mind* (1538), and *Prayers and Devotional Exercise* (1535).

Conclusion

The Renaissance represents the age of humanist education sparked by a renewed interest in the Classics. Though begun in a small city in Northern Italy, the Renaissance brought major changes to Western Europe—the way people viewed the world, life, and God changed dramatically. Furthermore, scholastic pedagogy was rejected, and new humanistic pedagogy called the "new" learning became the major paradigm in Christian education.

What Can We Learn from Renaissance Education?

- Starting in the fourteenth century, Europeans began defining the nature of reality solely based on an anthropocentric worldview, placing human dignity and its potentiality at the core of thinking.

- The medieval ideal of spiritual virtue and piety as the goal of education was eradicated, and human wisdom became the most desirable outcome in Renaissance education.

- Renaissance educators introduced a humanist curriculum encompassing Quintilian's theory of education.

- The general principles regarding knowledge shifted toward the subjective arena of introspection where the harmony and compatibility of truths, better known as syncretism, became the central method of intellectual inquiry.

- A newfound interest in the world of humanity led to the development of ethics, which sought to synthesize morality under the guidance of philosophical naturalism and theology.

- Renaissance scholars sought to separate religion from society and led a humanistic crusade against the church and Christian schools.

- Combined with medieval darkness set off by the Catholic church, the effect of the Renaissance was deleterious to the ministry of Christian education.

- Unlike Italians, Northern educators viewed the Bible in its original language as the source of all human intellect.

- The exclusive emphasis of Renaissance education was on learning classical language and literature, in particular the philosophy of Cicero, Plato, and Quintilian.

- General trends and themes of the Italian and Northern Renaissance as follows:

Southern Renaissance	Northern Renaissance
‣ Context: Italy	‣ Context: Germany, Holland, England, and France.
‣ Emphasis: Return of Greco-Roman classicism	‣ Less concerned with the ancient Classics.
‣ Anthropocentric focus on human virtue: human value, dignity, and capacities	‣ Influenced by the Italian Renaissance

- Emphasis was on individuality and self-consciousness of the human
- Content: grammar, history, poetry, and moral philosophy
- Cultural advancement: arts, architecture, politics, business, etc. Rejected scholasticism
- Cicero and Plato were enthroned in the intellectual arena

- Did not reject God; rather sought to renew and reform the church through education
- Content: Integrated study of Christianity and humanities (e.g., grammar, history, poetry, and moral philosophy)
- Forerunner of the Reformation

Study Helps

Reflection Questions

1. What do historians mean by the term "renaissance"? What was the basic meaning of the term?
2. Why was this term used to describe Europe during the fourteenth to sixteenth centuries?
3. What caused the Renaissance? How did the movement change over time?
4. What were the most significant changes that occurred in Europe during the Renaissance period?
5. What were the general trends and themes of the Italian and Northern Renaissance?
6. In what ways was the Northern Renaissance different from the Italian?
7. What main points did Petrarch, Feltre, Groote, Erasmus, and Vives make in their assertion of education? What are their similarities and differences?
8. How did humanism affect religious thinking and the development of Christian education during the Renaissance?
9. What was the impact of humanism on the theory and practice of Christian education?
10. What was the essence of humanism's contribution, whether positive or negative, to the development of educational thought?

11. Why do you think so-called "Christian humanism" became an important value to Northern Europeans during the Renaissance?

12. Can we reconcile humanism and Christianity in education? Offer your criticism of the relation between humanism and Christianity.

Technical Terms

Cicero
(106–43 B.C.)
One of the greatest Roman orators, philosophers, and senators. Cicero believed that the purpose of education was preparing culturally developed individuals who could promote moral, social, and political progress and better the condition of humanity.

Didacticism
The term literally means the art of teaching in Greek. Often the term refers to traditional classroom, teacher-centered, content-driven teaching.

Neoplatonism
A mystical philosophy developed by Plotinus in the third century A.D., based on the synthesis of Platonic philosophy, mysticism, and Judeo-Christian concepts. Neoplatonism had great influence on medieval mysticism and Renaissance humanism.

Quintilian
(A.D. 35–95?)
His full name is Marcus Fabius Quintilianus. He was a Roman educator, philosopher, and rhetorician who wrote *The Instruction of Orators*, the most comprehensive work on the education and profession of an orator. Quintilian's ideology and pedagogy were so similar to that of Cicero that people called him "an imitator of Cicero."

Recommended Bibliography

Brady, Thomas A., Heiko Oberman, and James D. Tracy. *Handbook of European History, 1400–1600: Late Middle Age, Renaissance, and Reformation.* Grand Rapids: Eerdmans, 1996.

Estep, William R. *Renaissance and Reformation.* Grand Rapids: Eerdmans, 1986.

Moore, Ernest Carroll. *The Story of Instruction.* New York: MacMillan, 1938.

Notes

[1] Francesco Cordasco, *A Brief History of Education* (Totowa, NJ: Littlefield, Adams, 1976), 46.

[2] Glenys Patterson, *The University from Ancient Greece to the 20th Century* (Palmerston North, NZ: Dunmore Press, 1977), 103.

[3] Ibid.

[4] Ibid., 104.

[5] Edward J. Power, *A Legacy of Learning: A History of Western Education* (Albany: State University of New York Press, 1991),170-178; Cordasco. *Brief History*, 47.

[6] Power, *Legacy*, 183.

[7] William K. Medlin, *The History of Educational Ideas in the West* (New York: The Center for Applied Research in Education, Inc., 1967), 48.

[8] L. Glenn Smith and Joan K. Smith, *Lives in Education: A Narrative of People and Ideas* (New York: St. Martin's Press, 1994), 97.

[9] Ibid., 98.

[10] Ibid., 100.

[11] Merritt M. Thompson, *The History of Education* (New York: Barnes and Noble, 1951), 102.

[12] S.E. Frost, Jr., and Kenneth P. Bailey, *Historical and Philosophical Foundations of Western Education*, 2nd ed. (Columbus, OH: Charles E. Merrill, 1973), 185.

[13] Source: **http://www.ncl.ac.uk/lifelong-learning/distrib/reform10.htm** (Accessed on Oct. 23, 2002), 7.

[14] Joseph Sauer, "Desiderius Erasmus" trans. by W.G. Kofron, in *The Catholic Encyclopedia*, V:1-8, ed. by Kevin Knight, online edition, **www.newadvent.org** (New York: Robert Appleton Company, 1999), 1.

[15] Source: **http://www.florilegium.org/files/EDUCATION/GSRE-art.text** (Accessed on Oct. 24, 2002),

[16] Smith and Smith, *Lives*, 113.

[17] Ibid.

[18] Medlin, *History*, 56.

Chapter 9
The Reformers as Educators (16th Century A.D.)

James Riley Estep, Jr.

Overview of Period

The Renaissance serves as the immediate impetus for the Reformation. The renewed spirit of freedom within classical humanism, scientific and geographic exploration of the world, and the development of the university model of education produced suitable ecology for the Reformation to occur.

> "Education in these centuries in both Protestant and Catholicism followed in the footsteps of Renaissance humanism and its ideals."
> —John L. Elias, A History of Christian Education, 97

The ecclesiastical, spiritual, and political status within the Roman Catholic Church and the Holy Roman Empire likewise made reformation an inevitable necessity for the survival of Christianity. Even prior to Luther's *Ninety-Five Theses*, generally acknowledged as the beginnings of the Protestant reformation (October 31, 1517), calls for reform in the Church by such men as Peter Waldo, John Wycliffe, and John Hus had been rejected, thwarted, and even cost them their lives.

It was an era of unprecedented discovery. The voyages of exploration made by such figures as Columbus, Magellan, and Cortez were contemporary events. The invention of the printing press facilitated a 15th-century information explosion paralleled only by the introduction of the Internet. Astronomical discoveries, such as those made by Copernicus, sparked a new revolution in science. A revolution in the Church, and in education, was inevitable. "Their

[Protestant leaders] writings and actions offer sound guidelines for modern believers concerned about the place of education in a Christian view of life. . . . The impact of the reformation was particularly strong on the theory and practice of education. . . . In the first blush of the Reformation all of this was called into question—the purpose of education, its structures, its content, and its method."[1]

The State, the Church, and the School

Who controls education? The State? The Church? A combination of the two? We often consider this issue to be a modern concern within American education. However, during the Reformation the same issue arose and received three different responses. Three models of schooling in relation to the Church and State were present in the Reformation.

- Luther (Germany) favored Christian education through the State, with the Church in support.
- Calvin (Switzerland) favored Christian education through the Church, with the State in support.
- Jesuits (Catholic, Europe, particularly Italy, Spain, and France) favored Christian education through the Church-State, regarding the two as inseparable.

Linda Cannell commented on the views of Luther and Calvin as follows:

> The greatest control over education by the state occurred in those countries most influenced by Luther and Calvin, however, for different reasons. Luther pictured the Church as an arm of the State. Therefore, it was the responsibility of the *State* to see that its people were educated. Calvin, on the other hand, viewed the Church as the preserver and leader of the people and the State as the administrative and enforcement agent of the church.[2]

While it is readily understood why Calvin and the Jesuits placed emphasis on the Church's control over education, *why would Luther favor State control?* State control would make education compulsory, it would be designed to aid the society, and it would aid parents that lacked piety and learning.[3] He was, of course, also keenly aware of the Roman Catholic control on education in Germany,

Saxony specifically, and would be cautious not to place simply another ecclesiastical authority in its place over education. Gangel and Benson also note that Luther was "bypassing . . . the clergy," due to their "theological deficiencies" and hence "turned to the princes and city councils."[4]

Lutheranism: Education via the State

Purpose of Education

In general, Protestant education began with Luther, and advanced as it advocated public literacy as a means of reading and interpreting the Bible. The formation of personal piety, or character formation, was the principle concern of Luther's educational agenda. The purpose of Lutheran education was to develop children morally and intellectually so as to provide better service and stability to God, the church, State, and society. "Luther saw in schools the vehicle to inculcate Christian teaching, which in turn would enhance loyalty to the state and strengthen the emerging nationalist spirit among the people."[5] Christian education was to be understood within the context of three Reformation ideals: *Sola Gracia*, justification by faith alone; *Sola Scriptura*, supremacy of Scripture alone; and the principle of believer's priesthood, wherein every Christian was to serve in ministry, not just the ordained clergy. All these shaped Luther's education ideals, and were in direct opposition to the position of the Roman Catholic Church.[6]

Educational Contexts

Luther advocated education within the home, church, and schools. Luther never forgot the place of the home as an educational institution.[7] Painter comments that Luther believed that "by natural and divine right, authority is lodged in the parents, who occupy at once the threefold office of prophet, priest, and king. It is their function to instruct, to train, and to govern."[8] Luther sought to equip the family to be an educator by providing encouragement from the church and the small catechism for the parents' use with children. The establishment of schools provided instruction that was beyond the parents' capabilities.[9]

In regard to schooling, Luther advocated a two-tiered system of preuniversity instruction, followed by higher education at the university. Elementary instruction was provided in the student's vernacular, since it was designed for the common person. Luther advocated compulsory schooling for boys and girls. "Schooling became compulsory in Magdeburg in 1524, in Eisleben in 1525, and in the electorate of Saxony in 1528." Compulsory education and school standards developed throughout Germany throughout the 1520s and 1530s.[10] He and Melanchthon's vernacular schools did provide a more open environment for common girls to receive an education, though opportunities for the inclusion of girls in classical schooling probably narrowed.[11]

> *Vernacular* instruction means instruction in the language of the student typically, rather than Latin.

Latin or secondary school remained relatively the same as in Medieval and Renaissance models for upper classes; they were taught in Latin and Greek. Enrollment in secondary education was a sign of social status and formed the notion of formal classical studies for university studies and professional leaders. While Luther emphasized the necessity of elementary education, he did not oppose the Latin school because the advanced studies would aid in establishing social order and correcting the errors of the Catholic church by providing an educated leadership for the Reformation.[12]

Ultimately, the university provided higher education. The university was the context wherein Luther had begun his reforms while serving as a professor at the University of Wittenberg. Hence, he personally valued the place of higher education for the Christian. The classical humanistic model of higher education present in Northern Europe was adopted by Luther, as described in the previous chapter.

Other types of schooling were available during the Reformation. For example, guild schools for professional training, royal court schools for the instruction of nobility, vocational schools for acquiring a trade, and private tutors, often used to provide instruction for girls.

Educational Content

The two tiers of education, Elementary or Latin Grammar schools, each had their own curriculum. Elementary was for reading, writing, and arithmetic, with religion a primary subject matter. In his "Letter to the Mayors and Aldermen of All the Cities of Germany in Behalf of Christian Schools," Luther advocated the study of languages, including biblical Greek (🔊 9.1). Why? "He attributed his biblical language skills to his deliverance from Catholic bondage,"[13] and hence elementary education was a means of advancing the cause of the Reformation. As Kaufman comments, "An understanding of the essentials of Christian doctrine were necessary if the ideas of the Reformation were to be understood by the masses of Germany."[14] "While Luther at first advocated unlimited access to the Bible in schools, by the late 1520s he became convinced that catechisms were the best vehicle for religious education."[15]

The elementary school curriculum they developed was designed to provide the essential understanding Luther desired. "At the heart of elementary learning was reading, writing, and music," taught by catechism and hymns.[16] Luther's emphasis on music was from a personal as well as a liturgical conviction. He also valued Aesop's Fables for moral truths, and catechetical instruction not for memorization, but for understanding and application.[17]

The Latin schools studied the typical classical and humanist curriculum present in the Renaissance; with rhetoric and dialectic being added later. The curriculum consisted of the liberal arts, particularly history, music, both instrumental and vocal, and science. Additionally, biblical languages, Greek and Hebrew, were emphasized as tools for the study of Scripture, and gymnastics were included for the instruction of the nobility for knighthood.[18]

Educational Process

Teachers were to work with the students in the learning process. Luther valued teachers who knew how to use the child's natural curiosity and quizzical nature. Schoolmasters had to be able to sing, so as to provide musical instruction for liturgical purposes. More than memorization, instruction was comprised of oral language teaching, a trade work-study plan, catechism, and practical participatory approaches to learning. In Luther's mind, a teacher had to possess three qualities:[19]

> "Christ wished to educate men, became a man, and if we wish to educate children, we must become like children [and] the apple must lie next to the rod." Martin Luther —Theo. C. Braebner, *The Story of the Catechism*, (St. Louis: Concordia Publishing, 1928) 89

1. Personal spiritual and moral maturity

2. Physical capability, since teaching is a rigorous task

3. Intellectual acuteness, to understand the subject matter, educational practices, and the child.

Instructional methods used in the Lutheran educational agenda were similar to those used in Renaissance schools, but with a few modifications. Memorization of the catechism was a principle means of religious instruction. However, the emphasis was not merely on the rote memorization of the passage; rather, the focus was on the content and application of the Bible for understanding it, not simply reciting it. In addition to lecture, students were given individualized study plans and learned languages through oral exercises rather than written, and worship was conducted in the vernacular of the people. Also, no harsh discipline was used in schools under a Lutheran influence.

Lutheran Voices

Martin Luther (1483–1546) was born November 10, 1483, at Eisleben in Saxony (🌐 9.2). He entered the University of Erfurt at age seventeen, receiving a bachelors degree in 1502 and a masters in 1505. That same year he joined the Augustinian Order in Erfurt, Germany. He received his doctorate in 1512 from the University of Wittenberg, where he joined the faculty. Luther's disenchantment with Roman Catholicism, with its stress on works and the purchase of indulgences, became a matter of public debate on October 31, 1517, with the posting of his "Ninety-Five Theses," noting ninety-five points of Roman Catholic doctrine with which he no longer could agree. This was the birth of the Protestant Reformation, and with it came a reformation of the German educational system, which was no longer tied to the Roman Catholic Church.

One significant factor influencing the education in Luther's early work was the church/school survey of 1528. Luther and Melanchthon "visited many of the churches and schools of Saxony and some of the other German states. What he found was ignorance of Scripture and spiritual indifference," giving rise to the production of a short and large catechism completed in 1529.[20]

Luther produced several significant writings advocating the formation

October 31 is known for three holidays: Halloween (secular), All Saints Day Eve (Catholic), and Reformation Day (Protestants)

of a universal, compulsory system of schools throughout Germany. His earliest work giving some attention to education was his "Letter to the Christian Nobility of the German Nation" (1520), wherein he promoted the formation of a university system in Germany and hinted at the need for elementary and secondary education. The most significant was his "Letter to Mayors and Alderman of All the Cities of Germany in Behalf of Christian Schools" (1524), which included a call for elementary education for both boys and girls (See 🌑 9.1). However, universal education of every child does not mean equal. It only meant that education was available to every child (quantitative), not necessarily that it was qualitatively the same. The development of a comprehensive system of schools was further voiced in his "Sermon on the Duty of Sending Children to School" (1530), wherein he noted the spiritual and societal benefits of education. Noll summarizes Luther's line of argument as follows: "No schools, no Christianity. No schools, no good rulers. No Christianity and no good rulers, utter chaos and heathenism in Germany."[21] While Luther painted a portrait of German education with broad strokes, he delegated the implementation of his ideas to Melanchthon in southern and central Germany, and to Burgenhagen in northern Germany and Denmark.[22]

Luther also provided for the continuing Christian education of adults and children. He personally produced a translation of the Bible in German, placing God's Word into the vernacular of the common person. Between 1522 and 1534 over 20,000 copies of the German New Testament were printed.[23] Additionally, he also provided two catechisms (small and large) and the first Protestant hymn books.

Philip Melanchthon (1497–1560) was known as the "Preceptor of Germany" (🌑 9.3). He entered the University of Heidelberg at age 12, receiving his bachelors degree in 1511 and a masters in 1514. In 1518 he joined the faculty of the University of Wittenberg as professor of Greek, where he became a colleague of Martin Luther. As such he was uniquely qualified to write *Commonplaces* (1521), a compilation and summary of Lutheran teachings; as well as seven catechisms. He continued to serve as a professor at Wittenberg for 42 years. During his tenure at Wittenberg he served as a model of the Protestant (Lutheran) humanistic thought, and wrote Greek and Latin grammars.

Melanchthon initiated large-scale reforms to the German educational system by outlining modifications for all schools and developing the first system of public schools in Europe since the collapse of the Roman educational system. He combined the newly formed Protestant faith with the classical humanistic approach to education to provide a uniquely contemporary Christian education. He was the founder of the Saxony State school system, as described in his 1528 work, *Visitation Articles*, which articulated major principles of the faith, a model for schooling, reasons for children to be sent to school, and standards for teachers.

John Sturm (1507–1589) in 1537 developed a gymnasium in Germany at Strassburg, where he served for 40 years. He designed a classical humanistic education, which included the study of Latin for ten years and Greek for five.[24] His was the first graded model of education similar to today's graded structure. This model of education was heavily influenced later by the rise of Lutheranism.

Johann Burgenhagen (1485–1558) was professor at Wittenburg and the town's preacher. Reed and Prevost comment that he "more than either Luther or Melanchthon aided the cause of Protestant schools in Germany."[25] He formed extensive school plans for the cities of Brunswick, Hamburg, Lübeck, Bremen, and throughout northern Germany and Denmark.[26]

Legacy of Lutheran Education

The positive impact of Luther's reforms on the educational system and culture of Germany is without question. Luther advocated a theological orientation to education, without distinction between Christian and public education, since all education was ultimately in the service to the church. His translation of the Bible into German virtually created the modern German vernacular. His advocacy of school reform led to an expansion of public education throughout Germany, the first of its kind in modern Europe. This included opening educational opportunities for girls, previously excluded from educational endeavors. Luther also restored the family's place in Christian education, providing support for familial instruction in the faith. Most unique was the Lutheran notion of the Church and State in joint educational ventures, which ultimately led to the decline of the Christian distinctive in education and the Church in Germany.

Calvinism: Education via the Church

As with Lutheranism, education in the Calvinist tradition was also for the purpose of advancing literacy of the masses, as a means of individual reading and interpreting of the Bible. While Lutheranism tended to be limited to Germany, Calvinism was the most widespread Protestant group throughout Europe (e.g., Scottish Presbyterians, French Huguenots, English Puritans), and even the early European settlements in America (e.g., the early American schools of New England). With the widespread influence of Calvinism came not only a theological framework, provided through Calvin's *Institutes of the Christian Religion*, but an educational agenda.

Purpose of Education

Whereas Luther linked the purpose of education to service of the State, "Calvin saw education as a means to the glorification of God and the edification of the church through the exposition of God's truth in such a way that the people of God might learn to worship and serve him as they ought."[27] Calvinistic education was basically for the purpose of developing personal piety. This was narrower than the focus of Medieval education, but this was also an emphasis often *omitted* from Medieval education, and hence was a reformation of education for personal piety.[28]

Educational Contexts

As previously noted, education in the Calvinist tradition is primarily the work of the Church, and secondarily the work of the State. "Both the magistrate and the home were to have their roles in the work of education, but it was to be primarily through the church that this task would be organized and accomplished."[29] In Calvin's Geneva (Switzerland), a city wholly adoptive of his theology and sociopolitical ideology, education had two basic forms: education in the church (worship and catechism) and education in the schools of Geneva, which were administrated by the Church.

The Geneva Academy was Calvin's crowning educational achievement. While the Academy operated a girls' school, very little is known about it. The instruction of boys was provided in two schools: the university preparatory school and the university itself. Geneva's education system consisted of private schools (through age

16) and then public schools that served as the university, but only for boys. "The primary purpose of the university was eminently practical, to prepare young men for the ministry or for service in the government."[30] Unlike Luther, Calvin was not as open to the notion of the education of girls, though he did associate with several women of influence throughout his life.

How was the Academy administrated? Education in Geneva was operated by the Church, with a *serious* theological litmus text. The *Pastors* of Geneva served as the school board, even over parents and the government, while the teachers, known as *doctors,* were simply charged with providing instruction. Calvin divided the administrative and instructional functions, even though the pastors also provided instruction. Pastors were instructors *and* congregational ministers, while doctors were instructors, but not necessarily ministers (though they should approach their task pastorally).[31]

While this may sound like the ideal Christian education, the theological litmus test was also the cause of the darkest day of the school. The most notable incident involved Michael Servetus, an instructor at the Academy, who, in 1553, was burned alive at the stake over a doctrinal controversy on the nature of the Trinity. Another instructor, Sebastian Caroli, fared better than Servetus, being expelled from his teaching position for questioning the author-ship of the Song of Songs.[32]

Educational Content and Process

School-based education was likewise Christian in character. Every class began with prayer and ended with the Lord's Prayer, and twice daily singing of the Psalms (noon and 4:00 p.m.). Consistent with Calvin's background, a classical humanistic curriculum was used in the school. The university preparatory school studied lan-guage, classics, and philosophy. The university focused its attention on theology, science, and mathematics.

Unlike in Lutheran schools, discipline was more harsh in Cal-vinistic areas due to belief in total depravity. "The ideal Calvinistic teacher knew the art of physical punishment; the student needed to know that the instructor's best efforts were mild compared to the burning fires of hell."[33]

Teachers were moral models of education; they embodied the ethics of the Christian leader. "Teaching was for Calvin the means of constantly setting forth the unadulterated truth of God's Word, which alone would result in the edification of the church," in opposition to the Roman sacramental practices.[34] Moore has identified Calvin's understanding of the learner's responsibility and the teacher's responsibility in the learning process.

Learner's Responsibilities [35]	**Teacher's Responsibilities** [36]
"faithful and active attendance at public assemblies for instruction"	*Methods of Instruction*: "the lecture, catechesis, simple reading, perhaps private tutoring"
"diligent over their personal study of the Scriptures"	*Learning Objectives*: Oral presentation and summation of the Catechism, and personal affirmation of faith in the presence of the congregation
"exercise vigilance over his own life . . . full fruition in obedience"	

Calvinist Voices

John Calvin (1509–1564) was born on July 10, 1509, in Noyon, France (9.4). He received the best education available at his time, the University of Paris. While there he entered the College de Montaigu, where he encountered Mathurin Cordier, a gifted instructor who impacted Calvin so much that he later dedicated a book to him. In Paris he studied theology, law, and classical humanism. Calvin regarded humans as being learners, inquirers into the revelations of God; however, he believed all to be limited by human brokenness, and hence dependent on the work of the Holy Spirit in order to reach a full understanding of God and man's relation to Him.[37] Calvin wrote more than other Protestant leaders, the most notable being his *Institutes of the Christian Religion* (1536, first edition) (See educational excerpts in 9.5). Calvin's most significant contribution was the founding of the Geneva Academy, which became a model for Calvinistic educational institutions throughout Europe and colonial America. It taught a basic elementary education (reading, writing, and arithmetic), as well as religion and grammar; secondary education for leaders included Latin, Greek, and Hebrew, and Christian theology. Later, logic and rhetoric were added to the curriculum.

Huldreich Zwingli (1485–1531) was born near St. Gall in Switzerland (9.6). An ordained Catholic priest and disciple of

Erasmus, Zwingli voiced a concern for reform in the church as early as 1518, when he halted the sale of indulgences in Zurich and openly began preaching against celibacy of priests, monasticism, and other teachings of the Roman Catholic Church. A predecessor of Calvin, he was the chief Swiss reformer, centered in Zurich, and a forerunner to the Anabaptists, who separated from his leadership in 1525. He wrote *Short Christian Instruction* (a small catechism), *On the Education of Youth* (1523), which advocated reform in the schools of Zurich and was adopted by the Zurich city council in September of that year, and *The Manner of Instructing and Bringing Up Boys* (1523). He regarded education as a means of reforming the church and society. Zwingli met his end in the battle of Kappel while serving as a chaplain and standard bearer in a Protestant army on October 10, 1531, when he was killed after being mortally wounded.

John Knox (c. 1505–1572) is another early figure associated with the spread of Calvinism and its educational agenda (❧ 9.7). As a Calvinist reformer in Scotland, Knox advocated the establishment of schools throughout Scotland patterned after the Geneva Academy. His *Book of Discipline* raised the level of literacy and biblical knowledge among the population to an all-time high.

Legacy of Calvinistic Education

Calvin's greatest legacy was twofold: publication of the *Institutes* and the founding of the Geneva Academy. These two contributions provided a model for schooling and a consistent theological framework through which a distinctively Christian education could be theorized. Calvinism also placed the responsibility for Christian education exclusively in the hands of the church, with the state in a solely supporting role. Like Luther, Calvin both advocated and implemented a comprehensive system of schools, elementary to university, in Geneva. One final note on the educational legacy of Calvinism is that its legacy is more influential than any other Protestant reformation.

Roman Catholic (Jesuits): Education via the Church-State

The initial impact of the Protestant Reformation was *devastating* on the existing educational system in Europe. Since the Protestants opposed Catholicism, and the educational systems of the era were dominated by the Roman Catholic Church's influence, the educational institutions of the era initially suffered staggering losses. For example, the University of Erfurt in 1501 had 2000 students enrolled. By 1529, only twelve years after the posting of Luther's *Ninety-Five Theses*, the enrollment was 20 (a 99% reduction in enrollment!). Similarly, in 1500 the University of Leipzig had a comparable enrollment and was down to 100 students enrolled in 1529 (over a 93% reduction).[38] The Roman Catholic Church was faced with a crisis, and they responded with their own brand of reformation. What Protestants call the Catholic *counterreformation*, some Catholic historians of education call "the Catholic Revival."[39]

Three educational innovations were initiated by the Roman Catholic Church during this period: (1) the educational reforms dictated by the Council of Trent (1545–1563),

> *Orders* refers to a group of clergy in the Roman Catholic Church, usually named for their founder.

(2) the teachings of several individuals and new teaching orders, particularly in France, but most influentially (3) the formation of the Society of Jesus, the Jesuit Order in 1540. While most of this discussion is devoted to the educational work of the Jesuits, it will briefly touch on the educational initiatives of Trent and the teaching orders.

Council of Trent on Education

The Council of Trent provided a fresh expression of the teachings of the Roman Catholic Church and even produced the *Catechismus Romanus* (Lat., *Roman Catechism*), "intended to aid pastors in their preaching and teaching."[40] It also standardized the training of clergy, a standard that had waned following the Medieval era. Additionally, the Council sought to place restrictions on academic freedom through the Inquisition (arrest, detainment, questioning, and even torture of those identified as a threat to the Church) and the production of the *Index of Forbidden Books*, limiting the theological and ideological exposure of faithful Catholics. All of this was an effort to stem the tide of the Protestant Reformation.

Teaching Orders in the Church

While other orders did indeed have instruction as part of their charter, these new orders were formed specifically for the purpose of instruction. While these orders were established throughout Europe,

France seemed to be a focal point of their endeavors. Perhaps the most successful was the Confraternity of Christian Doctrine or CCD, established in 1571 in Milan (Italy), which taught men and women how to teach the catechism. (*Constitution and Rules of the Confraternity* and *School of Christian Doctrine* both by Charles Borgave, outlined its pedagogy and structure for education. At the death of its founder, Charles Borremeo in 1584, it had 3000 teachers and administrators with 40,000 pupils (children and adult). Its success was so evident that Pope Pius V made it a global educational initiative in 1560.

Other newly authorized orders also enjoyed success in fulfilling their educational agendas. The Christian Brothers (1684–present) founded by Jean Baptiste de La Salle focused on the education of poor boys in reading, writing, singing, and Christian belief. La Salle's *La Conduite des Ecoles Chretiennes* (1695) was its foundational manual. Similarly the Pairists (1602) established schools for the poor and destitute boys in Italy, and then in Spain and France. The Ursulines (1535), founded by Angela Merici (1474–1540), encouraged and equipped nuns to become more active in education, medical work, and service to the poor. Their work in France, initiated by Anne de Xaintonge (d. 1621) in 1609, was the most noteworthy. The Oratorians were similar to the Ursulines, founded in Italy by Philip Neri (d. 1695), but it too soon moved to France. (See ❀ 9.9 for list of all new Roman Catholic orders established during this period.)

However, of all the new educational orders, the most significant and successful one was the Jesuits (1540–1773, 1814–present). The rest of this section will focus on the educational work of the Jesuits as the leading educational body of the Roman Catholic Church.

Jesuit Educational Voice

It is impossible to remove the nature of the Society of Jesus from the personality of its founder, Ignatius Loyola (❀ 9.9). "Luther tried to reform by *revolution*, . . . Loyola by a real *reformation*."[41] *Ignatius of Loyola* (1491–1556) was born in Spain as the youngest of thirteen siblings. Born Don Iñigo Lopez de Loyola, he later adopted the name Ignatius. His life's desire was a career in the military. However, in 1521 his career was cut short with a leg injury from a French

> Two most recognized Jesuit universities in the United States are Loyola and Xavier . . . named for the two dominant voices in Jesuit education.

cannonball in the defense of the city of Pamplona. During his long and arduous recovery and readjustment to a civilian life, he was heavily influenced by two books: *The Life of Christ* and *The Lives of the Saints.* Following his recovery he spent a period of asceticism in a cave near Manresa, Spain. In 1522 he began writing *Spiritual Exercises,* the foundational document for the creation of a new monastic order: The Society of Jesus, the Jesuits. The following year (1523) he began his pilgrimage to Jerusalem. He completed his education, including studies in Alcala and Salamanca, and even became acquainted with Juan Luis Vives, an influential educator during the Renaissance. He arrived in Paris, France, in 1528 and received his MA in 1534 in theology and philosophy from the University of Paris.

The Society of Jesus, or the Jesuits, was founded by Loyola in 1534. On August 15, 1534, he took a vow to God for poverty, chastity, and service to God in the Holy Land or to the Pope. The Society was officially recognized by the papacy on September 27, 1540. The three principle documents that capture the intent and composition of the Jesuits are *Spiritual Exercises,* Loyola's spiritual discipline, written in Spanish but by order of Pope Paul III translated into Latin in 1548 and printed for the first time; the *Constitutions* (written in 1556), emphatically details the education emphasis innate to the Jesuit order, and the *Ratio Studorium* (Lat., *Sequence of Studies;* see ❀ 9.10 for excerpts), outlining the order of study for a Jesuit student (which will be discussed later).

Francis Xavier (1506–1552) was a friend of Loyola, and one of the original members of the Society of Jesus. Xavier emphasized the missiological dimension of the Society, having done missions work in Bombay and Calcutta, India. He made use of education as a means to further the mission work of the church.

Purpose of Jesuit Education

The purpose of the order and its educational agenda, is summarized in one phrase: *Omnia Ad Majorem Dei Gloriam* (Latin, "All to the glory of God"). Education in the Jesuit tradition was designed to advance the Church and Christian society (like that of the Middle Ages). In essence, it was to remove or replace the Protestant influence in Europe and restore the Roman Catholic

> While the Society was dissolved by Pope Clement XIV in 1773, it was reinstated 41 years later, in 1814.

Church to its early prominence in the political, economic, and spiritual life of the culture. It sought to produce a distinctively Catholic intellectual. "Jesuit education aims at forming a man before attempting to form a specialist."[42]

Jesuit Educational Contexts

The Jesuits focused their attentions on secondary schools and higher education for male students, to the intentional exclusion of women. These schools were primarily designed for the training of Jesuits and the indoctrination of Catholic nobility. Secondary education was from ages 10-16, with higher or philosophical education from ages 16-18, with additional studies to follow. The secondary schools were designed after the classical model of schools. The first Jesuit educational institution was opened in Coimbra, Portugal (🌑 9.11). A Jesuit university was opened in 1540 in Paris, and prior to Loyola's death in 1556 thirty-nine additional colleges were opened. By 1584 the Jesuits had established more than 160 colleges. From this point their endeavors rapidly expanded: 400 colleges by 1626, 612 by 1710, 800 with an estimated student population of 22,589 by 1749.[43]

Jesuit Educational Content

After fifteen years of study on educational systems, the Jesuits produced the *Ratio Studorium*, which remained unchanged from 1599–1832—that's unchanged for 233 years. The *Ratio* outlined a system of education, objectives, content, and methods, forming a comprehensive curriculum guide. It is an addition to *Constitutions*, ten items providing instruction for those serving as instructors or schoolmasters. The instructions given were divided into four sections for each of the four kinds of instructors:[44]

- Administrative Officials (Provincials, Rectors, and Prefects of Studies)
- Professors of the University teaching biblical, theological, and dogmatic studies
- Professors of the University teaching other subjects, such as arts, philosophy, mathematics, or natural sciences
- Professors of the Humanities

The early or lower course of studies in the Jesuit institution, called the *Studia Inferiora* (Lat., "Lower Studies"), would be compatible with late high school/early college. It consisted of five courses of study: Lower, Middle, and Upper grammar; followed by studies in the humanities and rhetoric. The schools provided an additional course of study for upper-level students in philosophy and the arts.[45]

Jesuit Educational Process

The perceived excellence of the Jesuit education system arose through the excellence of their faculty. Jesuit institutions had two kinds of students: potential Jesuits, having passed the *Novitiate*, the first course of studies, and externs, simply pupils without priestly aspirations. Admission to the order required a pupil to be in excellent health, demonstrate a capacity for study, unquestioned character, talent, or aptitude for advanced study, and possess prior education (equivalent to high school and even college).[46]

A total of twenty-one years of study was required to be a school teacher among the Jesuits, and twenty-nine to be a college instructor. The teacher education program alone was a minimum twelve-year program of instruction, with a minimum of six years of preparatory study before the final stage of their teacher education program. Their preparatory studies were divided into three phases over a typically twelve-year course of study: The *Novitiate* stage of training extended for two years, consisting of studies in doctrine, teaching catechism to children, classical and vernacular languages, rhetorical exercises, and spiritual training through Christian service. The *Juniorate* studies consisted of up to a one to three-year review in the classics and an additional three years for the study of math, science, philosophy with discussions in Latin on the subjects of the course. The *Scholasticate* extended for three to four years, similar to supervised student teaching, teaching with guidance from masters. Then he returned to the Provincial House of Studies for a final four-year study of theology prior to ordination, typically at age 32. Additional optional studies could be taken at this point for two more years for specialization.[47]

Loyola had adapted content and methodology of instruction from a variety of sources. The most commonly utilized methods of instruction were lecture, memorization and drill, military discipline and structure, debate within a competitive atmosphere, repetition and recitation. Schools were large and used assistants to help teachers with class. Classes were taught in Latin, so as to preserve the Medieval tradition of education.

Jesuit schools also provided additional studies like law and medicine if it would serve to further the influence of the church politically or on the mission field.

Legacy of Jesuit Education

The Jesuits demonstrate better than any other group of instructors in the Reformation the power of Christian education. The educational endeavors of the Jesuits stalemated the advance of Protestantism, and reasserted a Catholic presence in education and society. They likewise provided the most highly regarded scholars of the era, as well as highly trained instructors. Even today the Jesuits are considered among the best educators and institutions, providing a Catholic voice in the higher education community.

Conclusion

"The first educational lesson we might learn from the Reformation, then, is that there can be (at least there has been) no long-term flourishing of the church apart from a concern to educate each generation."[48] Education became one of the most crucial vehicles for the *reformations* of the 16th century. It became an effective tool in the hands of both Protestants and Catholics to propagate their message and defend their teachings. The Church of the 21st century could perhaps learn a vital lesson from this era of history.

What Can We Learn from the Reformation?

- No theological reformation is complete witout reforming educational theory and practice.
- Reformers are not just theologians, but educators.
- Christian education and loyalty to one's theological tradition are connected.
- Education is a tool for reform in the Church.
- Christian education is not limited to the walls of the church building.
- Christian education can and should address the needs of society.

Study Helps

Reflection Questions

1. How could the church of the 21st century better use education as a vehicle for change within congregations, colleges, and seminaries?

2. Who do you agree with on the Church, State, and Education debate (Luther, Calvin, or the Jesuits)? Why?

3. If you could have studied in any of the types of colleges mentioned (Luther's Wittenberg, Calvin's Geneva Academy, or the colleges of the Jesuit order), which would you have picked? Why?

4. How would ministry have to change if 90% of the congregation were illiterate? What would worship be like? What would be different from our current worship, which assumes literacy among the people?

5. Under what conditions could Luther's model work in our country? What would have to change? How are the religious norms of 16th-century Germany different from those of 21st-century America?

Technical Terms

Augustinian Order	Roman Catholic order which follows the life and teachings of St. Augustine
Institute of the Christian Religion	Authored by John Calvin, it is the primary text of Calvinism
Juniorate	Second level of teacher preparation among the Jesuits.
Novitiate	First level of teacher preparation among the Jesuits.
Orders	A monastic group, typically named for its founder or aspirate saint
Preceptor	Leader, originator
Priesthood of Believers	Every Christian a minister, as opposed to clerical authority; one of three Protestant principles held by Luther and Calvin.
Ratio Studorium	Curriculum of Jesuit education
Scholasticate	Third level of teacher preparation among the Jesuits.
Solo Fidelis	"Faith alone," as opposed to salvation via works; one of three Protestant principles held by Luther and Calvin.

Solo Gracia	"Grace alone," as opposed to work and judgment; one of three Protestant principles held by Luther and Calvin.
Vernacular	The common language; education in the vernacular was among the most significant educational issues during the Reformation.

Recommended Bibliography

Kaufman, Steven. "Luther's Educational Ideals." *Presbyterion* 9 (1-2), 37-51.

Moore, T.M. "Some Observations Concerning the Educational Philosophy of John Calvin." *Westminster Theological Journal* 46 (1984), 140-155.

Noll, Mark. "The Earliest Protestants and the Reformation of Education." *Westminster Theological Journal* (49): 97-131.

Painter, F.N.V. *Luther on Education.* St. Louis: Concordia, 1889.

Schwickerath, Robert. *Jesuit Education.* St. Louis: B. Herder, 1903.

Notes

[1] Mark A. Noll, "The Earliest Protestants and the Reformation of Education," *Westminster Theological Journal* (49): 97, 98, 101.

[2] Linda Cannell, "Summaries of Historical Periods for DES936," Trinity Evangelical Divinity School (Spring 2000).

[3] Steven Kaufman, "Luther's Educational Ideals," *Presbyterion*, 9 (1-2): 42.

[4] Kenneth O. Gangel and Warren S. Benson, *Christian Education: Its History and Philosophy* (Chicago: Moody Press, 1982), 140.

[5] Kaufman, "Luther's," 41.

[6] Noll, "Earliest Protestants," 107-108.

[7] F.N.V. Painter, *Luther on Education* (St. Louis: Concordia, 1889), 113-127.

[8] Ibid, 127.

[9] Noll, "Earliest Protestants," 108-113.

[10] Jo Ann Hoeppner Moran (Cruz), "Education," *The Oxford Encyclopedia of the Reformation* (New York: Oxford University Press, 1996), 21.

[11] L. Glenn Smith and Joan K. Smith, *Lives in Education* (New York: St. Martin's Press, 1994), 134-135.

[12] Cannell, "Summaries."

[13] James E. Reed and Ronnie Prevost, *A History of Christian Education* (Nashville: Broadman and Holman, 1993), 193.

[14] Kaufman, "Luther's," 44.

[15] Moran (Cruz), "Education," 21.

[16] Kaufman, "Luther's," 44.

[17] Ibid., 45-47.

[18] Ibid., 45.

[19] Ibid., 48.

[20] Ibid., 46.

[21] Noll, "Earliest Protestants," 105.

[22] Merritt M. Thompson, *The History of Education* (New York: Barnes and Noble, 1951), 38.

[23] Smith and Smith, *Lives,* 130.

[24] Thompson, *History,* 108.

[25] Reed and Prevost, *History,* 195.

[26] S.E. Frost, Jr., and Kenneth P. Bailey, *Historical and Philosophical Foundations of Western Education,* 2nd ed. (Columbus, OH: Charles E. Merrill, 1973), 199.

[27] T.M. Moore, "Some Observations Concerning the Educational Philosophy of John Calvin," *Westminster Theological Journal,* 46 (1984): 143.

[28] Noll, "Earliest Protestants," 124.

[29] Moore, "Observations," 144.

[30] Ibid., 147.

[31] Ibid., 145-146

[32] G.R. Elton, ed., *The Reformation (1520–1559),* The New Cambridge Modern History, vol. II (Cambridge: University Press, 1958), 116-117.

[33] Reed and Prevost, *History,* 198.

[34] Moore, "Observations," 142.

[35] Ibid., 151-153.

[36] Ibid, 153-154.

[37] Ibid., 148.

[38] Noll, "Earliest Protestants," 102-103.

[39] Pierre J. Marique, *History of Christian Education,* vol. 2 (New York: Fordham University Press, 1926), 122.

[40] John E. Elias, *A History of Christian Education* (Malabar, FL: Krieger, 2002), 98.

[41] Robert Schwickerath, *Jesuit Education* (St. Louis: B. Herder, 1903), 60.

[42] Marique, *History,* 139.

[43] Reed and Prevost, *History,* 207.

[44] Marique, *History,* 137-138

[45] Thompson, *History,* 108; Marique, *History,* 138-140.

[46] Robert Herbert Quick, *Essays on Educational Reformers* (Cincinnati: Robert Clarke and Company, 1874), 5.

[47] Marique, *History,* 144-146.

[48] Leland Ryken, "Reformation and Puritan Ideals of Education," *Making Higher Education Christian,* ed. by Joel A. Carpenter and Kenneth W. Shipps (Grand Rapids: Eerdmans, 1987), 40.

Chapter 10
Enlightenment Education
17th–19th Century A.D.
Part 1: Background Events and Philosophers

Alvin Wallace Kuest

The Enlightenment was a transitional period as radical as the transition from a modern to a postmodern culture. The transformation of education accompanied the philosophical and societal changes of the Enlightenment. Chapters 10 and 11 address education in the Enlightenment. Chapter 10 will focus on the background events and early philosophers that initially shaped education in the Enlightenment, while Chapter 11 will focus on the educational theorists that have left an indelible mark on the history of education, even today. Together, these chapters provide a thorough overview of education during the Modern era. As such, Chapters 10–11 provide the stage upon which Christian education in Europe (Chapter 12) and early America (Chapter 13) developed.

Overview of the Period

An adaptation of Robert Frost's "The Road Not Taken" perhaps will give a sense of what happened to education in England at the beginning of the historical period known as The Enlightenment.

> Two roads diverged in England's wood,
> And sorry they could not travel all,
> And be one educator, long they stood
> And looked down the two as far as they could
> To where they bent in the undergrowth;
> Then took the other, as just as fair. . . .

I shall be telling this with a cry
Somewhere ages and ages hence:
Two roads diverged in England's wood, and, sigh,
They took the one John Locke traveled by,
And that has made all the difference.

[Adaptation by Alvin W. Kuest]

The dating of the Age of the Enlightenment varies with the recorders of history. "For those who like a dramatic and specific date, the simple but far-reaching phrase of Descartes, 'I think, therefore I am,' will do very well for the beginning: 1637."[1] Some date the Enlightenment with the signing of the Treaty of Westphalia, which ended the Thirty Years' War in 1648. Hugh Black begins the Enlightenment in 1642 with "one of the momentous decisions in modern history which opened up the Great Divide in social and educational history."[2] For it was in 1642 that the British Parliament

> **FYI:** The term *pansophic* means "all wisdom or knowledge."

failed to support the Pansophic Institute of Jan Amos Comenius. Instead they would later throw their support to John Locke's view of learning and teaching as presented in his 1693 work *Thoughts Concerning Education*, and his 1697 memorandum on the reform of the Poor Law.[3]

Cultural Transitions: From Renaissance to Enlightenment

At this point in time France was the most powerful nation in Europe. With a desire for the extravagant, Louis XIV, King of France, very successfully promoted the arts and literature. "All across the continent, leaders powerful and petty, imitated him by posing as gentlemen of refinement and benefactors of culture."[4]

Among those who benefited from this indulgence into the arts and literature were philosophers and scientists. Kant, Voltaire, Diderot, Newton, Descartes, and others became known as *philosophes*—a French term used to describe those who were fervent followers and promoters of the philosophy of John Locke and the new science of John Newton. They were philosophers, but more so. Not satisfied with presenting their ideas through academia, they unashamedly sought out followers, popularizing their views by use of the press.

Aggressive and self-promoting, they lead very precarious lives, never knowing whether they would be courted by leaders of government for their forward-looking views, or thrown into dungeons because of their outspoken views about the mysticism in religion.[5]

The *philosophes*, much like the Humanists of the Renaissance, tended to be of the educated, socially, and affluent elite. The two groups differed in how they viewed themselves: the Humanists saw themselves as the protectors/guardians of truth, whereas, the *philosophes* saw themselves as pioneers, great discoverers of truth. They could spread the truth so that all could know it. Truth was not meant for libraries, it was meant to improve mankind and change society.[6]

Their work was a declaration of freedom. No longer was mankind bound to accepting the teaching of another, especially to those teachers found in antiquity, the one of most significance: Aristotle. Humanity was mature enough to find his own way without paternal authority. Humanity was urged to understand his own nature and the natural world by methods of science.[7] Scientific reasoning was the cry of the day. Humanity was free to discover itself. The age received its greatest influence from the discoveries of Sir Isaac Newton. His discovery of universal gravitation brought forth the thought, if man could unlock the laws of the universe through scientific reasoning, which were the very laws of God, why could he not also discover the laws underlying all of nature and society?[8]

One of the major developments in education during the Enlightenment was the new way in which to think of nature and how man fit into the scheme of the universe. The church had heavily influenced educational practice in past ages in the Western world; the system of learning was based on the supernatural. The world and all therein was created and set in motion by God, and humanity just had to draw close to God to gain an understanding of how it worked, how he fit into its design. According to the *philosophes*, man was constantly looking to the past in order to understand the present and the future would just happen.

Enlightenment *philosophes* and educational theorists saw nature as holding the clues on how life was to be lived. Education was the avenue by which nature could be understood and from which the principles of how to live could be drawn. By drawing on the principles of nature mankind could prepare for the future and not have to depend on a deity to possibly provide it. The principles of the natural universe could be discovered by means of science and the use of the scientific method.[9] "The Judeo-Christian tradition with its emphasis on theism, a personal God, and revealed truth represented a strong and continuing part of this [Western] heritage. Now, the Enlightenment introduced a new way of thinking—a naturalistic and secular way of thought that insisted on the role of human intelligence to find ways of knowing everything."[10]

> **Deism**: believing an impersonal force created the universe, then left it to function in perfection.

Although the *philosophes* (most were Deists) moved in a secular direction away from God as the primary source for all knowledge, the general public of Europe and the Americas were loyal attendees of local churches and read and followed their Bibles. God and the tenets of Christianity continued to be the source of truth and meaning for most people.

The wave of prosperity brought about by the collapse of feudalism and expansion of economic opportunity yielded a greater degree of confidence to those of the middle class.[11] One of the elements now available to those of the middle class was education. Before the reformation it was only available to those with money or those who would become a part of a monastic order. By 1750 the public, not just the scholastics and wealthy, became increasingly literate. This phenomenon belonged mostly to the middle class who now had the leisure time to read.

Historical Influences on Education

With a name such as the "Enlightenment" one would think that all was peaceful and grandiose, however this was not to be the case. Born out of the Thirty Years' War, the Enlightenment was to see many local battles as the Catholic Church tried to destroy or convert smaller religious groups. King Louis of France drove the Huguenots out of France, while the Moravian Brethren were forced to flee Moravia and

> **Question:** In the Thirty Years War, when the peasants stormed the palace at Prague, where did they throw the governor?
>
> Answer: pit of manure

Bohemia. Thousands died during this period of persecution, but those who survived took their message with them.

The Treaty of Westphalia, which ended the Thirty Years' War, impacted much of Europe. The position of the Austrian Hapsburg Emperor, who had been the exalted Holy Roman Emperor, was weakened to the position of a European monarch. While France and other major powers gained some territory, Germany felt the biggest impact. Germany's prince could now determine the religion of his subjects. Calvinism and Lutheranism were given religious recognition along with the Catholics. However, smaller groups, such as the Church of the Brethren gained no recognition and their plight deepened.

Warfare brought in the Enlightenment and warfare took it out. Some see the social and political ferment of this period as being responsible for the Revolution. While embodying many of the ideals of the *philosophes*, the Revolution in its more violent stages (1792–94) served to discredit these ideals temporarily in the eyes of many European contemporaries.[12] (See 🌐 10.1)

The Aim of Education during the Enlightenment

During classical Greek, Roman, Medieval, Renaissance, and Reformation periods, education looked to the past to find truth, beauty, and wisdom. During the Enlightenment educators looked to the future, spending little to no time with the ancient texts or sacred writings. Dwelling on the past limited the student and did not allow for the progression of society. Enlightenment *philosophes* believed they could "reconstruct or rebuild social, political, and economic conditions to get the kind of consequences they desired."[13] The future destiny of mankind was in the hands of the student, and it could not be found in the past. The focus of attention was on the individual; his ability to reason and rationalize and control his future became the dominant thought in philosophy.

The Educational Contexts of the Enlightenment

In spite of the work of philosophers such as Juan Luis Vives during the Renaissance, little had changed as to educational methods when Europe entered the Enlightenment. Education was designed for the wealthy and positioned student. The church generally controlled *elementary education*, whether called vernacular, common, parochial, or private schools. Children were taught so that they would be able to read the catechism and Bible in order to gain knowledge of God. Luther encouraged the development of home schooling of children to prepare them for elementary school. Many parents whether Lutheran or not did educate their own children at home. In England and the colonies the Dame School became popular after the Reformation. These schools were operated by a woman who was willing for a fee to take children into her home and educate them.[14]

Secondary education was supplied by grammar schools, which were overseen by clergy under the auspices of the church. These schools prepared students to enter the universities. The secondary schools existed primarily to prepare young men to enter the clergy and their chief purpose was to point to the primacy of God.[15]

The *universities* were for the select few who proved themselves capable of continuing on in various subject areas (theology, law, medicine, science, and soon education). W.B. Boyd writes of Comenius:

> The university in his opinion, should make provision for the study of every branch of human knowledge and should be reserved for those "select intellects" who had proved their fitness to profit by it in a public examination at the end of the gymnasium [grammar school] course. The more exacting demands of advanced study at this stage would compel most students to confine themselves to the particular subject for which their natural gifts most evidently fitted them. Only those of exceptional ability should be permitted to pursue all branches of learning.[16]

In spite of Comenius's insight and wisdom into the educational process only a few followed his writings and for the rest of the educational world his writings became "closed books" upon his death. The work of Locke too was ignored, not lost as Comenius, by educators in schools and universities. A great gap developed between those who wrote about educational philosophy and those who practiced it. Often, as was the case with Comenius, there was a shortage of schools established based on these educational concepts, and with the loss of direction these too fell into obscurity.[17]

The lack of direction by the educational philosopher was not the only reason for the decline of education in the seventeenth century. One of the main problems was that dreams were big, but money was short. The lack of funding prevented the attraction of teachers who could effectively use the new philosophies. Monies were available only in meager amounts for public education and the general public could not afford private tutors. This lack of funds led to the second problem for elementary and secondary schools, poorly trained teachers. If a school was to be operated, they had to take whatever teachers they could get, and often these teachers were inept and could not teach the simplest of subjects.

The universities were not exempt from this crumbling of education. The loss of funding and poorly trained teachers had a direct influence on the universities. Fewer students were able to make the transition to higher levels of education. Classical curricula and traditions used in most of the elementary and secondary schools no longer fit the needs of contemporary society. The educational weaknesses would lead to an educational slide, which would reach into the 18th century. Universities, unable to attract professors of outstanding merit, became feeble and inert. This would lead to the time when the University of Paris and Oxford University sank to their lowest depths in their histories.[18]

Out of this darkened hole of education shone a bright light. In France LaSalle began the Christian schools in 1682. He was able to establish these schools because of Louis XIV's edict that all children of "those who had made a profession of faith" be instructed in catechism and prayers, along with reading and writing.[19] In England James II allowed the dissenting and Anglican churches to set up charity schools for the same purpose. These schools did well but were soon eclipsed by the Society for Promoting Christian Knowledge set up in 1698. Within forty years the Society had 2,000 schools and 40,000 students.

The Free Schools of England, as promoted by the Bishop of Landtaff, had grown to over 5,000 students by 1788. The schools were opening quickly under the tutelage of Joseph Lancaster. Nobility, wealthy, and common folk, supported each of them financially. They were located in buildings that had been abandoned; for example, one school met in a Quaker Meeting House that was no longer used as it inhabitants had left England under persecution. Another school met in the "old palace of the Archbishop of

Canterbury: — in the very place where the primitive martyrs used to be *imprisoned, examined,* and *tortured.*"[20] Also, as funds came available, new school buildings were constructed.

Classrooms were a long square shape with all desks facing forward. Each desk held only one boy. The teacher was prominently placed at the front so that he might have a good view of the students. Everything had its place—even hats had to be worn and stored in a certain manner. (🔊 10.2)

Private grammar schools and those started by religious groups not associated with the Church of England were the exception.[21] The institutions of higher learning were just as bad off as the system of Elementary and Secondary schools that fed into them. William Boyd writes,

> The most hopeful feature in the situation was undoubtedly the fact that most people were under no delusions about the badness of the schools and universities, and were anxious to see them reformed. This made it easy for men of idealistic temper to plan grand schemes involving radical changes in educational outlook, and for more practical men to attempt to bring about improvements in the existing order of things; and in both respects much was done to make straight the way for the educational advances of the nineteenth century.[22]

The Content of Education

Vernacular education, which had made a tremendous impact on education in the Reformation and Renaissance, was on the wane. Latin and Greek once again rose to ascendancy. The grammar school, which gave instruction in Latin and religion and made no provision for vernacular education, plodded along and maintained its position. Indifferent to the winds of education, it preserved its place, especially in countries where either Catholicism or Protestantism had gained in dominance. Reading and writing in Latin was taught primarily from the Bible or the classics. Math generally included simple mathematics and geometry. Depending on the school, art, music, philosophy, and science may be added. (See 🔊 10.3)

In the universities the study of theology continued to dominate the curriculum. The traditional curriculum consisted primarily of the

Seven Liberal Arts (grammar, rhetoric, dialect, geometry, arithmetic, astronomy, and music), theology, Bible, Church Fathers, philosophy, law, science, Latin, Greek, Hebrew, and the Classics. Humanism had moved the focus from Mysticism (seeking a direct personal communion with God), and Nominalism (the emphasis of the human experience and opposition to the suppression of individual opinion) and centered it on the present physical life more than the spiritual life. Humanism valued the inwardness of humans and called for them to pursue self-understanding.[23]

The Educational Process of the Enlightenment

Humanism advanced in Northern and Southern Europe because education had become disconnected from society. Before the Enlightenment, education had become pedantic, students were not encouraged to learn and understand a subject; the only thing the teacher wanted was a simple regurgitation of the facts. Rote memorization and recitation were the main teaching methods used in schools, both elementary and secondary.

Church-related elementary and secondary schools were the predominant schools. Their educational philosophy saw children as basically evil and corrupt; children are born in sin and have a predisposition to commit sin. Therefore, the teacher had the responsibility to instill correct knowledge from the classics and the Bible to replace this bent to sinning. Furthermore, the teacher also had free reign to use the rod, both in encouraging proper learning and in punishment for wrongdoing; literally giving rise to the saying that education was pounded into you.

The Enlightenment brought a different concept into the classroom. The teacher became more of a friend or guide. Rousseau, in his classic work *Emile*, saw the teacher as a private tutor who would be a guide working closely with the student to help him discover knowledge. Pestalozzi and Froebel looked at the teacher as a loving parent, especially a mother. They saw the teacher as one who would become concerned with the child's development and as an observer find ways to teach that would meet the child's needs.

The Enlightenment began to move away from the traditional view of the teacher/professor as a well of knowledge that was to pour that knowledge into the minds of their students. Students began to be seen as an integral part of the learning process. Memorization, recitation, and the rod would slowly be replaced in the classroom.

Voices

In mentioning an educational parallel to Frost's "The Road Not Taken," two voices are put forward as having a major impact on education at this time. However, their voices would not be limited to the Enlightenment but would continue into contemporary education. The two voices are those of Comenius and Locke. England chose not to develop Comenius's Pansophic University, but later opened its arms to John Locke's educational philosophy which impacted the future educational systems there and in America. Comenius was not lost as his philosophical influence was felt through the rest of Europe.

Johann Amos Comenius [1592–1670] (10.4) was born into a time of turmoil. His family were members of a Hussite movement known as The Unity of the Bohemian Brethren, a group heavily persecuted by the Catholic Church, and persecution would become a constant part of his life. Little is known about his early life until the age of 11 when he began his education in a poor village school.

His entry in Latin school was delayed by the death of his parents; it was not until age fifteen that he was able to attend the grammar school at Prerau. Once in school he developed a voracious appetite for learning. He learned rapidly and with much enthusiasm. However, he was frustrated with the laborious learning concepts of the 'grammar-grind' typical of European Latin schools, and openly wrote about finding a new way of teaching Latin. Later in the introduction to his book *Prodromus* he wrote an expression of hope that, "the youth might be brought by a more easy method, unto some notable proficiency in learning."[24]

Comenius suffered from persecution, plague, and war. At age twelve he lost both of his parents and two sisters to the plague. Later he would lose his first wife and two sons to the plague also, though there is some speculation that they died due to persecution. The Thirty Years' War would drive him out of his beloved Bohemia and see many of his fellow churchmen killed for their faith. He appealed to the Swedish government to allow the freedom of the Brethren in

Moravia and Bohemia as a part of the Treaty of Westphalia when the war ended, but in the embroilment known as politics, they were left out. They fled to Poland where Comenius began forty-two years of exile and persecution during which he lived in England, Prussia, Hungary, and Amsterdam. However, forty-two years later he was once again faced with war. During a raid on the town of Leszno, Poland, his house, including his library of manuscripts and books, was burned. All of these events would play an important part in the educational philosophy known as Pansophia.

In 1632 he published his *Janua Linguarum Reserata* which was an immediate success and translated into all European languages and several Asiatic languages. He followed this with *Vestibulum*, an elementary book meant to precede the *Janua*. With these texts his fame began to grow as an educator. In 1638 he was invited to revamp the Swedish school system; however, feeling that he did not have the time as he was now Bishop of the Moravians, he made himself available to offer advice and suggestions.[25]

During his education at Latin school and Herborn High School he met two men who would have a profound influence on his future. Wolfgang Ratke (1571–1635), who achieved some notoriety as an educational motivator, put forth the concept that "there should be no rote learning of words without knowledge of the things represented by words. Learning should follow 'the order and course of nature,' and should be pursued all the time by personal examination, experiment and analysis."[26] The other man who influenced Comenius was Johann Heinrich Alsted (1588–1638) who was one of his high school teachers. In Alsted's great work, the *Universal Encyclopedia*, he pleads for education to be taught in the vernacular, and that vernacular schools should exist everywhere for boys and girls. Unfortunately, he had no great opinion of the capacity of girls to learn, but he said that some noble women might take it up as a hobby.[27]

Ratke would be the primary influence in Comenius's texts on teaching Latin. Ratke's influence is evident in Comenius's approach to teaching which stressed group learning in teaching children, allowing them to use their natural curiosity to make discoveries. Comenius discouraged the use of rote memorization and recitation saying they were a waste of teaching time. Children should be allowed to discover the meaning of things, not just be told what they were to believe. To encourage this he grouped the children into four age groups for different levels of teaching:

- Birth to six years old: educated by their parents at home
- Six through twelve years old: taught in primary or vernacular schools
- Twelve to eighteen years old: Latin grammar school, a secondary school where they learned Latin, Greek, Hebrew, and the vernacular
- Eighteen years old and older: Attended a Pansophist university. The Pansophist university was only for the brightest of students.[28]

The crown jewel in Comenius's theory of education was the Pansophist university. The concept was to have students study the entire range of knowledge embraced in the Pansophist philosophy of education. It was to be a synthesis of all principles derived from theology, philosophy, and science. Course work leaned heavily on Protestant reformist theology, especially that of John Huss.

Philosophy was to be based on realism, what he termed Sense Realism—there are real objects that could be known through the use of a person's senses. Comenius believed as did Bacon that education should not be an emphasis on words but should place its importance on matter. Comenius believed the sciences were complementary to the Bible as science provided a way for mankind to know God's universe.[29]

> **Sense Realism** – Knowledge is best derived from induction not deduction. Learning is more effective from sensory perceived data than from abstract reasoning alone.

It has been surmised that Comenius's pansophic views were a direct result of the turmoil in his life. He believed war and persecution were a result of the ignorance of mankind. If mankind was to have complete knowledge, it would bring them closer to God and each other and as a result would bring peace. "Pansophism, an early form of international or peace education was an argument for universal knowledge and education."[30]

It was this pansophic philosophy that drew the attention of Samuel Hartlib (1596–1662), an English education reformer and associate of Oliver Cromwell, to Comenius. In 1641 he invited

Comenius to come to England to supervise the foundation of a pansophic college. Though Hartlib and many other English educators were excited about the possibilities of a pansophic college, parliament had its attentions focused elsewhere, insurrection in Ireland and a developing rebellion at home. They had given general approval for a college but never gave an official invitation to Comenius to come to England and establish one. So when Comenius came, he had to try to find patrons to support his work. He stayed less than a year and failed to establish the college, but his conversations with educators helped impact English education for a long time.

Comenius was a prolific writer. During his lifetime he published 154 works and it is unknown how many works in progress were destroyed in the fire. One of the works was his pansophic encyclopedia. His greatest works were: *The Labyrinth of the Worlds and The Paradise of the Heart*, which is reminiscent of *Pilgrims Progress*; his Latin texts *Janua Linguarium Reserata* and *Vestibulum*; *Opera Didactica* (or *Didactica*) was his major educational work; perhaps his most famous and popular work was *Orbis Pictus* (*The World in Pictures*). *Orbis Pictus* was not the first picture book created for children but it was the most useful and teachable one published. Illustrated by Comenius himself, the book had a careful arrangement of pictures with descriptive text. The pictures and text were placed in parallel columns so that the learning of the meaning of words could be gained through the sense of sight. To further facilitate learning the descriptions were in two different languages with matching numbering between the pictures and definitions to ensure proper learning.[31] (See 🔍 10.5)

Comenius's Pansophism promised universal knowledge, which would lead students to God who was the source of all knowledge, goodness, and truth. God as truth enabled the learner to find pure truth, not the truths of humanity. Humanity's truths brought hate and destruction, whereas, the truths of God would bring peace to humanity. The Bible coupled with the sciences and humanities would give humankind greater insights into God and world peace.

John Locke (1632–1704) was but a child of ten years of age when Comenius came to England (🔍 10.6). Born in Somerset (England), he was raised by his Puritan father who was a lawyer in the Parliamentary army. Because of delicate health and the outbreak of civil war in England, Locke's father tutored him at home until the age of 14 at which time he entered Westminster School. During a study of Descartes he openly criticized the practice of disputation because it was artificial and deceptive. However, it is interesting to note upon receiving his Master's degree, he became a tutor at Christ Church, Oxford, where he was also a reader in Greek and rhetoric.[32]

His father died while he was a tutor at Christ Church, Oxford, and the inheritance he received allowed him the time and resources to seek out his future career. After investigating the three fields, he settled on the study of experimental medicine. For a year or two he practiced as an amateur doctor, having never completed his qualifications due to a disagreement with university authorities. It was in this practice that he met Lord Ashley, the Earl of Shaftsburg, upon whom he had performed a delicate and successful operation. He became the Earl's private secretary and tutor to the Earl's son.

However, the experience of tutoring the Earl's son and later his grandson, played a great part in an essay published after his death, *Some Thoughts Concerning Education*. This essay, written after his work *Some Thoughts Concerning Human Understanding*, was intended to show how a young man could best develop his mind.[33] In the essay he set himself against the grammar schools, or any school, because they do not care if the students really learn, they only care if the students can feed back the information given to them. Words without meaning or understanding are just words and are therefore worthless. He recommended fathers as tutors, as his own father had been a tutor to him. He stressed the importance of understanding the child's needs. He believed the four outcomes of education were virtue, wisdom, good breeding, and learning, with the foundation of virtue being good religious training.[34] (See ✺ 10.7)

Locke's most influential educational idea was his theory of knowledge. Consistent with sense realism, Locke was an empiricist. He attacked the thoughts of Plato and Descartes regarding innate ideas within the human mind, promoting the opposite, that the mind began as a blank slate. Ideas are the result of sensation or reflection and are recorded in the mind, which serves as a piece of blank paper.[35]

Locke believed learning was experiential. It is because of this concept that he developed his view of *tabla rasa*, that a child's mind is a blank slate when it is born and learning is the impressions made on that slate. As children begin to sense their environment it makes an impression on their minds and the children learn. Learning is divided into the simple and the complex. Simple learning takes place among the senses, it may be by one sense (the color is orange), by several senses (the eating of the orange provides a sensation of taste, smell, touch, and satisfaction), by reflection (hunger before eating the orange), or by the combination of sensation and reflection (pain and pleasure).[36] Ideas derived from experience are the first elements written on the slate.

The mind is passive in receiving simple ideas, but once the ideas have been received it is able to act upon them in various ways. It can use them in simple form (as with the orange) or it can combine them to formulate complex ideas, or to set them aside in order to reflect on them for future usage. The mind can then note the relationship between differing experiences or separate them from differing experiences—abstraction. In this way complex ideas are formed, such as: beauty, essence, and that of relationships. These are complex ideas which have grown from the simple ideas impressed on the *tabla rasa* which sprang from experience.[37] However, some note a similarity between *tabla rasa* and Sense Realism. Note the following from Locke's *Of the Conduct of Understanding*.

> Knowing is seeing, and if it be so, it is madness to persuade ourselves that we do so by another man's eyes, let him use ever so many words to tell us what he asserts is very visible. Till we ourselves see it with our own eyes and perceive it by our own understandings, we are as much in the dark and as void of knowledge as before, let us believe any learned author as much as we will.[38]

Locke believed that mankind could know with certainty that God exists. We can also know about morality with the same precision as mathematics, because we are the creators of moral and political ideas.[39]

Etienne Bonnot de Condillac (1714–1780). Born Etienne Bonnot in Grenoble, France, he later took the surname of Condillac from a family estate after the death of his father. Rousseau was a tutor of Condillac's older brother and from this a lifelong friendship developed between Rousseau and Condillac. Though he was ordained a priest in 1741 he apparently never pursued the position. As a philosopher his work was based on Locke and Newton, preferring the reliance on observation and experience. He was the tutor for the Duke of Parma and his educational philosophy was a result of developing a learning system for the young duke.

As with Locke, he saw the mind as devoid of innate ideas, however, he did not separate the mind from the sense organs in describing sensations. He differed from Locke in several crucial ways:

- First, he claimed that all mental operations could be derived from sensation alone, rejecting reflection as a source of ideas.

- Second, he took Locke's attack on innate ideas a major step further, by denying the existence of any innate faculties. Mental faculties too (e.g., attention and memory) were themselves generated from the occurrence of simple sensations.

- Third, when Locke claimed that the function of language was to communicate ideas which could exist independently of it, Condillac insisted that the function of language was constitutive in their formation.

- This claim culminated in the view that knowledge itself is a well-made language, and that the basic form of a well-made language is algebra, which consists of tautological propositions.[40]

Condillac divided the process by which sensations lead to learning as a five-step process:

- Observing primary steps,
- Noting the relationship among these objects,
- Observing the intervals between the objects,
- Observing the secondary objects that fill the intervals, and
- Comparing all that has been observed and noted.[41]

Conclusion

Comenius believed that "mankind is one fellowship, one society, bound together by the common purpose of using intelligence for the making of a common life."[42] Whereas, John Locke believed "mankind falls into groups, classes, sets, factions, nations, individuals, which seeking each its own ends inevitably tend to plunge into hatred and strife, one against the other,"[43] thus they should be taught separately.

Locke believed in a two-part educational system: One for the lower economic level in which they are taught a trade and a second for the aristocratic class in which the student learned how to win friends and influence people, how to be a gentleman, thus promoting a class system in education. Whereas, Comenius saw the first concern of education to be the type of learning that leads to piety and understanding, that which draws mankind together and promotes peace through knowledge.[44] Thus England stood and looked long down Comenius's road but took the other Locke traveled by and that has made all the difference.

Early in the Enlightenment philosophers such as Comenius, Locke, and Condillac began to make some radical changes in the way people learn. Instead of a disciplinarian, the teacher was to be more of a friend or a guide, observing students and designing lessons to meet student's needs. Instead of the classics and Bible as curriculum, the world around the student became their classroom. The observation of nature and the scientific method replaced memorization and recitation. The church moved from the center of education to be replaced by mankind. The influence of the Enlightenment is still felt in 21st-century education.

What Can We Learn from Education in the Enlightenment?

- Learning is experiential, but not subjective; meaning that learning occurs through all of our senses.
- A learner cannot fully know simply by being verbally told. He or she must discover meanings, joining the learning process.
- While previous generations of Christian educators had focused on human sinfulness, the Enlightenment provided a counterbalance, emphasizing human worth and potential.
- Education can change not only individuals, but societies as well.
- One cannot separate philosophical shifts from educational agendas; they are interactive.
- Christians, such as Comenius and Locke, can disagree on educational theory, and yet still be Christians.

Study Helps

Reflection Questions

1. In what ways does your college education compare to Comenius's pansophic college?

2. John Locke's concept of *tabla rasa* simply put is that a student learns from personal experience. Do you agree or disagree? Why?

3. Comenius believed that mankind is one fellowship, one society, whereas John Locke believed "mankind falls into groups, classes, sets, factions, nations, individuals," which of these two have you seen in your education? How has it affected you?

4. How did your education compare to that of the vernacular schools?

Technical Terms

Constitutive   Forming an essential element of something.

Deism   Believing an impersonal force created the universe, then left it to function in perfection.

Humanists   A philosophy first developed in Italy which presented the theory that man was in control of his destiny and that his exposure to the classics and nature would create a moral being

Pansophic   All knowledge or wisdom. Comenius wanted a college that would be pansophic.

philosophes   A French term used to describe those who were fervent followers and promoters of the philosophy of John Locke and the new science of John Newton.

Sapere aude!   Dare to know! Immanuel Kant believed you should have the courage to use your own intelligence!

Sense Realism   Knowledge is best derived from induction not deduction. Learning is more effective from sensory perceived data than from abstract reasoning alone.

Tautological   In logic—a statement that is true by necessity or by virtue of its logical form.

Vernacular   The native language or dialect of a country or place.

Recommended Bibliography

Black, Hugh C., Kenneth V. Lottich, and Donald S. Seckinger. *The Great Educators: Readings for Leaders in Education.* Chicago: Nelson-Hall Co., 1972.

Boyd, William. *The History of Western Education.* Rev. by Edmund J. King. New York: Barnes and Noble, 1969.

Curtis, S.J. and M.E. Boultwood. *A Short History of Educational Ideas.* London: University Tutorial Press, 1970.

Gay, Peter. *Great Ages of Man: A History of the World's Cultures: Age of Enlightenment.* New York: Time-Life Books, 1966.

Gutek, Gerald L. *Historical and Philosophical Foundations of Education: A Biographical Introduction.* Upper Saddle River, NJ: Merrill Prentice Hall, 2001.

Notes

[1] Crane Brinton, *The Portable Age of Reason Reader* (New York: Penguin Books, 1956), 1.

[2] Hugh C. Black, "A Missing Chord in Educational Theory," in *The Great Educators: Readings for Leaders in Education,* ed. by Hugh C. Black, Kenneth V. Lottich, and Donald S. Seckinger (Chicago: Nelson-Hall, 1972), 770.

[3] Black, "Missing Chord," 771.

[4] Peter Gay, ed., *Great Ages of Man: A History of the World's Cultures—Age of Enlightenment* (New York: Time-Life, 1966), 12.

[5] Ibid., 11.

[6] Gerald L. Gutek, *Historical and Philosophical Foundations of Education: A Biographical Introduction.* (Upper Saddle River, NJ: Prentice Hall, 1991), 111, 112.

[7] Gay, *Great Ages,* 11.

[8] Timothy N. Tackett, "Enlightenment, Age of," *Microsoft Online Encyclopedia 2003* (http://encarta.msn.com, Microsoft Corporation, 1997–2003), 2. All Rights Reserved.

[9] Gutek, *Foundations,* 110.

[10] Ibid., 111.

[11] Rempel, Gerhard. *Age of Enlightenment* (http://mars.acnet.wnec.edu/~grempel/courses/wc2/lectures/enlightenment.html), 1.

[12] Tackett, *Enlightenment,* 5.

[13] Gutek, *Foundations,* 112.

[14] Charles Benton Eavey, *History of Christian Education* (Chicago: Moody Press, 1964), 194.

[15] Ibid., 203.

[16] William Boyd, *The History of Western Education*, rev. by E.J. King (New York: Barnes and Noble, 1969), 252.

[17] Ibid.

[18] Ibid., 281.

[19] Ibid.

[20] www.constitution.org/lanc/epitome.htm, 1.

[21] Boyd, *History*, 283.

[22] Ibid., 281.

[23] James E. Reed and Ronnie Prevost, *A History of Christian Education* (Grand Rapids: Baker, 1993), 169.

[24] S.J. Curtis and M.E.A. Boultwood, *A Short History of Educational Ideas* (London: University Tutorial Press, 1970), 174.

[25] Ibid., 175.

[26] Ibid., 171.

[27] Ibid., 173.

[28] Gutek, *Foundations*, 104, 105.

[29] Ibid., 102.

[30] Ibid., 103.

[31] Curtis and Boultwood, *Short History*, 180.

[32] Ibid., 223.

[33] Boyd, *History*, 274.

[34] Linda Cannell, *Summary of Historical Periods for DES936* (Deerfield, IL: Trinity Evangelical Divinity School, Spring, 2000).

[35] Ibid.

[36] www.findarticles.com/cf_dls/g2699/0005/2699000534/print.jhtml. *Gale Encyclopedia of Psychology.* 2001, 2.

[37] Curtis and Boultwood, *Short History*, 228.

[38] Reed and Prevost, *History*, 238.

[39] Oregon State University, "Locke," www.Orst.edu/instruct/phl302/philosophers/locke.html

[40] E.C.T. Moore, "Condillac," www.hku.hk/caut/Timmoore/papers/condill/cpage1.htm

[41] Reed and Prevost, *History*, 239.

[42] Black, "Missing Chord," 772.

[43] Ibid.

[44] Ibid.

Chapter 11
Enlightenment Education Part 2: The Progressive Educators

Alvin Wallace Kuest

Overview of Period

The progressive education movement begins during the Enlightenment with Jean-Jacques Rousseau (1712–1778) and continues through the work of Friedrich Froebel (1782–1852). It was a time that began in relative peace, but in 1789 the Bastille in Paris was stormed by the people who protested the monarchy's lack of reforms. Louis XV had tried but failed to make needed reforms. His son Louis XVI tried to bring about reform in order to better the lives of the commoners by making Anne Robert Jacques Turgot Controller-General of France. Though considered to be a brilliant intellectual and the *philosophe's philosophe* his reforms angered the vested interests and he was dismissed one and a half years later in 1776.[1] His dismissal caused Voltaire to remark, "The dismissal of this great man crushes me. . . . Since that fatal day, I have not followed anything, I have not asked anyone for anything, and I am waiting patiently for someone to cut our throats."[2]

In an attempt to maintain appearances, France had bankrupted itself politically and financially. Appearance had become everything—beautiful buildings, beautiful people, the arts, *philosophes*, and an air of financial self-indulgence had drained the treasuries. The people were taxed to almost financial exhaustion. In maintaining a proper appearance the political leaders became more concerned with themselves than in the running of the country. They borrowed huge sums of money from European bankers and then falsified national records in order to hide the true condition of the country. The commoners finally pulled away from the monarchy, formed the National Assembly, and then, with the storming of the Bastille, began the French Revolution, which many say ended the Enlightenment. The German poet, Goethe in 1792, was a part of the Prussian-Austrian army that invaded France during the French Revolution. When the French defeated the German armies at Valmy, Goethe remarked, "Here and today begins a new age in the history of the world. Someday you will be able to say—I was present at its birth."[3] In 1792 a new French Republic had been formed and Louis XVI was guillotined in 1793.

Revolution was not just occurring in France though. The American Revolution began in 1776 and ended in 1783. Germany was a country of 300 separate sovereign states in 1782 and by 1806 had been reduced to 100.[4] The upheaval that had begun in the Enlightenment had not ended. With the establishment of the French Republic, France's troubles were not over yet. Napoleon rose to power in 1799 and tried to conquer all of Europe. The resulting wars kept all of Europe in political upheaval until 1812 when Napoleon was defeated in Russia and finally fully defeated at the battle of Waterloo in 1815.

Though the countrysides were often disrupted because of war the artistry that had developed in the Enlightenment continued on through the eighteenth century. Europe, especially France, wanted extraordinary artistry from their craftsmen. Works of wood, carved and inlaid rivaled the artistry of the painter's palette; glass, tile, furniture, cutlery, and tableware became art in themselves. Walls, that at one time were painted or covered with tapestries, became the artist's canvas. They were painted, inlaid with gold and porcelain, and covered with wood, bronze, and plaster reliefs. Such was the artistry that it is still in demand in the 21st century.

The prosperity that had begun early in the Enlightenment continued with the rise of the bourgeoisie. There were fortunes to be made and with development of the bourgeoisie national economies blossomed. At the turn of the seventeenth

> **Bourgeois**—French, a person of the middle class [bourgeoisie] whose social behavior and political views are influenced by wealth.

century a new morality had appeared among the general public. Labor, which had been a frustration, became a new way to glorify God with the development of the Protestant work ethic. Poverty came to be viewed as something evil, not as way to draw near to God. France by the early eighteenth century was one of the world's richest nations. England developed a shipping industry that brought sugar, spices, and other treasures from around the world. Among those "treasures" were slaves from Africa that helped build the American and English economies.

During the late eighteenth century the Industrial Revolution occurred in England, producing more wealth. However, France failed to capitalize on the early industrialization and was still seen as an agriculturally based economy. The slow development of industry only added to its economic woes. England, though, with its colonization, both home and abroad, generated tremendous profit that was used to finance the new technologies that brought the Industrial Revolution to its fullest in the nineteenth century (🔵 11.1).

Wealth in the middle class also produced a new phenomenon—leisure. Until this point leisure had been only accorded to the wealthy aristocracy. Now more people had time in which to pursue other avocations; one of which was reading. The Gutenberg press had made more books available and the cost of books had dropped. Wealth, leisure, and literacy had created a reading public.

T.M. Tackett wrote the following concerning the philosophical advances of this era:

> During the first half of the 18th century, the leaders of the Enlightenment waged an uphill struggle against considerable odds. Several were imprisoned for their writings, and most were hampered by government censorship and attacks by the church. In many respects, however, the later decades of the century marked a triumph of the movement in Europe and America. By the 1770's second-generation philosophes were receiving government pensions and taking control of established intellectual academies. The enormous increase in the publication of newspapers and books ensured a wide diffusion of their ideas. Scientific experiments and philosophical writing became fashionable among wide groups in society, including members of the nobility and the clergy. A number of European monarchs also adopted certain of the ideas or at

least the vocabulary of the Enlightenment. Voltaire and other philosophes, who relished the concept of a philosopher king enlightening the people from above, eagerly welcomed the emergence of the so-called enlightened despots, of whom Frederick II of Prussia, Catherine II of Russia, and Joseph II of Austria were the most celebrated examples. In retrospect, however, it appears that most of these monarchs used the movement in large part for propaganda purposes and were far more despotic than enlightened.[5]

The Aim of Education

The Bishop of Landtaff in 1788 wrote the following concerning education in England:

> All nations indeed, of which we have any account, in becoming rich, have become profligate: a torrent of depraved morality has, in every opulent state, borne down with irresistible violence those mounds and fences, by which the wisdom of legislators attempted to protect chastity, sobriety, and virtue. If any check can be given to the corruption of a state, increasing in riches, and declining in morals, it must be given *not by laws to alter the inveterate habits of man*, but by education adapted to form the hearts of children to a proper sense of moral, and religious excellence[6] (✸ 11.2).

The schools the Bishop wrote of were a system of Free Schools for young boys of poverty. The schools were being set up in England to provide free education for all young boys. Each school would provide instruction in reading, writing, the elements of arithmetic, and the knowledge of the Holy Scriptures. Instruction in these were to be the blessing of every Christian and loyal Englishman.[7] The aim was to keep the children out of prison, provide the peace brought by doing well in life, to impart a knowledge of Scriptures and doctrines of the church, and to show them a way to rise above the poverty into which they had been born.

The Context of Education

In spite of the wealth garnered by the new middle class, poverty was still rampant. And many of the common people received no education at all. The only areas of Europe in which the common people were educated were Scotland and portions of Germany. In other areas schools, including elementary, secondary and universities, had become corrupt. Students were taught in the worst possible conditions—crowded, dirty, and generally in the living room or work area of the teacher. Teachers were underpaid and generally had little education themselves. Many teachers only took the position because they could not do anything else; they had failed in every other attempt to earn a living. Subjects were reading, writing, and religion. Seldom was math taught because the teacher found math too difficult to understand.[8] Education had lost all contact with contemporary needs. The classics, which many schools were limited by law to teach, and Latin were no longer of any need in society. "Whether, for example, we consider the complaints about the barrenness of the Jesuit schools which came from every part of France in 1762 or the condemnation of the grammar schools of England by Lord Chief Justice Kenyon in 1795—'empty wall without scholars and everything neglected but the receipt of salaries and endowments'—we get a painful impression of the sorry estate into which the old-time schools had declined."[9]

The Educational Content and Process

The content and process, particularly in reference to the role of the teacher, differed between institutions of education and educational theorists. In the *common schools* the role of teacher was a sad plight in the annals of education. Qualified teachers were not available and the salaries were too low to attract anyone with good credentials; therefore the teachers were the leftovers, sadly giving rise to the saying, "Those who can't, teach." Often the teachers were described as ignorant men and women whose only qualification was their unfitness for any other occupation.[10] The Grammar schools fared a little better. Here and there, one could find teachers of outstanding ability who maintained the quality of learning. But they also were of small numbers, discouraged by the small wages.[11]

The teacher in the *grammar schools* was a taskmaster. He would stand before the class

---

The Common School— established to teach vocations and common people to be good citizens.
The Grammar School— taught Latin and the Classics

---

demanding perfection in reciting the daily lessons. Tests would be given to show competency, and the only passing score was a perfect score. Classes were generally small and crowded into one room with all ages and abilities working together at the same time.

The better teachers became tutors to the families of the wealthy. Here they would live with the family and work with the children, sometimes with the benefactor as well. While teaching they were allowed to develop writings and philosophies. Rousseau tutored the two children of Madame de Mably, and though he disliked being a teacher, he grew fascinated with the broad issues of education. During the time he spent as tutor, he wrote his first treatise on education. Johann Herbart and Friedrich Froebel also began their educational careers as tutors.

Rousseau saw the teacher as a guide and coach. The teacher was to inspire the student as a youth to discover for himself from nature how the natural environment functioned and to discern how to live and survive in society. As the student grew older and questions about life began to become personal as how to live life and what was happening to their emotions and bodies, the teacher was to wait for the student to ask questions and force the subject.

To *Pestalozzi* the role of the teacher was that of a patient and loving parent. Above all the teacher was to be observant of the growth and development of each student, creating a planned environment suitable for the developmental level of each student.[12] The teacher's role was that of a guide and resource person.

An enabler was *Herbart's* view of the teacher. As an enabler the teacher was to awaken within the student the desire to learn and to assist him in analyzing and synthesizing information. Instead of being told what to learn, the student was to be lead in making independent just and moral judgments. Similar to Pestalozzi, the tools of psychology were to be applied in order to understand the natural functions and capabilities of the students.

Froebel conceived of the teacher as an idealized loving mother, which was very similar to Pestalozzi's concept of the teacher as a patient and caring parent. Teaching was similar to a religious vocation and the teacher was to be an agent who cooperated with God and nature to facilitate growth and development.[13] Teachers were to be observers of how the children's lives developed through games, play, and activities. Drawing on their own childhood and personal observations, they were to structure their teaching to facilitate the child's growth and development.

Voices

Jean-Jacques Rousseau (1712–1778) (11.3)

An out-an-out charlatan, an individual swayed by successive waves of emotion, stable in one thing only, his own self-love, a writer whose thought teemed with inconsistencies and contradictions, who relied on paradox to hold his readers, a thinker who when not giving expression to his feelings of the moment, utilized other men's ideas, a man who can be held responsible for most of the wrong turnings taken by education in the last hundred years. On the other hand, a highly original thinker who burst the bonds of convention, who in his political philosophy may be termed the father of modern democracy, and whose views on education were so revolutionary that they have influenced theory and practice ever since.[14]

The real Rousseau lies somewhere in between. His character and personality were so complex, that groups of people over time have accused him of being both innovator and charlatan and have been known to change their views of him as they study his works.[15]

His life began in uncertainty and continued into adulthood. Born in Geneva, Switzerland, his mother, Suzanne Bernard, died when he was nine days old. His father, Isaac Rousseau, a watchmaker, was known as a self-indulgent and violent-tempered man. When Jean-Jacques was only ten years old, his father's temper caused an incident which would have lasting consequences for Jean-Jacques. An altercation with an army officer forced him to leave town quickly. He would never be a part of Jean-Jacques's life again.

While Rousseau's father was a part of his life, he took an active interest in his education. As his first tutor he and his son spent hours reading books together. The readings ranged from love stories to the classics. It would be the experiences of his mother's early death and his father's reading with him that would make major influences on the educational theories he would later develop.

When his father left, his uncle, Gabriel Bernard, raised him. Under the tutelage of his uncle Jean-Jacques received a conventional primary education. After his primary education he was apprenticed to a notary and a coppersmith (engraver). The notary dismissed him because he was not disciplined enough to keep up his duties.

After leaving the engraver he traveled for a while living off his inheritance and the generosity of benefactors (generally thought to be women). He gave up his passion for women for a time to study for the priesthood, but was discouraged from his studies by the Bishop. He quickly became the secretary and companion to Madame Louise de Warens. She was twelve years his senior and became a mother figure, friend, and a lover. Under her patronage he was able to further his education. He developed a taste for music and became a music teacher in Chambery. He also wrote several operas, a ballet, and offered himself to Paris as a music teacher[16] (11.4).

He left the de Warens household to become a tutor of the M. de Mably's two children. While tutoring the children, Rousseau began to develop an interest in educational philosophy. The desire to teach was never strong but the interest in education would grow. It was here that he wrote his first educational essay, *Project of the Education of M. de Sainte-Marie*.

Leaving the de Mably's he went to Paris, earning a living by copying music. Paris at the time was the intellectual center of Europe. One of the amenities of Paris was that it was the nerve center of the *philosophes*. Here he was able to mingle with the likes of Condillac, Diderot, and d'Alembert. The association would aid him in receiving a position as secretary with the French Ambassador in Venice. However, his inability to work as a subordinate would cut short his career in politics.

Returning to Paris, Rousseau began a love affair with Therese Levasseur, an illiterate servant at the hotel where he stayed. Therese has been described as a rather pathetic unattractive woman and even though Rousseau tried to educate her she remained illiterate. The affair would produce five children, each of which was placed in a foundling home shortly after its birth.[17] Rousseau would leave Therese, and later he would return to take her as his common-law wife. Many believe it is ironic that this philosopher of child education, who encouraged the permissiveness of children, would discard his own children. Rousseau would later seek to justify his actions by saying that he lacked the money or expertise to raise children and declaring his sorrow over his decision.

While imprisoned for his own writings, Diderot encouraged Rousseau to write an essay for the Academy of Dijon in 1749. In the essay, *Discours sur les sciences et les arts*, he proclaimed that humans are by nature good and that it is society's institutions that corrupt them. The essay brought him considerable recognition and opened many doors for him. He moved to Montmorency and continued his writing under the patronage of the Duke and Duchess of Luxembourg. It was here that he did his best work including: *The New Heloise*, probably the most read novel of this time (based on his affair with the Comtesse d'Handetot of Paris); *The Social Contract*, his most influential writing on political theory; and *Emile* in 1762.

> **FYI:** This was the legitimizing of the notion, "Society is to blame" for human fault.

Emile is his greatest writing about education, and its influence has continued into the 21st century. However, even during his lifetime the essay would bring him much notoriety. *Emile* was acclaimed by the *philosophes* but cursed by the church and the French government. Because of his "heretical" discussion of religion in *Emile*, Rousseau had to leave France. The French government at the behest of the Church ordered the book burned and Rousseau arrested. He fled to Switzerland where he had citizenship in Geneva; however, because of the uproar over his book, his citizenship there had been revoked. He went to Berne and then to England at the invitation of David Hume.

Symptoms of paranoia, which had first appeared in an earlier visit to Geneva during a public infatuation with Mme d'Houderot showed itself and turned Rousseau against Hume, causing his early departure from England. The paranoia would get worse in his final years, driving him away from Diderot and the other *philosophes*. His volatile and angry outburst at being abused and misunderstood alienated him from most of his upper-class friends.

Leaving England, Rousseau had to sneak back into France under an assumed name in 1767. France let him stay under the promise that he would not publish his work. However, he still had problems subjecting himself to someone else's authority, even the government of France. He wrote *Confessions* and began holding readings of it in 1770. He was banned from the readings in 1771, and the book was not published until 1782 after his death.[18]

His remaining years were spent in relative peace as he copied music to make a living. During this time, in 1778, he wrote his ten classic meditations, *Reveries of the Solitary Walker*. The book opens: "So now I am alone in the world, with no brother, neighbor or friend, nor any company left but my own. The most sociable and loving of men has with unanimous accord been cast out by all the rest."[19] He died shortly after he finished the writing. It is said that he died of apoplexy, but the death was so sudden that many felt he committed suicide during a bout with paranoia.

The most complete portrayal of Rousseau's educational agenda is *Emile*, the fictional story of a child growing into young adulthood. It appeals to more than education, and reaches into social and political areas as well. More than likely, Rousseau did not intend the story to be taken literally, but as a novel that would illustrate principles of education. *Emile* reinforces Rousseau's belief in the innate goodness of a child. The book begins, "Everything is good as it leaves the hands of the Author of Things; everything degenerates in the hands of man."[20] In search of religion he had gone from a Catholic to a Calvinist to nothing and back to Calvinism, but at this time he was writing against the Calvinist doctrine of spiritual depravation. He did not believe the Supreme Being created a child as evil; it was the institutions of man that corrupted him. Children are not born as liars and cheats, rather they learn these things from the people with whom they associate. If Emile is educated naturally, not in the conventions of man, perhaps he can be the catalyst that allows a new natural education with which it might be possible to create social, political, and economic institutions that function naturally.[21]

In *Emile*, Rousseau develops five stages of human development The first is infancy, birth to five years. During this time the mother is the teacher and model. Stage two is from five to twelve years. Learning at this stage is primarily through the senses and development of physical strength. The third stage is adolescence, 12-15. The study of *Robinson Crusoe* is paramount at this stage as it teaches awareness of natural things and how the environment works. Puberty is the fourth stage, 16-20. Here the student will learn to deal with the dangerous emotions of adolescence, morals issues, and religion.[22] The final stage is ages 20-25. Here Emile meets Sophie and it is time to learn about marital rights and duties.

However, Rousseau did not believe the present school system could bring about a natural education. Elementary schools were in the control of the church, which he regarded as corrupt. Secondary schools were the agencies of miseducation, stressing a learning process that ignored nature and science. The answer was a tutor, one who would take the child for long walks on a country estate and speak of the things of nature as they encountered them, drawing from nature the lessons that would help the child in his personal development and understanding of the world around him.

The concept of a tutor reveals Rousseau's belief that education prepares students for specific stations in life. The wealthy are destined to rule and enjoy the luxuries of life while the other classes are to be subservient (🌑 11.5).

Johann Heinrich Pestalozzi (1746–1827). Pestalozzi was born in Zurich, Switzerland (🌑 11.6). His father, a surgeon, died when Pestalozzi was five years old leaving the family destitute. Johann, a sister, and a brother (who soon died) were raised by his mother, Susanna, and a trusted servant, Barbara Schmidt (or Babeli Schmid). Johann's grandfather, a minister noted for his work with the poor, became the male influence in his life. During the time he spent with his grandfather, he grew to appreciate the natural beauty of the outdoors and the work of farmers, which influenced his later work.[23]

Pestalozzi was a sickly child who was kept inside much of his childhood. Unable to socialize with other children before attending school, he was easily manipulated by the other children once he entered school. It was not until he entered the University of Zurich that he developed as a scholar. It was during his studies at Zurich that he came into contact with the writings of Rousseau. He avidly read every work of Rousseau's. *Emile* would make a lifelong impact on his life's work.

Then directly influenced by the writings of Rousseau, he became a farmer. He married Anna Schulthess and they had one child, Jean Jacque. He tried to improve on the practice of neighboring farmers who used orphans as field hands. Pestalozzi instituted a plan to establish an industrial school with twenty destitute children.

They would work in the fields during the summers and weave and spin in the winters. The plan lasted for five years and ended in bankruptcy due to poor management.

For the next twenty years he supported his family by writing. His first work was *How Father Pestalozzi Instructed His Three-and-a-half-year-old Son*. During his son's life Pestalozzi had observed his son's education and kept records of the results. He then built on those observations, developing and explaining his use of Rousseau's philosophy of natural education.

War opened the way for Pestalozzi's new methods of teaching. In 1797 French troops had massacred most of the adults in the village of Stans. The revolutionary government offered him an official post as head of the government-established orphanage. He was only able to work with the orphans for five months before war closed the orphanage. But it was long enough for him to utilize some of the ideas he had developed. He had to manage eighty children of differing ages by himself; and while he was not able to establish a form of systematic education, he was able to create a school designed after the home and was able to provide a number of educational experiences for his students. He found good results in the development of moral character when he took on the role of a quasi-father for the children. Intellectually his goal with these children was to cultivate their powers of attention, observation and memory as they prepared for their adult years. The most valuable discovery he made was that it was possible to teach a large number of children at one time without having to resort to physical punishment.[24]

The closing of the orphanage provided Pestalozzi a great, but frustrating opportunity to compare and contrast his methods with those of traditional education. Leaving Stans he was given an assistant teaching position with Samuel Dysli, the village schoolmaster in a working-class primary school in Burgdorf. Dysli was a teacher of the old traditional style. A shoemaker by trade, Dysli's school was in his shop and the children would recite their lessons while he made and repaired shoes. Memorization of the alphabet and catechism was his sole aim for the children. If a child missed a portion of the recitation, he was slapped across the back of the hand with a rod as punishment.

Pestalozzi opposed the use of corporal punishment as a means of instilling fear into the children. He also opposed memorization as the main thrust in learning. To Pestalozzi, à la Rousseau, memorization and recitation just involved the children saying words they did not understand and learning concepts that meant nothing to them. Instead, he believed that children should begin their learning by interacting with the environment around them and exploring objects close at hand. It was here in Burgdorf that Pestalozzi began to develop his renowned object lessons, allowing the children to hold and observe an object. From this he taught shape, function, counting, weight, and the names of objects. The physical involvement with the natural environment was his goal. The feud that erupted between the two resulted in Pestalozzi's resignation.

The Swiss government once again came to his rescue. By now his reputation as an educator had grown through his research and publications, so the government appointed him head of the teachers college at Burgdorf. While at the farm in Birr and at Stans, he recorded his observations of how the children learned. At Burgdorf, Pestalozzi developed his theory of sensory learning called *anschauung*, a concept which would revolution-

> **Anschauung**—German: *forming a concept or understanding from sensory impressions.*

ize education. Pestalozzi believed that the world is full of physical objects and people learn of them as they interact with them, seeing, touching, tasting, smelling, and hearing the objects. He fully developed his concept of object lessons not only to include handling the objects, but field trips into the countryside where students could observe nature, collect plants, animals, and minerals for closer study, and note the movements and cycles of plants and animals. Studies were to be done with nature close at hand; the concept of faraway places was left to later years when the student understood what was around him and could relate that to the unseen places.

Pestalozzi believed that children are naturally active. Their bodies require them to move in order to grow properly. Their minds are gathering information at an amazing rate. Thus when they are taught, they need to be able to use activity to increase their level of learning. This activity encompasses language, math, reading, writing, and geography. The wise teacher would encourage the students to use their active bodies and minds to grasp ideas and learn from them. Active learning compelled him to add music and physical education to his curriculum.

It was while he was at Burgdorf that he published one of his most well-known works in 1801, *How Gertrude Teaches Her Children*. The book expounds on the *anschauung* methodology in teaching. Also, in this work he divides education into two parts: the general method and the special method. The general method involved creating a climate of emotional security for the student. The special method involved the object lessons of form, number, and sound or name.[25]

Though Pestalozzi greatly admired and expanded Rousseau's ideas, he was much more concerned about Christianity. Though he too believed that people did not suffer from original sin, he believed that people had sinned against God and God's grace could redeem them from their sin. The role of the educator was to help students develop their natural gifts and this coupled with God's grace would create students who could reform the world.

The government took the building back and the school closed at Burgdorf after four short years. Pestalozzi moved the school to Yverdon to a castle given to him by the government. Pupils and teachers came to him from all parts of Europe and even from America. Among those who were influenced by Pestalozzi were Friedrich Froebel, Johann Friedrich Herbart, Horace Mann, and Henry Bernard. The school continued for twenty-one years, closing only after contention arose among his helpers over his management and business affairs of the school. He left the school in 1825 and died of a broken heart shortly afterward. The inscription on his tombstone reads, "Man, Christian, Citizen. Everything for others, nothing for himself. Blessings be on his name."[26]

Johann Friedrich Herbart (1776–1841). Born in 1776 in Oldenburg, Germany, Herbart's father was a lawyer and his mother was reported to be very brilliant (11.7). They divorced when he was young and his domineering mother raised him. She arranged and supervised his education with a tutor, Hermann Uelzen, even sitting in on some of his classes. At age twelve he began studies at the Latin School at the same time he was tutored by Hermann. Then in 1794 he entered the University of Jena (his mother went with him) where he became an enthusiastic student of philosophy. Herbart had been a fan of Kant, but after two years of study began to develop his own philosophy built on realism.

After three years at Jena, Herbart left without finishing his degree in 1797 to take a position as a tutor with the von Steiger family in Switzerland. He was entrusted with the education of three boys, ages 14, 10, and 8. His mother started to go with him, but turned back before getting to Switzerland. The boys were completely under his care, and he saw this as an opportunity to develop his own educational approach. It soon became apparent to him that his presupposed educational method was ineffective. By 1798 he had reformulated an educational system that remained unchanged throughout his life.

Excited by the new ideas he had developed, Herbart planned on staying on with the boys to further develop his ideas. It was during this time that he met Pestalozzi and visited him in Burgdorf. He was impressed with Pestalozzi's emphasis on the student's ability to learn through the natural employment of the senses. Herbart's belief was that educational methods should be based on psychology and ethics. He suggested that psychology would furnish the necessary knowledge of the mind and ethics would be used as a basis for determining the social ends of education.[27]

Called home by his mother, Herbart left the von Steiger family after two years. He spent his time at home caring for his mother and doing extensive writing on education including some pieces that showed an understanding of Pestalozzi's work. His mother died two years after he returned home, and Herbart was free to pursue his dreams. He went to Bremen to study at the University of Göttingen and received his degree in philosophy. He traveled, giving lectures until he was called to teach at Göttingen. After three years he was asked to fill Kant's vacant chair at the University of Königsberg. He would lecture on philosophy and pedagogy here for over twenty years. His greatest disappointment came when Hegel died and he was not called to fill his position at the University of Berlin. He remained at Königsberg until 1833 when he returned to Göttingen as Dean of the philosophy department. He continued writing and lecturing until his death in 1841.

Herbart's philosophy presented education as comprised of three parts: 1. government—the control that existed in the classroom either through teacher imposition or student self-control; 2. discipline—the development of personal self-control and self-government by the student; and 3. instruction—drawing the student's interest to the material to be learned. These parts can be seen in Herbart's four steps of teaching:

- *Presentation*: the teacher presents the new material to the students.
- *Association*: the teacher helps the student analyze the new material and compare it to ideas they have already learned.
- *Generalization*: the teacher and the class use the materials already learned to develop a new rule or principle.
- *Application*: the teacher helps the student apply the information to other situations in real life applications.

These steps in teaching were adopted by many of the colleges and universities in Europe and North America. Later his followers added an additional step preceding the others: *Preparation*—the student is prepared for learning by recalling past experiences.[28]

Herbart saw the teacher as an enabler, one who would provide assistance in analyzing and synthesizing information, but would not give the answer. To be a teacher of excellence he must be able to apply the tools of psychology. Teachers had to be observers who could understand the capabilities of each student's mind and be able to adjust their teaching to meet these needs.

Friedrich Wilhelm Froebel (1782–1852). Known as the father of the kindergarten, Froebel was born in 1782 in Oberweiss-bach, Germany (❂ 11.8). His father was a Lutheran minister in Oberweissbach; however, his mother died when he was nine months old. The youngest of five children, he grew up as a lonely and introverted child. His father taught him to read and then sent him to a school for girls because he was too backward to survive in a boys' school. At age four his father remarried a woman who already had a child of her own. Froebel complained of the treatment he received from the stepmother, even into his adulthood. Gerald Gutek writes:

> Froebel's memories of an unhappy early childhood had a pronounced effect on the theory of kindergarten education that he developed later in his life. It is interesting to note that Froebel, like Rousseau, lost his mother to death when he was so young that he could not have had a clear memory of her. He also had a stepmother whom he disliked intensely. When

he developed his theory of early childhood education, he, like Pestalozzi, created a version of the teacher who was a loving, kindly, and gentle motherlike figure. His concept of kindergarten teacher undoubtedly came from his idealized affection for his own lost mother.[29]

Froebel went to live with his mother's brother in 1793 who enrolled him in a school for boys. Not a good student in Oberweiss-bach he began to develop his skills as a scholar in the school for boys. He also began to make his first friendships with other children. He would later describe his uncle as a kind and gentle man.

Froebel's education continued until he was fifteen and appointed as an apprentice to a forester. He remained in the apprenticeship for two years leaving because the forester neglected him and all the practical parts of his work, teaching Froebel nothing. Two years later, at age seventeen, he entered the University of Jena to study, but after making a bad loan to his brother he ran out of funds and spent time in the school's debtors prison.

In 1803 he received an inheritance from his uncle that allowed him to go to school in Frankfurt, and this time he studied to be an architect. His studies proved to be unsuccessful in leading to a career. Froebel's efforts at finding a career, however, were not unfruitful. His experience with nature and architecture would provide a basis for some of his greatest educational developments.

While in Frankfurt Froebel met Anton Gruener, headmaster of the Frankfurt Model School, a school developed on Pestalozzian concepts. Friedrich accepted the invitation to teach at the school and spent two weeks at Pestalozzi's school at Yverdon to prepare. From the first moment in the classroom he knew that this would be his life's work. "It seemed as if I had found something I had never known, but always longed for—as if my life had at last discovered its native element. I felt as happy as a fish in the water or a bird in the air."[26]

He left the school after three years to study with Pestalozzi for two years. He was deeply influenced by Pestalozzi's work, but he identified areas that he felt could be improved. One of the areas was the play of children. He was convinced that play was a key to how a child learned. He wanted to find the meaning of play and how to use it to create learning.

From 1812 to 1816 he served as an assistant to Professor

Christian Samuel Weiss, a noted expert in mineralogy. However, in 1816 he opened the Universal German Educational Institute in Darmstadt. The curriculum for the school consisted of religion, reading, writing, arithmetic, drawing, German language, singing, mathematics, nature knowledge, geography, Greek, piano, and physical exercises.[31] The next year he moved to Keilhau where he attempted to establish an elementary school, but the school struggled with enrollment. At its peak it enrolled sixty students, and when it closed thirteen years later in 1829 it had only five students.

During the thirteen years he was able to test many of his theories and write about them. The most important of his writings was *Education of Man* (1826), followed seventeen years later by the top selling *Mother's Songs, Games, and Stories* (1843). As the school in Keilhau failed, he was asked to open a school in the castle at Wartensee, Switzerland. The physical environment of the castle proved to be unacceptable for a school, and it was moved to Willisau. Here the school prospered, and Froebel was able to gain the reputation as a quality educator.[32]

His next school was in Burgdorf where Pestalozzi had once operated a school. He opened a school for the town children, a boarding school for those who lived in outlying areas, and a school for three- and four-year-olds. His attention gradually began to focus on the preschool children. He left the school when his wife became very ill, and they returned to Germany where she died.

In 1837 Froebel opened his first kindergarten in Blankenburg, Germany. A second kindergarten was opened in Keilhau. Even though this one would only last three years, it became a training institute for kindergarten teachers. The growth in the number of kindergartens was only slowed when the Prussian government falsely accused Froebel of being an atheist and a revolutionary (it was his cousin Karl Froebel) and thus banned kindergartens in Prussia. However, within sixty years the kindergarten had spread throughout Europe, North America, and Japan.[33]

Froebel believed that play was a child's work, and he developed teaching methods that used play to help the children learn. His work in architecture and mineralogy helped him to design special play materials that were used in teaching. The materials were divided into two categories: gifts and occupations. Gifts were objects that represented what Froebel called fundamental forms (❀ 11.9). The gifts are described as follows:

- Six soft balls, colored red, blue, yellow, violet, green, and orange.
- A wooden sphere, cube, and cylinder.
- A large cube divided into eight smaller cubes.
- A large cube divided into eight long blocks.
- A large cube divided into twenty-one whole, six half, and twelve quarter cubes.
- A large cube divided into eighteen whole oblongs, with three divided lengthwise and three divided breadthwise. (Gifts 3 through 6 could be used for construction and building activity, for measurement and geometry, and to develop the sense pattern, balance and symmetry.)
- Quadrangular and triangular tiles to arrange and make patterns.
- Sticks for outlining figures.
- Whole and half wire rings for outlining figures.
- A variety of materials that could be used for drawing, perforating, embroidering, paper cutting, weaving or braiding, paper folding, modeling, and interlacing.[34]

The occupations were items that could be used in making and constructing activities. Among the occupations were paper, pencils, wood, sand, clay, straw, sticks, and other items children could use in creating projects and pictures.[35] Paper-folding was an occupation that Froebel developed. His patterns resembled origami and when the kindergartens went to Japan the projects were extremely popular.

Kindergarten teachers were to be observers of the children's lives as they interacted with each other, their play, and their activities. This allowed them to structure the environment and the lesson plan to meet the child's developmental needs. The teacher was also to be a warm and caring parent figure providing the attention that many did not receive at home and thus aiding in the natural development of the child.

Froebel felt that God was at the core of the universe and therefore should be at the very core of education. Religious sensitivity was natural to children; therefore, they were to be encouraged to give expression to their feelings about religion, God, and God's creation. To ignore their religious development would render them hollow in their lives.[36]

Friedrich Froebel believed that humans are essentially productive and creative—and fulfillment comes through developing these in harmony with God and the world. As a result, Froebel sought to encourage the creation of educational environments that involved practical work and direct use of materials. Through engaging the world understanding unfolds.[37]

Conclusion

The Progressive Movement comes at a time in the Enlightenment when education was at a virtual standstill. Basically it had lost its significance to humanity. It was empty and what there was of it was of poor quality. However, there were those who saw the importance of learning and desired that all would learn to love learning as much as they did. These philosophers sought to change the direction of education. No longer was knowledge or the church at the middle, but they placed man at the center of the educational process. The focus changed from knowledge that was based on the classics and the past to natural learning, which included man learning from nature and the scientific method which looked forward to the future. Teachers were no longer stern taskmasters, but guides for the student's natural development. After the influence of Rousseau, Pestalozzi, Herbart, and Froebel, schools would change forever.

What Can We Learn from the Progressive Movement?

- Humans, as developmental and learning beings, must be placed within the learning process. While the Progressive theoreticians made humans the center of education, perhaps overemphasizing their place, they at least provided a corrective to the medieval model of education and further expanded the ideal of human potential.

- Each person's individual development is important. During the Enlightenment educators began to acknowledge that persons are more than their "nature," fallen or innocent, and needed to be understood as individuals rather than groups.

- Lessons from nature as Creation can help students understand their culture, world, future, and faith. This aided the Church in emphasizing the idea of natural revelation in education.

- Students learn best when they are actively involved in their learning. While student participation was always valued, in previous eras it was limited or even curtailed.

- The learning environment is important to education, and hence the context of education cannot be taken for granted.

- God is always a vital part of education, traditional or progressive. His presence in the process of education and the maturity that results from it is undeniable.

Study Helps

Reflection Questions

1. In your educational experience how did your teachers compare to what Rousseau, Pestalozzi, and Froebel advocated?
2. How would the concepts of the Progressive movement prepare you for ministry? Would they be of benefit to you?
3. Rousseau can be seen as either a saint or a sinner, how would you view him and why?
4. In the Reformation Calvin saw a child's play as the devil's playground. Froebel saw it as a child's work, and the main method he used in learning. Whom do you agree with and why?
5. Herbart said that a teacher must use the tools of psychology in order to aid the learning process. What elements of psychology are necessary in the modern classroom?

Technical Terms

Anschauung German meaning "forming a concept or understanding from sensory impressions."

Bourgeois French, "a person of the middle class whose social behavior and political views are influenced by wealth."

Common School Established to teach vocations and common people to be good citizens.

Grammar School Secondary education, taught Latin, Greek, and classical literature

Protestant Work Ethic Calvinist philosophy that our work is a gift to the Lord and we honor him with it.

Recommended Bibliography

Boyd, William. *The History of Western Education.* Rev. by Edmund J. King. New York: Barnes and Noble, 1969.

Curtis, S.J., and M.E. Boultwood. *A Short History of Educational Ideas.* London: University Tutorial Press, 1970.

Gutek, Gerald L. *Historical and Philosophical Foundations of Education: A Biographical Introduction.* Upper Saddle River, NJ: Merrill Prentice Hall, 2001.

Reed, James E., and Ronnie Prevost. *A History of Christian Education.* Nashville: Broadman & Holman, 1993.

Internet Sites

Rousseau—www.infed.org/thinkers/et-rous.htm

Pestalozzi—www.infed.org/thinkers/et-pest.htm

Froebel—www.50megs.com
   www.infed.org/thinkers/et-froeb.htm

Notes

[1] Peter Gay, ed., *Great Ages of Man: A History of the World's Cultures—Age of Enlightenment* (New York: Time-Life, 1966), 167.

[2] Ibid.

[3] Ibid., 168.

[4] Gerald L. Gutek, *Historical and Philosophical Foundations of Education: A Biographical Introduction* (Upper Saddle River, NJ: Prentice-Hall, 1991), 231.

[5] Tackett, T.M., "Enlightenment, Age of," www.encarta.msn.com/encnet/refpages/Ref Article. aspx?refid=76171670, 4,5.

[6] www.constitution.org/lanc/epitome.htm, 1.

[7] Ibid., 4.

[8] William Boyd, *The History of Western Education* (New York: Barnes and Noble, 1969), 280.

[9] Ibid., 281.

[10] Ibid., 280.

[11] Ibid.

[12] James E. Reed and Ronnie Prevost, *A History of Christian Education* (Nashville: Broadman & Holman, 1993), 247.

[13] Gutek, *Foundations*, 240.

[14] S.J. Curtis and M.E.A. Boultwood, *A Short History of Educational Ideas* (London: University Tutorial Press, 1970), 262.

[15] Ibid.

[16] Reed and Prevost, *History*, 242.

[17] Gutek, *Foundations*, 114.

[18] "Jean-Jacques Rousseau on Education," www.infed.org/thinkers/et-rous.htm, 4.

[19] Ibid.

[20] Gutek, *Foundations*, 115.

[21] Ibid.

[22] www.infed.org/thinkers/et-rous.htm, 11.

[23] Gutek, *Foundations*, 131.

[24] Boyd, *History*, 321.

[25] Gutek, *Foundations*, 137.

[26] Reed and Prevost, *History*, 246.

[27] Nick Jankoviak (N/A), www.nd.edu/~rbarger/www7/herbart.html.

[28] Adapted from Reed and Prevost, *History*, 250.

[29] Gutek, *Foundations*, 234.

[30] Boyd, *History*, 351.

[31] Ibid., 352.

[32] Gutek, *Foundations*, 238.

[33] Ibid., 239.

[34] Ibid., 243.

[35] Ibid.

[36] Reed and Prevost, *History*, 253.

[37] www.infed.org/thinkers/et-froeb.htm, 1.

Chapter 12
Christian Education in 18th–19th Century Europe

James Riley Estep, Jr.

Overview of Period

Renaissance humanism, the reformations of Luther and Calvin, and the Enlightenment all provide a backdrop for Christian education in Europe during the 18th–19th centuries. "Men had found humanism insufficient, and they were weary of the deadening effects of dogmatic theology."[1] It was a time of a new series of reforms within the church, and with these new reforms came new and renewed educational endeavors. This chapter will focus on the three primary educational reforms that occurred during this period in Europe: German Pietism, the Sunday school movement, and the educational endeavors of John Wesley and his movement. While there were a variety of other movements, such as the Salvation Army, this chapter will focus on those endeavors that were specifically educational in their purpose.

German Pietism and the Moravians

The movement known as Pietism refocused attention away from theology and toward spiritual formation. Pietism began in western Germany as an outgrowth of Lutheranism. As Eavey observes, "Pietism combined Luther's emphasis on the study of the Scriptures, prayer, and faith with the Calvinistic stress on puritanical conduct."[2] With this focus on personal piety came a new form of education as advocated by the three principal voices in German Pietism: Spener, Franke, and Zinzendorf. Later Pietists, such as

Daniel Schleiermacher (1768–1834), continued in their educational endeavors. The Moravians were the most organized tradition within the pietistic movement.

The Purpose of Education

Pietistic education was reflective of Johann Amos Comenius's (1592–1670, ✪ 12.1; see Chapter 10) approach to education. Pietistic education was a call to personal spiritual devotion to God, not clerical, institutional, ecclesiastical, or political Christianity, but a personal faith. Just as the movement itself was a call for the restoration of personal piety within the church, education was a means to this end. In addition to

> **FYI:** The Moravians sustained a 24-hour prayer chain for world missions . . . that lasted 100 years! A family's prayer time became a generational affair.

personal piety, cooperate piety was exemplified by an emphasis on international missions, with education seen as a means of preparing global workers and reaching a global people.[3]

Educational Contexts of Education

While the educational contexts of the Pietists were indeed academically sound, they likewise focused on the spiritual vitality of their students. As with previous generations of Christian educators, elementary and secondary education were the principle contexts of instruction, as well as higher education. However, shifts within the focus and curriculum of these institutions demonstrated the Pietist's radical commitment to spiritual formation. For example, Phillip Spener, an early Pietist educator, initiated the *Collegia Pietatis* (1670), literally "College of Piety."

Pietism became the model for the Prussian elementary school, based on August Franke's approach to education, as well as several state orphanages.[4] Franke's *Pedagogium Regium* or secondary school in Halle became a paradigm for Pietist education, as well as for many of the states in eastern Germany. In his institution students learned Greek and Hebrew for biblical study, as well as participated in an on-site workshop for vocational training. He also provided opportunities for the study of nature, with little emphasis on classical studies common to other schools of his era.[5] Franke advocated the formation of home Bible studies and small groups, even involving laity in priestly functions, demonstrating the Pietists' far-reaching commitment to the Protestant concept of priesthood of believers. Later, Count Zinzendorf had classes twice a week for Bible study and pietistic instruction, initiating this program prior to the initiation of the Sunday school.

Educational Content and Process

It is essential to remember that in Pietistic education doctrine was *subordinated* to piety. Theological studies were a means toward achieving the end of spiritual formation, not the ultimate objective of Christian education. Living a pious life was considered more important than doctrinal perfection. Spener outlined the essential educational agenda of Pietistic education in his *Pia Desideria* (1675), translated *Pious Desires* (🖝 12.2). It can be divided into three parts:

- *Part 1* critiques the current spiritual level of the Church, society, clergy, and laity. Lack of piety is acknowledged.

- *Parts 2 and 3* represent his program for reforming the church with personal piety, which is a qualitative reformation focused on spiritual formation rather than what he perceives as a wholly theological reformation.

For Spener, personal Bible reading, as well as Bible study within the family and within groups, was essential for spiritual vitality in the Church. The Bible would be the central content and process of instruction as the congregation sponsored such studies.

As previously mentioned, Franke was the leading educational theorist of the Pietists, influencing even state-sponsored educational and social institutions in eastern Germany, specifically Prussia. 🖝 12.3 contains an outline of Franke's curriculum. Franke regarded teachers as the central educational component, and hence provided a Teacher's Seminary, a prototype for modern teacher education programs. The *Seminarian Praeceptorum* trained elementary teachers while the *Seminarian Inselectum* was for the preparation of teachers at the secondary level. It not only provided professional training for students as instructors, but it endeavored to instill behaviors within the life of a teacher as a Christian example, such as dress expectations and the limited use of alcohol and tobacco.[6]

Following in Franke's work, Zinzendorf provided a childhood curriculum consisting of catechism, hymnals for singing, and Bible study. He likewise established a means of providing Christian instruction throughout the community, not simply within the church or to a select few who could afford it.[7] Hence, the common themes within pietistic education were Bible study, personal application of biblical truth, and an emphasis on living faithfully, not simply learning the content of faith.

Voices

Phillip Jacob Spener (1635–1705) is regarded as the father of pietism in Germany (12.4). He was born in Rappoltsweiler, a German-French town. At the age of 16 he entered the University of Strasbourg to study theology with Lutherans. He later became a professor at the University of Strasbourg. In 1659 he left for Basel in Switzerland for further theological studies with the Waldenses and at Tübingen, Germany, where he received his doctorate. During this period he became increasingly influenced by Christian mystics and began placing an innate valuing on spiritual experience. In 1699 he assumed a pastorate in Frankfurt, Germany, and began to develop an emphasis on pietism within the congregation. His ministry, both within the congregation and throughout Germany, improved the quality of catechetical instruction by focusing on the lives of his students rather than looking at the theological content as did everyone else. His best known work is *Pia Desideria*, discussed above.

> Spener's contributions to Christian education are not sufficiently recognized in evangelical literature."
> —Gangel and Benson, *History and Philosophy of Education*, 173

August Hermann Franke (1663–1727) was the most influential pietistic educator. He wrote *Brief and Simple Treatise on Christian Education* where knowledge is depicted as a means of advancing faith, "knowledge an adjunct to godliness."[8] "The link between theology and education was so obvious to Franke that he spent very little time delineating a formal relationship. . . ."[9] 12.5 contains sample statements reflecting Franke's educational theory. The Pietist movement influenced Franke when he studied under Spener, which is evident when he united personal godliness (pietism) and wisdom (education). Christian wisdom, which was based on a relationship with Jesus Christ and not simply theological constructs, had four expressions: personal piety, prayer, Bible study, and evangelism. Franke opened the *Armenschule*, an orphan school in 1695, and the *Lateinschule*, or "Latin school," as well as the *Paedagogium Regium*, a boarding school for boys.

Nikolaus Ludwig Zinzendorf (1700–1760) was born in Dresden, Germany, and attended the University of Wittenberg in 1716 (✸ 12.6). He met Moravians in 1722 when they settled on his estates in Saxony (northeastern Germany). He was so impressed by their teaching and lifestyle that he embraced their pietism, and soon became acquainted with Franke's educational works. Zinzendorf was eventually made a bishop of the Moravian church, a newly formed church tradition established in 1727. He wrote *Plan of a Catechism for the Heathen*, advancing the missionary agenda of the Moravians.

> **FYI:** Saxony was also the German state that was first sympathetic to Luther's reformation and the location of the University of Wittenberg.

He gave special attention to the instruction of underprivileged children and adolescents. "Zinzendorf was careful to include the entire community in education. He developed a plan for paternal education and organized the community into educational units (called 'choirs') along developmental and gender lines."[10]

The Sunday School Movement in England

The Purpose of Education

It is fair to assume that most Christians are aware of the Sunday school. However, it is critical to remember that the Sunday school of the late eighteenth century was *radically* different from the Sunday school experienced by most of us in the twenty-first century. It is impossible to understand the original design and intent of the Sunday school without understanding first the social conditions of eighteenth-century England. Most of the English population was poverty stricken. Children were among the workforce, which prohibited them from attending any of the conventional schools of the era. Two-thirds of England was rural, and the remaining third was urban, with only 3500 common schools throughout the entire country. *In short, education was not readily available for the masses.*[11] The Sunday school, originated by Robert Raikes in 1780, was formed to address the social concern for literacy, morality, and hygiene; all from a Christian perspective.

Prior to the Sunday school other forms of instruction had been made available to the underprivileged or as a means of social reform, but it was this movement that became the most successful and long-lasting of all the Christian and state-sponsored endeavors to provide instruction to the masses.[12] Hence, the Sunday school began as a mission of the church for the purpose of addressing the social ills of the era through education.

> **FYI:** *Time* magazine in December 2002 ran an article on the Sunday School, demonstrating its continued vitality in ministry and church outreach!

Contexts of Education

"The history of modern Christian education is to a great extent the history of the development of the Sunday school. . . ."[13] Prior to 1799, only the Church of England was allowed to operate schools, and hence education was under ecclesiastical control, which was in turn under state-control. However, with the passing of the Enabling Act that same year, it enabled any qualified individual or group to sponsor a school.[14] Robert Raikes had a three-year period of experimentation (1780–1783) wherein he tested his model of the Sunday school prior to releasing the information publicly in his newspaper on November 3, 1783. Sunday school was not in a church building, nor was it even a ministry of the church. Rather, it was anywhere children could gather for instruction. The first Sunday school was established in 1780 in Mrs. Meredith's kitchen on Sooty Alley. Mrs. Meredith was paid for her provision of instruction and rent on the location of her kitchen. However, Mrs. Meredith soon resigned due to frustration with the children, and Raikes moved the Sunday school to a house on Southgate owned by Mrs. Chritchley, located near Raikes's own home.[15]

The Sunday school was advanced in England primarily through two institutions. The Sunday-School Society, established September 7, 1785, which planted 3730 Sunday schools within 27 years and paid teachers until 1815.[16] The aim of the London Sunday School Union, established July 13, 1803, saw to the improvement of the Sunday school as well as the formation of a religious curriculum.[17] By 1785, just five years from the Sunday school's inception, it crossed the Atlantic Ocean and was established in the English colonies in America. However, by the 1820s the American version of Raikes's Sunday school had shifted toward a denominationally controlled means of providing instruction rather than an outreach ministry to the impoverished (see Chapter 13 for the Sunday school in America).[18]

The establishment of the Sunday school was met with immediate acceptance and rejection. The Wesleys (John and Charles), as well as other educators and social reformers such as George Whitefield, William Fox, famous abolitionist William Wilberforce, and James Hamway, immediately accepted and endorsed the Sunday school. They accepted the Sunday school as a means of religious and social reform. However, opposition was raised from both ecclesiastical and social voices. The Sunday schools were regarded as "dangerous, demoralizing, bad institutions, and agents of the devil."[19] The Archbishop of Canterbury viewed it as an affront to the authority of the clergy. Also, the Sunday school caused economic pressure for the English aristocracy, fearing they would have to pay workers higher wages if they were able to read and write.

Educational Content and Process

"The Bible was the center of Raikes' instruction."[20] The Bible was used as a textbook for literacy (originally for reading only, with writing added to the curriculum later), morality, and hygiene. In addition to these studies, the Sunday school required Bible memorization and catechism, as well as mandatory attendance in worship services, since it met on Sunday. Participants were both boys and girls between 6 and 14 years old. Discipline was a necessary evil. "Many were reluctant to attend the school. Some were brought by their parents hobbled with heavy weights, logs, or shackles bound to their ankles. Discipline was strict. Those who misbehaved were immediately taken by Raikes to their parents, whom he expected to immediately punish their children. Raikes would then return the children to the school."[21]

> It was a *Sunday* school not just because of the worship opportunities, but because children didn't have to work on that day.

However, rewards for favored behavior and academic performance were also given. Bibles, books, games, clothes, shoes, and other items were distributed to support their interest in learning.

Originally, teachers were paid one shilling per day for instruction, but later the movement became dependent on volunteers for instruction, due to financial efficiency and the value of altruistic motives of volunteers.[22] More advanced students began serving as monitors or tutors in the Sunday school.

By 1803 William Brodie Gurney, founder of the London Sunday School Union, published formal curriculum and several resource manuals for teachers in the Sunday school. Four major works were developed to support the establishment of Sunday schools and instruction by 1805: *Plan for Forming Sunday Schools, Guide to Teaching, Catechism in Verse,* and *Reading Primer.* Additionally, *The Repository* or *Teacher's Magazine* served as a periodical for instructors in the Sunday school.[23]

The Founding Voice

Robert Raikes (1736–1811) of Gloucester, England, was born into a family of clergy (12.7). He was a career journalist, the editor of the *Gloucester Journal.* The Sunday school movement spawned from Raikes's work with prison inmates. Assessing their educational background, he linked a lack of education to the cycle of poverty and crime that lead to their imprisonment. He rhetorically asked, "Is vice preventable? If so, it is better to prevent crime than to punish it. Can these ignorant masses be lifted out of this ragged, wretched, vicious state?"[24] Raikes's educational maxims reflect his optimism to change the personal and social conditions within England (12.8):[25]

- "Vice in the child is an imitation of familiar sights and sounds.
- There is a time in the child's life when it is innocent. Then the faculties are active and receptive.
- Good seeds cannot be planted too early.
- The child takes pleasure in being good when goodness is made attractive.
- The Sunday school may be the instrument under God of awakening spiritual life in the poorest children and, supplemented by day classes, can form the basis of national education."

By 1811 (the year of Raikes's death), the number of Sunday schools in England reached over 400,000, and by 1831 the number grew to 1,250,000.[26] To what does the Sunday school owe its success? Three elements have been identified as keys to its success: (1) *Publicity* and promotion; remember, Raikes was a newspaper editor and hence had a readily available avenue for promoting his new institution of social change. (2) The Sunday school was considered *contemporary*. For example, it addressed immanent social needs and was supported by the contemporary leaders of English religious reform, such as the Wesleys. Finally, (3), the movement was well *organized* and supported. The formation of Sunday school unions in cities and nations, such as those in England and America, led to the success of the Sunday school by providing the architecture for the expansion of the movement.

The Reforms of John Wesley

John Wesley (1703–1791), the founder of the Methodist tradition, was born into a pastoral family (❧ 12.9). His mother, Susanna, was an early influence on Wesley. She actually articulated rules for parenting, which Wesley published in his journal. Wesley was also heavily influenced by the English Enlightenment thinking of John Locke (Chapter 10).[27] He came into contact with the pietistic movement, specifically the Moravians, while serving as a missionary to the colony of Georgia (America), along with his brother Charles. He was so impressed by them that he adopted pietism as a means of addressing the spiritual condition of the Church of England. In fact, his conversion experience in 1738 at Aldersgate Street in London occurred while Wesley was participating in a pietistic society. He even visited with the Moravians, namely Count Zinzendorf, touring their educational institutions, hoping to model them in England. The Methodists never left the Church of England, but sought to be a spiritually reforming component of it.

The Purpose of Education

"He [John Wesley] viewed education as a means of grace—as an instrument through which the Holy Spirit worked," e.g., for conversion and continual maturation.[28] Hence, the intent of education was a pietistic matter, but it also was essential for his reformation. Wesley "realized that the result of his revival would be permanent only if the revival was united with education."[29] Hence, Wesley viewed education as a means of advancing personal piety and the

Methodist movement within the Church of England.

In regard to the sustaining of his movement, he provided extensive training for lay leaders to serve as preachers and teachers. The equipping of these leaders was based on self-study, not seminary, and consisted of an aggressive reading plan, attendance at annual conferences, and mentored involvement in ministry (like internships). In so doing, Wesley was able to field lay ministers at an impressive rate and with some degree of quality assurance.[30]

> Wesley's reading plan for lay leaders consisted of 11,000 pages of reading . . . 7300 of which was from the pietistic tradition.

Contexts, Content and Process of Education

Wesley resisted the educational theories of Rousseau, Voltaire, and Hume, even criticizing them openly in his publications, sermons, and speeches. For example, he argued that Rousseau's *Emile* was the "most empty, silly, injudicious thing that ever a self-conceited infidel wrote," noting that if his ideas were implemented in schools it would be "continually ruining fifty children at a time!"[31] Towns summarizes Wesley's instructional methodology into five points:

- Secure the students' attention before teaching.
- Use words that the children understand.
- Use illustrations from everyday life.
- Establish a relationship of love.
- Be patient, and repeat yourself many times.[32]

As previously noted, the Wesleys supported the Sunday school movement. The Wesleyans even formed the Wesleyan Sunday School Union. However, Wesley's educational endeavors were not limited to his support of the fledgling Sunday school movement. He also developed three other means of Christian education for laity. The *Class Meeting* was a group of 12 people, meeting at least once a week for the purpose of checking spiritual vitality and reporting on any concerns of a physical or moral nature. The *Band System* was copied from the Moravians, and consisted of six individuals, meeting weekly for the purpose of confession, discussing both physical and behavioral concerns among its members. Finally, the *Select Societies* were for the spiritual elite of the Wesleyan movement. Mainly consisting of lay preachers, it provided accountability and additional opportunities for study and advancement of abilities.

Kingswood School, a boarding school established near Bristol (England), was Wesley's crowning educational achievement. He provided a comprehensive sketch of the developments within Kingswood in his *Journals*, but in 1781 he published *A Plain Account of Kingswood School* which restated his motivation and plan for the establishment of the school (12.10). As a school, it paralleled the schools of the Moravians (particularly the curriculum and schedule of Franke) present throughout eastern Germany in schedule and curriculum, once again illustrating his affirmation of the pietistic model of education. Kingswood was founded May 21, 1739, along with a charity school for the children of poverty-stricken miners. The school was created for boys ages 6-12, with strict attention given to admission and enrollment. The schools later provided instruction and opened housing for girls. While the school experienced periods of decline and revival, and never reached its full potential in reality, in theory it represented Wesley's ideology of the Christian school.

Conclusion

We still live with the educational initiatives of Enlightenment Christian education. Methodism, the Sunday school, and even the pietistic movement are still vibrant in Christian education today. Methodism, represented today by numerous denominational bodies, still endeavors to maintain an emphasis on personal devotion and group study of the Scriptures. The Sunday school, now well over 200 years old and bearing little resemblance to its original intent, is part of virtually every congregation's educational ministry. Pietism reminds us that while Christian living is based on our beliefs and our theology, formal doctrinal constructs are not a substitute for genuine Christian living. Christianity is a relationship with Christ, not simply a religion with Christ as a central theme; it is a relationship that must be supported by Christian education.

What Can We Learn from 18th–19th Century European Christian Education?

- Doctrine is a means to an end, and not a substitute for spiritual formation.
- Personal piety is the primary expression of faith, not political, theological, or ecclesiastical Christianity.
- Christianity can address the concerns of society beyond the walls of the church, providing outreach ministries to the community and society.
- The Sunday school is an adaptable means of providing instruction, and is only stagnant when we allow it to be.
- Unfortunately, some of the most beneficial and innovative ideas in Christian education are met by resistance from within the Church.
- Education is a means of permanent reformation in the Church.
- Christian education should be both church-based and church-sponsored, e.g., Bible studies and Christian schools.

Study Helps

Reflection Questions

1. Do you agree with the pietists' focus on spiritual formation? What is the relationship between theology and personal faith?
2. How is spiritual instruction present in your institution of education? How is the pietistic spirit represented on your campus?
3. How does our Sunday school today differ from Robert Raikes's model?
4. Is there room for the original paradigm, social outreach, of the Sunday school in the church today?
5. Do you think the Sunday school has a future? Why or why not? What would have to change to change your mind?
6. How has education helped maintain momentum in your theological tradition? In your congregation?

Technical Terms

Armenschule	Franke's orphan school
Class Meetings, **Band System,** and **Select Society**	Wesley's three means of providing Christian instruction to the laity.
Kingswood School	Wesley's school located near Bristol, England
Methodism	Movement within the Church of England started by Wesley, so named due to the "method" of discipleship and piety he advocated.
Moravian	Pietistic denomination originating in Germany
Paedagogium Regium	Franke's secondary school
Pietism	Movement originating in eastern Germany valuing personal faith and faithfulness over doctrinal rigidity.
Prussia	Province in eastern Germany, known for its militaristic discipline
Sunday School Union	Organizations formed for the expansion or improvement of the Sunday school in the 18th–19th centuries, e.g., English Sunday School Union and the American Sunday School Union.

Recommended Bibliography

Rice, Edwin Wilbur. *The Sunday-School Movement and the American Sunday-School Union.* Philadelphia: American Sunday-School Union, 1917.

Towns, Elmer L., ed. *A History of Religious Education.* Grand Rapids: Baker, 1975.

Notes

[1] C.B. Eavey, *History of Christian Education* (Chicago: Moody Press, 1964), 178.

[2] Eavey, *History*, 179.

[3] Kenneth O. Gangel and Warren S. Benson, *Christian Education: Its History and Philosophy* (Chicago: Moody Press, 1983), 185-186.

[4] Cf. John Friesen, "Education, Pietism and Change among Mennonites in Nineteenth-Century Prussia," *The Mennonite Quarterly Review* (66.2): 155-166.

[5] John L. Elias, *A History of Christian Education* (Malabar, FL: Krieger, 2002), 112.

[6] Kenneth O. Gangel, "August Hermann Franke (1663-1727)," *A History of Religious Education*, ed. by Elmer L. Towns (Grand Rapids: Baker, 1975), 195.

[7] T.F. Kinloch, "Nikolaus Ludwig Zinzendorf (1700–1760)," *A History of Religious Education*, ed. by Elmer L. Towns (Grand Rapids: Baker, 1975), 202-205.

[8] Eavey, *History*, 182.

[9] Kenneth O. Gangel, "Franke," 193.

[10] James E. Reed and Ronnie Prevost, *A History of Christian Education* (Nashville: Broadman-Holman, 1993), 270.

[11] Edwin Wilbur Rice, *The Sunday-School Movement and the American Sunday-School Union* (Philadelphia: American Sunday-School Union, 1917), 12-13.

[12] Elmer L. Towns, "Robert Raikes (1735-1811)," *A History of Religious Education*, ed. by Elmer L. Towns (Grand Rapids: Baker, 1975), 226-227.

[13] Eavey, *History*, 215.

[14] Reed and Prevost, *History*, 257.

[15] Rice, *Sunday-School*, 15.

[16] Ibid., 21

[17] Ibid., 23.

[18] Cf. Jack L. Seymour, *From Sunday School to Church School* (New York: University of America Press, 1982) for an account of the American Sunday school divergence from the model presented by Robert Raikes.

[19] Rice, *Sunday-School*, 20.

[20] Ibid., 18.

[21] Reed and Prevost, *History*, 257.

[22] Rice, *Sunday-School*, 15-17.

[23] Eavey, *History*, 227-229.

[24] Rice, *Sunday-School*, 14.

[25] Ibid., 16.

[26] Reed and Prevost, *History*, 259.

[27] Cf. James Estep, "John Wesley's Philosophy of Childhood Education," *Christian Education Journal* (1 NS. 2): 45-46, for a discussion of Locke's influence on Wesley.

[28] Gayle Carlton Felton, "John Wesley and the Teaching Ministry: Ramifications for Education in the Church Today," *Religious Education* (92.1): 95.

[29] Elmer L. Towns, "John Wesley (1703-1791)," *A History of Religious Education*, ed. by Elmer L. Towns (Grand Rapids: Baker, 1975), 213.

[30] Bill Temple, "Preparation for 'Beating the Devil': Uncovering the Leadership Development Paradigm and Practices of John Wesley in Early British and American Methodism," unpublished paper (Deerfield, IL: Trinity Evangelical Divinity School, 1994), 4.

[31] John Wesley, *A Thought on the Manner of Educating Children* (1783), 2.

[32] Towns, "John Wesley," 221-222.

Chapter 13

Christian Education in Colonial and Early America

17th–19th Century Christian Education in America

James Riley Estep, Jr.

Overview of Period

America was not always the United States. At one point it was the *New World* and simply regarded as a vast wilderness for imperial expansion. Summarizing the history of Christian education in America must traverse three *Americas* relevant to the period:

- First, Colonial America, which would be educational institutions established prior to American independence from Europe, primarily England, in 1783 (end of the Revolutionary War).

- Second, early America, a period of the move for a distinctive American education, both public and Christian.

- Finally, the later nineteenth century, wherein the influence of Christianity in public institutions of education waned from the previous two periods, requiring the church to develop alternative forms of Christian education.

The eighteenth–early nineteenth centuries were characterized by two *Great Awakenings* (🕭 13.1), which brought about spiritual revival in America. Such men as Jonathan Edwards (1703–1758) and later Charles G. Finney (1792–1875) assumed the mantle of leadership of these periods of spiritual revival. It was during these periods that indigenous

> "Religion, morality, and knowledge being necessary to good government and the happiness of mankind, schools and the means of education shall forever be encouraged."
> —Northwestern Ordinance (1787)

religious traditions were born in America, for example the Stone-

Campbell Movement and Pentecostalism. While these men were not primarily educators, they did regard education as a means to accomplish their primary objective: conversion. Both awakenings spurred the advancement and establishment of educational institutions throughout the colonies and early United States. So influential were these awakenings that Martin Marty observes, "the enlightenment thinking on education of the nation's founding fathers gave way to the revivalism of the Great Awakenings."[1]

While the nineteenth century was the formative period for American public education, and hence many textbooks and studies have been focused on its movements and progress, this chapter will focus on Christian education. Hence, it will address public education and higher education in pre-twentieth-century America, but only as it relates to the subject of Christian education. In actuality, it is not until the late nineteenth century that the clear distinction between public and Christian education becomes readily evident.

The General Purpose of Education

Marianne Sawicki calls the nineteenth century "evangelizing a new nation."[2] The general aim of religious instruction, as well as many public institutions of education in the early nineteenth century, was conversion, Bible knowledge, and moral formation. "The aim of education in all of the colonies seems to have been primarily religious, the biblical material constituting a large part of the curriculum."[3] More specifically, "For the most part colonial schools were instruments of the Protestant Reformation."[4] Even after the colonial period, during the early Republic, such men as William Holmes McGuffey (1800–1873) published the "McGuffey Reader," which "preserved the stereotype of the true American as pious, patriotic, and Protestant."[5] (❧ 13.2). In short, the purpose of Christian education was for Christian formation. Even institutions of public instruction were in a recognizable degree influenced by Christian beliefs.

However, in public education institutions this purpose was narrowed and eventually lost over the course of the nineteenth century. Scotchmer notes that public education in New England, which was heavily influenced by the Puritan's Calvinism, had three dimensions to learning: piety, morality, utility. However, after the founding of the United States, in the early Republic, piety became absent, leaving only morality and utility. By the end of the nineteenth century and into the twentieth, with education being shaped by societal expectations and progressive educational theorists, the aim of public education was restricted to utility.[6]

The purpose of education in America was heavily influenced by the changing contexts in which Christian education was provided. The contexts of Christian education were interrelated with all the contexts of instruction in colonial and early America. Church-sponsored educational initiatives were not readily required since the public education institutions served this same purpose. For example, "Wherever the *New England Primer* was used there was no need for supplementary Sunday School or religious instruction, for the *Primer* was essentially a child's book of religion."[7] As public institutions became increasingly less influenced by Christianity, the necessity for the formation of distinctively Christian institutions of education increased proportionally. Hence, American education prior to the twentieth century had an innate religious presence in virtually every context.

Public Christian Education

Context and Purpose

Schooling in colonial America reflected the social structure and religious elements of the culture. The culture of colonial America was not homogeneous, particularly in religious beliefs. New England's colonies were almost exclusively Puritan (Calvinistic), while the Middle Atlantic Colonies were divided religiously and the Southern colonies were most typically affiliated with the Church of England. In addition to the religious differences came various social structures, which also gave a wide degree of latitude for the role of religion in public life. For this reason three different forms of schooling were established throughout the colonies.

Southern Colonies: Private tutors throughout the southern colonies were the means of providing education for the social aristocracy, with religious instruction frequently included. However, formal instruction was also provided or sponsored by the Church of England's Society for the Propagation of the Gospel in Foreign Places (SPGFP), which was founded in England in 1701. The Society sent more than 300 missionaries to the southern colonies. "The educational motive was religious indoctrination."[8] An example of their work was the provision of a schoolmaster for the city of Charleston, South Carolina, from 1705–1709, and the establishment of schools throughout major southern cities.

Mid-Atlantic Colonies: Parochial schools were established throughout the Mid-Atlantic colonies, which were states more religiously divided than the colonies of New England and the South, and hence had a less denominationally oriented instruction in public school.[9] In addition to parochial schools, academies existed to provide career training. Benjamin Franklin proposed a system of academies be established throughout Pennsylvania, but none of these were religiously based (⬤ 13.3). While religion did not play a central role in the states' plans for schooling, many denominational bodies (Quakers, Dutch Reformed Church, and the SPGFP) provided an elementary education, some focused more on the underprivileged.[10]

New England Colonies: Perhaps the most familiar form of public education in colonial America was that provided in the New England colonies, which were almost exclusively Puritan. The common schools of New England provided an integrated education of religion (Calvinism) and an elementary curriculum.[11] The New England common school paradigm was the most successful model of Christian public education in our nation's history. Prior to the establishment of schools, the town minister served as an educator. However, the advent of the common school in New England moved the educational ministry of the Church to the schoolhouse. It is from the New England schools we derive the traditional picture of the one-room schoolhouse. New England's Puritans operated thirty-four common schools (27 confirmed and 7 only possibly), with only one school failing to gain popular support (⬤ 13.4). The common schools were based on four factors: "Puritan ethic," "republicanism," Evangelical Protestantism," and "capital entrepreneurship," all of which were to one degree or another religiously motivated.[12]

The formation of such an advanced system of schools in New England was no accident. The "Old Deluder Satan Act" of 1647 required the establishment of a common school in every town of more than fifty families, with the addition of a Latin grammar school in a town of more than one hundred families. This law was not the first one in New England. The law of 1642 made education compulsory, but did not necessitate schooling as the means of delivering instruction[13] (🔍 13.5 for "Old Deluder Satan Act").

In addition to the common school, several other institutions provided education, including religious instruction. For example, the Dame school, an institution designated specifically for girls, copied from its earlier English model, taught literacy and religion.

Content and Process

"We can assume that in any polity that encourages homogeneity rather than celebrates diversity, teachers would have an easier time deciding what to teach. As in the early days of the republic, that was actually the situation in America: Only the majority Protestant faith was officially recognized."[14] This was nowhere more evident than in the New England common school. It first used the *Hornbook*, which preceded the ever popular *New England Primer* as a school textbook (🔍 13.6). It was in fact a paddle-shaped writing tablet that contained not only the alphabet, but the Lord's Prayer and other religious texts on it.

The New England Primer was the curriculum for the common school (🔍 13.7). "Next to the Bible the most influential book in New England during the colonial period was *The New England Primer . . .*"[15] The contents of the *Primer* were drawn almost exclusively from the Bible, Psalm books, and the popular children's catechism known as *Testament*, as well as other Christian materials. It taught syllables, spelling, and used mnemonics based on religious rhymes. It included the Apostles Creed, Lord's Prayer, a popular children's catechism, the Ten Commandments, religious poetry, as well as a religious rhyme for the alphabet.

Typical of the Puritan culture in New England, the *Primer* was overtly Calvinistic. As Frost and Bailey observe, "It was thoroughly Calvinistic, deeply religious, and stressed on almost every page the sinfulness of man, his danger of eternal damnation, and his duties toward God and man."[16] Despite its original popularity, the *Primer* entered a state of decline in 1790, with the publishing of *A New Guide to the English Tongue* by Dillworth, which lacked the religious emphasis of its predecessor.

Mission/Sunday School

Context and Purpose

As early as 1737 (over forty years earlier than Raikes) the Wesleyans in America had a form of instruction on Sundays, but it never developed into a formal movement like that of the Sunday school.[17] The first Sunday schools in America following Raikes's pattern were led by William Elliot in 1785. The second started a year later by Francis Asbury, famous Wesleyan missionary, for the instruction of slaves in the home of Thomas Crenshaw in Hanover County, though he could not teach them literacy by law. In 1790 the Methodist Conference in Charleston, South Carolina, officially recognized the Sunday school. That same year, the First-Day or Sunday School Society was organized in Philadelphia.

The Sunday school of the nineteenth century was "the primary setting for Protestant religious education of the laity . . . ,"[18] evidenced by its growth in the new nation. While there was little progress between the Revolutionary War and the War of 1812, the Sunday schools' advance was only temporarily hindered. During the early nineteenth century, "Sunday schools in the United states were to remain relatively free from denominationalism."[19] This gave rise to the development of the Sunday school unions, collaborative efforts at establishing Sunday schools. For example, Sunday school unions opened in New York (1816), Boston (1816), and Philadelphia (1817), and ultimately the American Sunday School Union was created in 1825 (which originated from the Philadelphia Sunday School Union).[20] Notably, the American Sunday School Union also equipped women to teach other women.

"During these years [mid-1820s] the Sunday school was both a mission school for the poor and a means of religious instruction for the faithful."[21] An emphasis of the Sunday school as a tool for missions, both to the underprivileged and international contexts, was evident. For example, the vast missions area

> "Religious instruction has been withdrawn from the common school and interested wholly to the home and the church; . . . the Sunday-school has arisen, not indeed to interrupt or displace parental and pastoral culture but to supply their unavoidable deficiencies and to act where they can not." Henry Barnard (1865) —Seymour, *Sunday School to Church School*, 35.

of 1830 known as Illinois was targeted by the American Sunday School Union with $145,000 ($25,000 the first year and $60,000 the next two years) for the establishing of Sunday schools throughout the territory.[22] However, in 1830 denominational groups began showing interest in the Sunday school as part of their church educational program. This signaled a radical shift from the original function of the Sunday school as a paracongregational outreach ministry to the poor and indigent to a congregational educational ministry to the congregation. By the 1860s, only the educational ministry aspect of the Sunday school remained.[23]

National S.S. Conventions
Philadelphia: 1832, 1833, 1859
Newark, NJ: 1869
Indianapolis: 1872.

One reason for the inclusion of the Sunday school into the denominations and for its success was that the Sunday school began to compensate for the religious losses made in the public schools. As religion was slowly moved out of the public arena of education, the Sunday school created a context wherein religious instruction could be provided. In short, when the "4 Rs" became the "3 Rs" (minus religion), the Sunday school assumed the role of religious instruction. The Sunday school continued to be a vibrant ministry within the Protestant congregations of the United States. Eventually the need for a National Sunday School Convention was realized, and five were held between 1832 and 1872.

How influential were the Sunday schools in the United States? By 1832, 8,268 confirmed Sunday schools were counted in the United States, and the American Sunday School Union was present in twenty-seven states and the District of Columbia. By 1875, there were 65,000 Sunday schools in 36 states and the District of Columbia. By 1889 it is estimated that 10,000,000 people attended Sunday school, representing 10% of the nation's population.[24]

Incidentally, the first Vacation Bible Schools were conducted in New York City and Traux Prairie, Wisconsin, in 1900 and 1901. They were an outgrowth of the Sunday School and an endeavor to recapture part of the outreach potential it had originally.

Content and Process

As a mission school, the curriculum had been focused less on Scripture and more on the practical necessities of life, e.g., hygiene, literacy, ethics, and Scripture served as the content for their instruction in these matters. However, in the denominational Sunday school programs (after 1830), the Bible and catechism were utilized as content. "The idea was accepted that the parental responsibility for religious education was enhanced by the ministries of the church and Sunday school."[25]

Two dominant developers of the Sunday school's curriculum and support materials were John Vincent and Edward Eggleston, who, while they had their differences, agreed that the Sunday school was to be formal instruction and the sole educational institution within the congregation.[26] By the late nineteenth century a full graded program of Sunday school curriculum and programming had developed, similar to the modern Sunday school. Often two levels of instruction were offered, direct and advanced. One popular feature of the era was the "Sunday-school Concert," which consisted of a midweek service with prayer, a pastoral address, and Scripture memory.[27] Lecture and memorization became the standard method of instruction.

Higher Education Institutions

Context and Purpose

"To be a college in America before the Civil War was to be a Christian college,"[28] meaning that "the typical old-time college, then, operated more as a Christian community college than as a denominational institution; and rarely did it reflect narrowly sectarian interests."[29] In 1776, only nine colleges were present in the United States; in 1861, more than 200, with the majority being denominationally administrated.[30] Gutek notes three reasons for the Protestant influence in American higher education:

- "American Protestants . . . generally valued an educated ministry."
- "The proliferation of religious denominations stimulated a competition that extended to establishing colleges."
- "Denominational colleges were viewed as a way to educate the faithful and build religious commitment in the young."[31]

The move to establish the institutions of higher education was an interdenominational effort. The Puritans sponsored Harvard College (1636), the Anglicans established William and Mary (1693) and King's College (1754, now Columbia), the Congregationalists established Yale (1701)[32] and Dartmouth (1769), the Presbyterians established Princeton (1746), the Baptists created Brown (1766), and the Dutch Reformed created Rutgers (1766). In fact, Princeton, Dartmouth, and Brown were all results of the first Great Awakening. The original mottoes of these institutions, which have now all been abandoned, demonstrate their Christian affiliation:[33]

Harvard College: "For Christ and Church"

Yale University: "Light and Truth"

Princeton University: "Under God's Guidance It Flourishes"

King's College: "In Thy Light Shall We See Light"

Brown College: "In God We Trust"

Rutgers College: "Sons of Righteousness, Shine upon the West"

Dartmouth: "Virtue Rejoices in Trials"

The Roman Catholic Church also founded Georgetown College following the Revolutionary War (1791). The College of William and Mary's charter (1692) explained its purpose "that the Church of Virginia may be furnished with a seminary of Ministers of the Gospel, and that the youth may be properly educated in good manners, and that the Christian faith may be

> "Most ministers in the Virginia colony were a sorry lot. . . . the less desirable [ministers] migrated to America [from England]."
> —Frost and Bailey, *Historical and Philosophical Foundations*, 282

propagated among the Western Indians to the glory of Almighty God."[34] Religiously oriented colleges for women were also available, even conferring degrees, e.g., Oberlin College (Ohio) and Judson College (Alabama).

However, the Christian orientation of higher education in America did not survive the nineteenth century. "This religious decline [in the late nineteenth century] can be seen in three areas: first, the curriculum; second, the profiles of faculty and administrators; and third, the nature of graduates."[35] Harvard University is a prime example of the decline in Christian influence in American higher education (❧ 13.8).

Harvard College was established in 1636, as the first institution of higher education on American soil. It later became a university in 1780. Harvard College was established for men entering

> In 1680, Harvard College's motto was *In Christi Gloriam*, Latin for "In Christ Glory."

Puritan/Congregationalist ministries. In the early years, enrollment rarely exceeded twenty students, but by 1696 over 87% of the ministers in Congregationalist churches were Harvard trained (107 of the 122).[36]

The most pivotal transition period in Harvard's history was under the leadership of President Charles W. Elliot from 1869 to 1909 (🖰 13.9 for the Harvard University web site). He and his administration were responsible for transitioning Harvard from a liberal arts college model to the modern research university for which it is now known. This transition also accompanied a diminishing of the Christian distinctive in its educational program. Hugh Hawkins's book *Between Harvard and America: The Educational Leadership of Charles W. Elliot* contains a chapter that adequately summarizes the religious effects of his presidency, entitled *"Christo et Ecclesiae?"* (Latin motto for Harvard, "Christ and Church," but notice the question mark!). He concludes this chapter with the observation, ". . . after Elliot had increased the scholarly stature of the divinity school and the variety and beauty of the morning religious service, he felt both lacking in richness and substance. What he [Elliot] called nondenominationalism was often, as critics charged, Unitarianism raised to the *n*th power."[37]

Mark A. Noll notes six shifts in higher education that occurred near the close of the nineteenth century, all of which minimized or eliminated the influence of Christianity in higher education: curriculum, faculty qualifications, teachers as scholars to teachers as researchers, professionalism, funding from industry not denominations, and overtly Christian to nominally Christian.[38] In short, the culture shifted toward a more secular orientation, and the institutions of higher education shifted accordingly.

Content and Process

As should be expected from the previous discussion on higher education, religious requirements decreased while curriculum broadened throughout the nineteenth century.[39] The curriculum of an eighteenth-century colonial college would have typically required the following:[40]

First Year: Latin, Greek, logic, Hebrew, and rhetoric

Second Year: Greek, Hebrew, logic, and natural philosophy

Third Year: natural philosophy, metaphysics, and moral philosophy

Fourth Year: mathematics, and review in Latin, Greek, logic, and natural philosophy

Note the inclusion of biblical languages throughout the course of study. This facilitated the theological component within every student's curriculum. (See ❧ 13.10 for diagram of curriculum in New England colonies.) However, the Bible did receive some additional attention in both traditional higher education as well as the Bible colleges during the nineteenth century. "Only rarely did a course in the English Bible appear in the official curriculum. President Alexander Campbell's Bethany College (of West Virginia) was an exception; it opened in 1840 as the only literary college in America to maintain a Department of Sacred History and Biblical Literature as an integral part of the curriculum," later followed by other colleges such as Geneva College in 1848.[41]

Bible Institutes/Colleges

Context and Purpose

As the influence of Christianity waned in the institutions of higher education, the need for distinctively Christian higher education, or at least a college-trained clergy, became apparent. The evangelical response to this need was the Bible institute or Bible college. The Bible institute or Bible college movement began as an evangelical, interdenominational movement, but later became denominationally oriented.

The first Bible institute was founded by A.B. Simpson in New York, and it was named the Missionary Training Institute (1882). However, perhaps the most readily recognized of these early educational endeavors was accomplished by D.L. Moody (1837–1899). As the founder of the Moody Bible Institute (Chicago, 1886), he has been acknowledged as the originator of the modern Bible School or Bible College movement (❧ 13.11). Following the establishment of Moody Bible Institute, the Boston Missionary Training School, now called Gordon College, was created in 1889.

> **FYI:** Over 600 Bible institutes and colleges exist in North America today. One hundred of them are members of the Accrediting Association of Bible Colleges.

According to Larry McKinney, current executive director of the Accrediting Association of Bible Colleges, forty Bible institutes/colleges were established in North America between the years 1882 and 1920, with six of them established prior to 1890 and eighteen more before 1900.[42] The content of these institutions was almost entirely a Bible and practical ministries curriculum, with general education lacking or absent until the mid-twentieth century. Brereton cites three advantages to the Bible institute, leading to its success: "Brevity, practicality, and efficiency."[43] In short, the Bible colleges were able to provide pastoral education from a Christian perspective and field more trained clergy than the typical institutions of higher education, which by the last decade of the nineteenth century had lost their Christian identity and moorings.

Content and Process

The comment regarding brevity, practicality, and efficiency could also be said of its curricular content. Bible institutes/colleges had a very focused curriculum. S.A. Witmer provides insight into the curriculum of early Bible colleges. He notes "three departments of the curriculum" as follows:[44]

1. *Literacy* – English, logic, philosophy, natural sciences, ancient and modern history, geography.

2. *Theological* – Christian evidences, Bible, New Testament Greek, systematic theology, church history, and pastoral theology.

3. *Practical* – homiletics, evangelism, Sunday school work, and vocal music.

The curriculum of Bible institutes was even more focused, minimizing or even omitting the literacy or general education component of the curriculum.

Voices

Horace Bushnell (1802–1876) was the most influential theological and Christian educator of the nineteenth century (🔊 13.12). He was born in Bantam, Connecticut, on April 14, 1802, into a community dominated by Calvinism. His youth had been filled with doubt and skepticism, but he joined the Congregationalist church in 1821. Bushnell then entered Yale College in 1823 and graduated in 1827, but he returned to serve as a tutor while studying law from 1829–1831 but then went into the divinity school to prepare for the ministry. Between his times at Yale, he then taught at Norwich, Connecticut, but gave it up for journalism in New York City. In 1831, during the second Great Awakening, he began preaching at the North Congregation Church, which was to be his only ministry. He was later ordained and married in 1833. He and his wife, Mary Apthorp, had five children, though two of them died in their youth.

> "He was a heretic in the eyes of the American Protestant ortho-doxy which suppressed one of his books, and a reactionary to the worshippers of science and the cult of industrial progress."
> —Robert Ulich, *A History of Religious Education* (New York: New York University Press, 1968), 245

Bushnell distinguished himself due to his stance on revivalism. He was unique in that he rejected both the more conservative New England Calvinists and the more liberal Unitarians. He openly opposed the revivalists' emphasis on emotionally driven religious fervor and conversion. Living and serving in Connecticut, New England, Calvinism was the immediate theological backdrop for him, and hence reaction to his approach to Christian education of children was immediate. He was charged with heresy for his unorthodox view of the Trinity, but made such a successful defense of it in his *Christ in Theology*, that any attempts to have a heresy trial were thwarted. Likewise, his *The Vicarious Sacrifice* presented an unortho-dox view of the atonement of Christ.

Christian Nurture (1846) is summarized in the phrase "the child is to grow up a Christian and never know himself as being other-wise," a stark rejection of the New England Calvinism so prevalent in his background (🔊13.12). In so doing, he also opposed the revivalist tendencies of the day, considering a gradual maturing to a spontaneous conversion experience. His book "challenged then con-ventional ideas of sin and regeneration by arguing for a steady development of a Christian within the organic structures of family and church."[45] The radical nature of this approach was evident by the objec-tions of Protestant ministers and the suspended publication of his book.

> "A man's theology is never divorced from his biography."
> — John M. Mulder
> Introduction to *Christian Nurture*, xviii

He viewed the child as a child, not a proto-adult as did the revivalists. Hence, Bushnell advocated graded curriculum for use in child educational systems, even the Sunday school. However, his curriculum called for an indoctrination of ideas, rather a discovery approach.[46] Families and the Church, as God's family, provided the context in which a Christian could be grown through nurture. Of all the educational theorists in nineteenth-century Christian education, Bushnell is the most profound and influential. His work spawned the Religious Education movement in the twentieth century. In fact, Yale University maintains the Horace Bushnell Chair of Christian Nurture to this very day. His work likewise became a dividing point within the Christian education community. "*Christian Nurture* served as a theological divide with the extreme individualism of older Puritanism."[47] Even today this divide continues among Christian educators who must ask, *Where do I stand on Bushnell?* He recovered the ministry of the Church to the child, and the role of the family as the principle educator of children. Much of his success stems from the context of Revivalism, Sunday School Movement, and Horace Mann's public education endeavors.[48]

Voices in Public Christian Education

Some of the early proponents for a national system of schools also favored the inclusion of Christian religious instruction. For example, Samuel Knox author of "Essay on the Best System of Liberal Education" (1799) and Benjamin Rush, a physician and signer of the Declaration of Independence and author of "A Plan for the Establishment of Public Schools" (Philadelphia, 1786), regarded public schools to have a political, social, and religious task. Noah Webster (1758–1843) regarded the historical and ethical teachings of the Bible to be invaluable to students, and hence while not wanting to teach sectarian doctrines, teaching the Bible historically and ethically was promoted. Benjamin Franklin (1706–1793), a Unitarian, favored moral education through the Bible an essential for the establishment of a new nation. Also, Simeon Doggett's "Discourse in Education" (New Bedford, 1797) advocated teaching Christianity as a historical religion.[49] In short, religious and public education were not seen as separate concerns in the early Republic.

The dividing point between public education and Christian

education came early in the nineteenth century with the work of *Horace Mann* (1796–1859) (🌐 13.13). Recognized as the father of public schooling in America, he served as Secretary of the Board of Education in Massachusetts in 1837. Mann advocated the establishment of publicly funded common schools administrated by the state government. He did not openly oppose the teaching of religion in public school classrooms, but said it could only be done when it did not cause friction or interdenominational squabbles. "The schools teach the moral doctrines of Christianity among which he included piety, justice, love of country, benevolence, sobriety, frugality, chastity, moderation, and temperance."[50] He advocated the reading of the Bible aloud in class, but without *any* commentary by *anyone*. This was, of course, virtually impossible with the denominational representations within a classroom. He tied school decisions to local populations and constituencies, and hence if religion was acceptable in the classroom, it was permitted, but if it was a source of contention, it would be omitted. Christianity, and religion in general, became an *option*. Hence, it was Mann's policy that eventually led to the omission of religion from the public school classroom. For him, the Bible was simply a means of social efficiency and morality, but he rejected its creedal and spiritual aspect.

Excursus: The Church Library Movement[51]

Though the Reformers consistently promoted the establishment of libraries for Christian and public education, it was the nineteenth century that witnessed the popular rise of libraries in congregations. The development of congregational libraries was spurred on by the formation of the Sunday school and public libraries in the United States. "The library was the true mark of a *bona fide* Sunday school."[52] Two educational efforts at establishing church libraries were the Sunday School Movement, in both England (1786) and America (1789), and the Methodist Book Concern, established in 1789.

Originally, congregational libraries were limited to stored Sunday school curriculum and materials, however, the New York Union Society "was foremost in the introduction of Sunday-school circulating libraries."[53] By 1830 the Sunday School Union

---

had circulated over six million pieces of printed texts for congregational libraries. By 1859 three-fifths of the libraries in the United States were started by the Sunday school.[54] In fact, in the twentieth century the use of libraries on the mission field became a standard missiological method.[55] Denominational bodies began to recognize the value of congregational libraries. For example, in 1927 the Southern Baptist Convention was the first to establish a denominational library service.

George Scofield (1810–1887) devised the "Ten Dollar Library" plan which allowed congregations to purchase a one hundred volume collection consisting of books varying from 72 to 250 pages each, for the sum of ten dollars to further stimulate the establishment of congregational libraries. Over the first ten years of the program's existence over ten million volumes were distributed. Programs such as these advanced the formation and expansion of the church library movement.[56]

The current status of the church library is somewhat less than ideal. However, in the nineteenth century, congregational libraries were vibrant supporters and providers of Christian education.

Conclusion

Just as the 18th–19th centuries were a transitional period in the history of the United States, so it was for Christian education. The advent of the Sunday school, Bible institutes or colleges, congregational libraries, and others provided prototypes for the future, such as the New England common school. It demonstrated that Christian education can effectively address the needs of the church and the society. It demonstrated Christian education beyond the walls of the congregation, providing an outreach to the culture.

What Can We Learn from Christian Education in Early America?

- Positive or negative, a symbiotic relationship exists between Christian education and state-sponsored, public education.
- Christian education is formed in direct response to the needs of both the church and the society.

- The Sunday school is an adaptive means of education that need not be abandoned in the 21st century.

- Theological shifts, such as revivalism and Bushnell's theory of childhood nurture, yield unique educational avenues.

- Unfortunately, it was the divisions within Christianity that eventually led to its exclusion from the public classroom.

- The Bible can have a place in the public school classroom, the determining factor being the religious homogeneity of the community.

- Bible colleges are a direct response to the need for qualified pastors, as they are today.

- Christian education is not restricted by the walls of the church building.

Study Helps

Reflection Questions

1. How would you describe your experience in Sunday school? How did it compare with the description of the Sunday school in this chapter?

2. Do you agree with Horace Mann's position on the place of the Bible and religion in the public school?

3. Do you think a model like the New England common school would work today? Why and why not? What has changed in America that would limit or advance its applicability?

4. What is the history of your institution (college, seminary, graduate school)? When did it start? Was it part of the response to the loss of Christian influence in higher education?

5. How does the curriculum of early Bible colleges compare to your college experience?

6. What kind of outreach educational ministries, such as the original Sunday school, exist today?

Technical Terms

Common Schools Tax funded public education, typical of New England colonies.

Conversion An approach to education common in the late eighteenth and early nineteenth centuries. It viewed the purpose of education as a means of conversion, and valued a sudden, radical experience of spiritual realization, i.e., conversion.

Dame School Adopted from England, it was a school for girls.

Great Awakenings Periods of spiritual revival in England and America, emphasis on conversion. Two periods of revival occurred during the 18th–19th centuries, one in each, known as the first and second awakenings.

Hornbook Original textbook of the New England common schools.

McGuffy Reader Most popular textbook in American schools, effectively replacing the *New England Primer*.

Mission or Sunday School Originating in England in 1780, it was the most common form of Protestant education in England and the United States. It originally served as a paracongregational outreach ministry, but in the 1820s was incorporated into the ministry of denominations.

New England Primer Textbook for the New England common school, used in the late eighteenth century. Calvinistic, it used Christianity as a means of providing elementary education.

Nurture An approach to Christian education first advocated by Horace Bushnell. It opposed the revivalist and conversion approach to education.

Parochial Schools Common in the Mid-Atlantic states, these institutions provided elementary education, though not as religious as the New England common school.

Puritans Calvinistic group settling in New England colonies.

SPGFP Society for the Propagation of the Gospel in Foreign Places, missionary society of the Church of England responsible for much of the educational establishments throughout colonial America, especially the South.

Sunday School Unions Societies formed for the purpose of promoting Sunday schools in America, which appeared in most major cities in the United States. The largest of unions was the American Sunday-School Union, which consolidated many of these unions.

Recommended Bibliography

Bushnell, Horace. *Christian Nurture.* Grand Rapids: Baker, 1991; reprint of 1861 edition.

Carpenter, Joel A., and Kenneth W. Shipps, eds. *Making Higher Education Christian.* Grand Rapids: Eerdmans, 1987.

Marty, Martin E., with Jonathan Moore. *Education, Religion, and the Common Good.* San Francisco: Jossey-Bass, 2000

Rice, Edwin Wilbur. *The Sunday-School Movement and the American Sunday-School Union.* Philadelphia: American Sunday-School Union, 1917.

Rudolph, Frederick, ed. *Essays on Education in the Early Republic.* Cambridge: Belknap Press of Harvard University Press, 1965.

Seymour, Jack L. *From Sunday School to Church School.* New York: University of America Press, 1982.

Notes

[1] Martin E. Marty with Jonathan Moore, *Education, Religion, and the Common Good* (San Francisco: Jossey-Bass, 2000), 38.

[2] Marianne Sawicki, *The Gospel in History* (New York: Paulist Press, 1988), 257.

[3] Arlo Ayres Brown, *A History of Religious Education in Recent Times* (New York: Abingdon Press, 1923), 40.

[4] John L. Elias, *A History of Christian Education* (Malabar, FL: Krieger, 2002), 120.

[5] James E. Reed and Ronnie Prevost, *A History of Christian Education* (Nashville: Broadman-Holman, 1993), 303.

[6] Paul F. Scotchmer, "The Aims of American Education: A Review from Colonial Times to the Present," *Christian Scholars Review.* 13(2): 99-119.

[7] Brown, *History*, 39.

[8] S. Alexander Rippa, *Education in a Free Society* (New York: Longman, 1988), 26.

[9] The Mid-Atlantic Colonies/States were religiously divided, for example: New Jersey and New York were settled by Anglicans; Pennsylvania by Quakers, German Lutherans and Pietists, and New Jersey also had Presbyterians.

[10] Kenneth Gangel and Warren Benson, *Christian Education: Its History and Philosophy* (Chicago: Moody Press, 1982), 246.

[11] Brown, *History*, 31-32.

[12] Gerald L. Gutek, *Education in the United States: An Historical Perspective* (Boston: Allyn and Bacon, 1991), 106.

[13] S.E. Frost, Jr., and Kenneth P. Bailey, *Historical and Philosophical Foundations of Western Education*, 2nd ed. (Columbus, OH: Charles E. Merrill, 1973), 266.

[14] Marty and Moore, *Education*, 35.

[15] Brown, *History*, 37.

[16] Frost and Bailey, *Historical*, 273.

[17] James Reed and Ronnie Prevost, *The History of Christian Education* (Nashville: Broadman-Holman, 1993), 260.

[18] Helen A. Archibald, "History of Religious Education 1850–1950: A Documentary Trail," *Religious Education*, 82 (3): 411.

[19] Reed and Prevost, *History*, 261.

[20] Cf. Edwin W. Rice, *The Sunday-School Movement and The American Sunday-School Union* (Philadelphia: American Sunday-School Union, 1917) for a comprehensive treatment of the Sunday school movement in the United States in the nineteenth century.

[21] Jack L. Seymour, *From Sunday School to Church School* (New York: University of America Press, 1982), 29.

[22] Brown, *History*, 56.

[23] Seymour, *Sunday School*, 29-30.

[24] Reed and Prevost, *History*, 263.

[25] Seymour, *Sunday School*, 33.

[26] Ibid., 71.

[27] Brown, *History*, 62.

[28] William C. Ringenberg, "The Old-Time Colleges, 1800–1865," in *Making Higher Education Christian*, ed. by Joel A. Carpenter and Kenneth W. Shipps (Grand Rapids: Eerdmans, 1987), 77.

[29] Ibid., 81.

[30] Gutek, *Education*, 137.

[31] Ibid., 137-138.

[32] In 1701 Yale was established in reaction to the change in focus at Harvard, the accusation that Harvard had moved away from its pastoral mission.

[33] Larry J. McKinney, *Equipping for Service* (Orlando, FL: Accrediting Association of Bible Colleges, 1997), 40-41.

[34] Frost and Bailey, *Historical*, 287.

[35] McKinney, *Equipping*, 53.

[36] Rippa, *Education*, 39-40.

[37] Hugh Hawkins, *Between Harvard and America* (New York: Oxford University Press, 1972), 138.

[38] Mark A Noll, "The University Arrives in America: 1870–1930," in *Making Higher Education Christian*, ed. by Joel A. Carpenter and Kenneth W. Shipps (Grand Rapids: Eerdmans, 1987), 100-102.

[39] Frost and Bailey, *Historical*, 342.

[40] Gutek, *Education*, 134.

[41] Ringenberg, "Old-Time," 87-88.

[42] McKinney, *Equipping*, 70. See pp. 70-73 for a list of institutions established prior to 1920.

[43] Virginia Lieson Brereton, "The Bible Schools and Conservative Evangelicals," in *Making Higher Education Christian*, ed. by Joel A. Carpenter and Kenneth W. Shipps (Grand Rapids: Eerdmans, 1987), 114-115.

[44] S.A. Witmer, *The Bible College Story: Education with Distinction*. (Manhasset, NY: Channel Press, 1962), 35.

[45] Conrad Cherry, ed., *Horace Bushnell: Sermons* (New York: Paulist Press, 1985), 3.

[46] John H. Krahn, "Nurture vs. Revival: Horace Bushnell on Religious Education," *Religious Education* (70.4): 379-380.

[47] Reed and Prevost, *History*, 320.

[48] John M. Mulder, "Introduction," Horace Bushnell's *Christian Nurture* (Grand Rapids: Baker, 1991; reprint of 1861), xxv-xxviii.

[49] Cf. Frederick Rudolph, ed., *Essays on Education in the Early Republic* (Cambridge: Harvard University Press, 1965).

[50] Elias, *History*, 155.

[51] Cf. James Riley Estep, Jr., "Church Library," *Evangelical Dictionary of Christian Education* (Grand Rapids: Baker, 2001), 144-145.

[52] Robert W. Lynn and Elliot Wright, *The Big Little School* (Nashville: Abingdon Press, 1980), 57.

[53] Rice, *Sunday-School*, 59.

[54] Lynn and Wright, *School*, 57.

[55] Rice, *Sunday-School*, 221, 233-234; Lynn and Wright, *School*, 57.

[56] Ibid.

Chapter 14

The "Early Days" of Religious Education: 1900–1950s

Mark A. Maddix

Overview of the Period

The history of Christian education in the twentieth and twenty-first centuries paints a diverse portrait. Those in the last century saw significant theological shifts within Christianity, and with each successive theological shift came an equally significant shift in the church's approach to education. Chapters 14 and 15 focus on education from 1900 to the present. Chapter 14 will focus on the first half of the last century, which was characterized by two theological developments: Classical Liberalism and Neoorthodoxy. With each of these two theological developments came educational agendas, which will be explained in this chapter.

At the turn of the century, religious education, as it was then called, was a vibrant and growing enterprise.[2] The psychology of religion had come into being as the new discipline for the scientific investigation of religious education. Theologians, denominational leaders, educators, and biblical scholars were joined in the excitement of determining the implications of biblical studies, religious experience, social concern and social action, and moral and character education for religious education.[3] It was in this atmosphere that the Religious Education Association (REA) was founded in 1903 by such religious educators as George

> "In the early decades of the 20th century the term 'Christian Education' meant Church-related higher education, while 'Religious Education' was used for Sunday School and related Organizations."[1]
> —D. Campbell Wyckoff

Albert Coe, William Clayton Brower, and Sophia Lyon Fahs (❧ 14.1). The REA was developed because of dissatisfaction with the Sunday school, and it mobilized academic and parish educators to professionalize the field of religious education.[4]

George Albert Coe was a prime mover in the religious education movement and influenced it for several more decades.[5] Coe's contribution to the field resulted in a movement toward what has been called the classical-liberal approach to Christian education.[6] In his book, *A Social Theory of Religious Education* (1917), he critiques current "tendencies" in Christian education and provides merits of liberalism for religious education. Coe states, "Here, then are three points in which liberalism has obvious significance for a theory of religious education: The effort to develop in each person an individual or independent attitude in all religious matters; the awakening of thought as contrasted with mental habituation; and the fusion of rightness toward God with rightness toward man."[7] Coe's liberal approach to religious education influenced much of the first half of the twentieth century. The term "liberal" refers exclusively to the optimistic, classical liberalism that shaped the religious education scene during the early decades of this century. The result of Coe's approach to religious education was an emphasis on the scientific approach to religious experience and a denial of the role of biblical revelation and theology as normative for religious education. The impact of the shift would become most evident in Coe's successors in the first half of the twentieth century.

Wilfred Evans Powell provided an immediate reaction to Coe's thesis in his book, *Education for Life with God* (1934). Powell provided a critical review of Coe's work and concluded that religious education needed a more direct relationship with God, which he expressed in terms typical of the pre-Barthian period. He stated that "religious education seeks to guide the pupil so that they will discover and enter into the best possible relationship with God. . . . the heart of this relationship is seen in Jesus Christ."[8] Powell's critique provided a precursor to Karl Barth's more serious consideration of a traditional theological approach. Barth had become a major force in German theological thinking since 1918, when his commentary on Romans was first published.[9] Barth was not well known in the United States, however, until *The Word of God and the Word of Man* was published and translated in English in 1928. The commentary on Romans was not available in English until 1933. The impact of Barth's work resulted in a movement that placed radical attention on the Bible, and this shook the theological world. Barth's theological influence placed a greater emphasis on the Bible as God's revelation as compared to the classical liberal model that placed its emphasis on social reconstruction.

Shifts and changes in theology always influence Christian education. These shifts are evident in the early twentieth century. In this chapter two distinct approaches will be explored with their implications for Christian education. The early years of the twentieth century were dominated by the classical liberal religious education as reflected in the writings of George Albert Coe, and the next quarter century provided a stark reaction to this movement as reflected in the reorientation of biblical revelation as normative for Christian education.

Classical-Liberal Religious Education

The new century introduced a new model of religious education. Whereas the previous generation emphasized individual salvation, the new generation emphasized immediate salvation through the reordering of society. The new model was an optimistic brand of classical liberal theology, linked with an optimistic attitude toward education. Harold Burgess in his book, *Models of Religious Education* (1996), states, "The single most important change was almost a complete reliance upon revealed truth and was superseded by a characteristic commitment to discover, and to test, truth through rigorous application of the scientific method."[10] This new model constitutes a radical departure from the historical educational endeavor of the Church. The primary attention was placed upon individuals functioning within society rather than upon the content of a divinely revealed message. Instead of proceeding primarily from the historical beliefs of the church, liberal thinkers proceeded upon the assumption that religious education theory and practice should be based on the best scientific knowledge available in regard to the nature of humans and the conditions for their growth.[11]

The religious education movement embraced the chief themes of Protestant liberal theology, which included the attempt to reconcile Christianity with the intellectual world that emerged after Darwin's *Origin of Species* (1859). Liberal theology took an evolutionary viewpoint on the world, accepted the application of modern historical methods to the study of the Bible, and agreed with the positive assessment of human nature reflected by the Enlightenment.[12] Liberal theology elevated ethics over dogmatics in the Church life, arguing that Christians were not to focus on individual salvation but were to struggle for a more just world. Hence, liberal theologians gave a humanistic and social interpretation to humanity, salvation, the Church, and Scripture.[13] Burgess identifies the following characteristics of the classical-liberal religious education:

- The position that theological constructs are open to continual change, thus human experience becomes normative for religion itself as well as for religious education theory and practice.

- The conviction that religious education is essentially concerned with social and cultural reconstruction, not with individual salvation.

- The view that the religion teacher's task is to create social consciousness and to develop social living skills by arranging situations in which learners participate directly in the social process.

- The doctrine that Christian personality and lifestyle arise from the development of latent personal and religious capacities.[14]

These characteristics of liberal religious education provided the primary foundations of religious education in the first half of the twentieth century.

Influence of Progressive Education

The liberal religious education of George Albert Coe and his predecessors were highly influenced by nineteenth and twentieth century educators: Johann Pestalozzi, Friedrick Froebel, Horace Bushnell, and John Dewey. Pestalozzi's educational theories followed the psychological movement of the nineteenth century. He argued that effective religious education included the replacement of historic education with a process based on relevant relationships capable of being comprehended by a child. Both Pestlozzi and Froebel argued that humankind's core nature was good. Froebel believed that this divine nature must be unfolded and lifted to consciousness through education.[15] Hence, religious education was viewed as the awakening of an already present religious element, not as a redemptive activity.

Horace Bushnell's book, *Christian Nurture* (1861), was the most influential book in religious education in the nineteenth century. Bushnell's famous quote, "That a child is to grow up a Christian, and never know himself as being otherwise," provides the primary thesis for his view of Christian nurture.[16] Bushnell, like Froebel, argued that religious education ought to nurture the religious bud that was already present in the child. Thus, Bushnell opposed the evangelism of children and suggested that the primary role of the family and the church was to nurture a child in the way children are expected to live (14.2).

John Dewey's emphasis on progressive education must be counted among the most significant of the factors that gave shape to liberal religious education. Dewey's emphasis on experience as the basis of knowledge was in direct opposition to the historical views of knowledge. Dewey taught that knowledge is best thought of as modified action based on experience, and learning may not be distinguished from the living of life's experience. His emphasis on experience and community clearly provides the framework for liberal religious education.

Even though Dewey separated himself from the Religious Education Association at its conception, progressive education was evident in the field of religious education.[17] It is most evident in the content of the articles presented in *Religious Education* from 1906–1940, reflecting both progressive education and liberal theology.[18]

Educational Purpose and Content

Classical-liberal religious educators are unanimous in their rejection of the historic notion that the content of religious education is essentially a divinely authoritative message that is to be transmitted from generation to generation.[19] This included their denial of the Bible and theology as central to religious education. This assertion is in complete contrast to a theological view of religious education that places the Bible central to faith and practice, and central to the primary content and subject matter for Christian education. For Coe and other liberal religious educators, the Bible was one of a number of resources for religious education. They were concerned that the transmissive approach to religious education would lead to indoctrination and irrelevance to life. Therefore, they believed that the Bible had a prominent place in religious education, not because it was viewed as the authoritative Word of God, but because it narrated valuable social experiences. They advised religious educators to foster the divine life in students by making use of the experiences recorded in the Bible, as long as they related these biblical experiences to the present experience of learners.

Since the classical-liberal approach or the sociocritical approach to religious education rejects the historic notions of religious education, it places primary emphasis on social interaction. For example, Coe proposes that religious education became a process of creative discovery in which students dealt with both their individual and social experiences.[20] Thus for Coe and other liberal religious educators, the chief content of religious education flowed from the lives and experiences of students as these were illuminated by the religious tradition of the church. This view is a result of the combination of both classical liberal theology and progressive education.

Since liberal religious educators also reject the historic notions of the Bible as central to their curriculum and place experience as central, they also provide a social interpretation to sin and redemption. Like the advocates of the Social Gospel, they believe that conversion is not an individual experience but the social reconstruction of society. Therefore, the goal of religious education goes beyond individual salvation and

> The goal of religious education goes beyond individual salvation and the well-being of the Church to encompass the reconstruction of society through social welfare, social justice, and a world society.

the well-being of the Church to encompass the reconstruction of society through social welfare, social justice, and a world society. For Coe and the liberal theorists, working for the democracy of God was the way of expressing traditional doctrines of redemption.[21]

Coe expresses this view of redemption: "Our generation has come to see that the redemptive mission of the Christ is nothing less than that of transforming the social order itself into a brotherhood or family of God. We are not saved each by himself, and then added to one another like marbles in a bag. . . ."[22]

Because the primary purpose and content of the liberal

approach to religious education is experience and social reconstruction, the role of religious education is to provide experiences where learners can participate in real life experiences. In this educational process, the role of the teacher is not to teach the transmissive aims of the Bible, but rather, the teacher is to promote growth through skillfully guiding the learner's participation in life experiences. The goal in this process is to "emancipate" the learner for full and active membership in the "democracy of God."[23] This includes such educational experiences as group interaction, personal interaction, and engagement in society.

Because the *process* and *content* are inseparable realities to the liberal approach, it has been suggested that content refers to material of experience, whereas process is the way of dealing with that content. One important example of this way of relating content and process is that religious beliefs, attitudes, and overt behaviors are considered influenced more by the shape of the experience itself than by the biblical or doctrinal subject matter. Thus, the teacher is to employ activities that foster social interaction as the overall method of instruction and the student is central to the learning process. The content of religious education includes social development of the student through social interaction. "The school experience that is most effective educationally," Coe explains, "is when the pupil experiences the least break between it and the life of the larger society."[24]

Coe and the liberal religious educators' view of content and process is supported by their view of the learner. Harold Burgess writes,

> The learner, as understood by the aid of modern science rather than by theological doctrine concerning human nature, may be the determining factor in the classical-liberal model. As a product of evolution, the learner is perceived to have received both 'good and bad' fruits from the experience of the race. Any doctrine of original sin which severs human relationship with God is rejected out of hand. The radical heritage is believed to leave the learner's religious capacities, rooted in instinctual nature, intact. Accordingly, the laws by which the learner may be educated for full participation in the 'democracy of God' are within the learner's own self.[25]

Thus, the primary task of religious education is to side with the creative evolutionary forces within the person through controlled observation and experimentation.

Summary

The liberal approach to religious education dominated the first three decades of the twentieth century and continues to impact religious education today. The combination of liberal theology and progressive education offered by George Albert Coe, John Dewey, and others profoundly impacted the life of the Church and the scope of religious education. Religious education once valued the historical validity of the sacred Scriptures and theology as central to religious education, but now has placed human experience and social reconstruction as central to the educational task.

Voices

George Herbert Betts (1868–1934). Betts was a Methodist educator who taught psychology at Cornell College in Iowa. He later was named Professor of Religious Education and taught at Boston University, the University of California, and Northwestern University. His most influential work was on church curriculum theory that embodied the social theory of religious education. Also, he applied empirical research to the study of religion and education.[26] He was involved in several notable projects including *The Beliefs of 700 Ministers and Their Meaning for Religious Education* (1929) and *The Character Outcome of Present-Day Religion* (1931).[27] The following books supported his social theory of religious education, *Social Principles of Education* (1912), *How to Teach Religion* (1919), and *Method in Teaching Religion* (1925).[28]

William Clayton Bower (1878–1954). Bower was a pastor in the Disciples of Christ churches in New York and California before moving to Lexington, Kentucky, in 1912 to teach religious education in the College of the Bible and Transylvania College. After teaching there for fourteen years he joined the faculty at the University of Chicago Divinity School until he retired in 1943.[29] Bower's primary contributions to religious education were in the fields of curriculum development, experiential education, and moral and spiritual development. Bower advocated that controlled experience would enable the curriculum to remain person-centered and assist the learner in the process of self-realization. His theory was heavily influenced by Rousseau and his contemporary John Dewey. His primary contributions to the field of religious education are reflected in his books, *A Survey of Religious Education in the Local Church* (1919), *The Curriculum of Religious Education* (1929), *Religious Education and the Modern Church* (1929), and *Church and State in Education* (1944).

Ernest John Chave (1886–1961). Chave served as a minister in Baptist churches in Vancouver, British Columbia, and Sioux Falls, South Dakota, before joining the faculty of the University of Chicago Divinity School as professor of Religious Education in 1926.[30] His most influential book was *A Functional Approach to Religious Education* (1947). In this book, he rejected the historical foundations of the Christian faith and argued that religious education cannot look to historical theology sources for its message, content, or incentives. For Chave, religious education flowed out of the present experiences of life more than from ancient historic traditions. He defined religious education as "a systematic, planned procedure for making religion meaningful and operative in individual and collective living."[31] Also, Chave was very influential in the development of the Religious Education Association and served as its president.

George Albert Coe (1862–1951). Coe was the founder of the Religious Education Association (REA) in 1903. He taught psychology and education at Union Theological Seminary in New York City for thirteen years and taught education at The Teachers College of Columbia University until he retired in 1927. Coe's impact on Christian education is varied. He believed that the Church had failed by making Christian education a purveyor of dogma and facts rather than a transmitter of Christian lifestyle characterized by deliberate and conscious obedience to God.[32] Coe was convinced that moral development was an important task of religious education because he believed that persons were by nature religious, thus, religious education should be made a part of general education. Coe emphasized scientific method and the psychology of religion over classical theology in his view of religious education. His primary contributions include *Education in Religion and Morals* (1904), *A Social Theory of Religious Education* (1917), *The Motives of Men* (1928), *Educating for*

Citizenship (1932), and *What Is Religion Doing to Our Consciences?* (1943).[33]

Gaines Dobbins (1886–1978). Dobbins grew up in southwestern Mississippi to a farming family. His father was a Methodist and his mother a Baptist. He earned his graduate degrees at Teachers College of Columbia University, Peabody College, and the University of Chicago. At the University of Chicago he studied under John Dewey and George A. Coe. Dobbins joined the faculty at The Southern Baptist Theological Seminary, Louisville, Kentucky, in 1920 and served there until 1956.[34] While at Southern, Dobbins developed a strong Christian education department. He is known for being the most influential leader in shaping Christian Education and church administration among Southern Baptists. He was a prolific writer publishing over thirty books and hundreds of articles for his denominational curriculum and in professional journals. His most influential works were *Can a Religious Democracy Survive* (1938), *A Ministering Church* (1968), and *The Improvement of Teaching in the Sunday School* (1943).

Sophia Lyon Fahs (1876–1978). Fahs taught at Union Theological Seminary, New York, in religious education (❧ 14.3). She is best known for her book *Today's Children and Yesterday's Heritage: A Philosophy of Creative Religious Development* (1952). In this book she develops the various dimensions of a curriculum that would foster creativity, freedom, and discovery. She utilized the social-cultural approach in developing a liberal approach to religious education in the curriculum of the Unitarian Church.[35] In 1959, at the age of eighty-two she was "ordained to the liberal ministry" in the Unitarian denomination.

Hugh Hartshorne (1885–1969). Hartshorne taught religious education at Union Theological Seminary, New York, the University of Southern California, Columbia University, and Yale Divinity School. Hartshorne was a student of George Albert Coe and followed Coe in his emphasis on moral development and character education. His most influential book *Childhood and Character: An Introduction to the Study of the Religious Life of Children* (1919) provides a rationale for his approach to religious education. He believed that Christian formation took place primarily through worship. He was president of the Religious Education Association from 1935–1939. He contributed widely to REA from 1914 through 1954.[36]

Hartshorne sought to improve the effectiveness of church school (Sunday school) by using the latest scientific technique. He researched the structures and modes of church school administration found among churches in a variety of settings. In 1933 he reported his findings in *Church Schools of Today*, a valuable guide for churches and church schools seeking their own model of administration.[37]

Neoorthodox Theology and Religious Education

The classical liberal theological perspective was the accepted foundation for religious education practice in mainline Protestant denominations until the 1930s.[38] However, after the great depression and World War I, a shift in classical-liberal thinking that supported an optimistic future began to change. During this time theological influences were shifting from classical liberalism, to a neoorthodox theology that focused on "God and the Church." The conflict between these theological positions and their resulting debate over religious education conception and practice came to a head in 1939 at the joint meeting of the Professors Section and the Research Section of the International Council of Religious Education. According to Kevin Lawson, "this event has come to symbolize a turning point in the theological foundations of the field of Christian education."[39] As the dialog between competing perspectives continued, the neoorthodox theological view came to dominate the mainline Protestant Christian education movement and provided a corrective for liberal religious education.

The emergence of Protestant Neoorthodox theology in the United States, was due primarily to the work of Karl Barth, H. Richard Niebuhr, Reinhold Niebuhr, and Paul Tillich (14.4). This "new" orthodox theology distanced itself from traditional Protestant orthodoxy by its acceptance of modern critical approaches to the study of the Bible. It criticized liberal theology for ignoring

> The theological shift of this period is described as a transition from "this-worldly" to a decidedly "God-and-church" orientation.

fundamental biblical doctrine in the liberal attempt to make Christianity relevant in the modern world. Barth provided a strong reaction to liberalism with his renewal on biblical revelation, the transcendence of God, awareness of sin, knowledge of the heavenly Father through Jesus Christ, and concern for eschatology. All of these renewals sounded very evangelical, but were not.[40]

Karl Barth, a prominent German theologian, challenged the foundations of the classical-liberal theology by reinstating the role of revelation. Whereas the attention of the liberal model was centered on social interaction, his revelatory approach placed a greater emphasis on a God who works in history. This theological shift is often described as a transition from "this-worldly" to a decidedly "God-and-church" orientation. Barth's influence is unparalleled in his focus on the Bible as the primary source of truth. He provided an alternative to liberal theology and opened the gate for the Bible and theology to return to the center of the Church and religious education.

The development of neoorthodox theology and its impact on the liberal religious education did not go without resistance. Harrison Elliott, professor at Union Theological Seminary, defended religious education based on liberal theological principles in his book *Can Religious Education Be Christian?* (1940). Elliott personally rejected the tendency to return to what he considered an inadequate, neoorthodox, version of Christianity and the authoritative approach to religious education that he believed would grow out of it.[41] He concluded that religious education can be Christian only if Christianity is understood in terms of the continuing liberal position.[42] He rejected the appeal to the Bible as transcendent authority, contending that for religious education to be truly Christian it had to rest intrinsically on human experience and not on an appeal to the extrinsic authority of divine revelation.

H. Shelton Smith's book *Faith and Nurture* (1941) provided support for Christian education to be reformulated along neoorthodox lines. It is important to note that Smith's book was not written as a reply to Elliott's question, but was critiquing the assumptions of liberal religious education which had been unchallenged for some decades in mainline Protestant churches.[44] Smith made the Bible and

> "The term 'Christian Education' became the label for those writing and speaking about religious education who proposed a more theologically oriented religious education."[43]

not the life situations proposed by liberal religious educators the heart of religious education. He critiqued liberal education for the overemphasis on social sciences at the expense of Christian theology. He even went so far as to argue that liberal religious education had rejected the true Christian faith. Smith's book was a watershed in the history of Protestant religious education and provided a basis for a more theologically oriented religious education.

Paul Vieth's report entitled, *The Church and Christian Education* (1947), defined the aims and objectives of Christian education based on an examination of the writings of prominent Protestant educators. Vieth's thesis of Christian education was, "The purpose of the curriculum of Christian education is to confront individuals with the eternal gospel and nurture within them a life of faith, hope, and love, in keeping with the gospel."[45] The influence of Vieth's report provided a significant shift in a movement from liberal religious education toward a more theologically informed religious education.

By the 1950s many Protestant religious educators espoused a more theologically oriented religious education. Randolph Crump Miller's *The Clue to Religious Education* (1950) provided a foundation for moving theology back to the center of religious education. Miller stated,

> The clue to Christian education is the rediscovery of a relevant theology which will bridge the gap between content and method, providing the background and perspective of Christian truth by which the best methods and content will be used as tools to bring the learners into the right relationship with the living God who is revealed to us in Jesus Christ, using the guidance of parents and the fellowship of life in the Church as the environment in which Christian nurture will take place.[46]

For Miller, the task of Christian education was not to teach theology but to make theological truth relevant through the interpretation of experience. Theology is instrumental in bringing learners into a right relationship with God and the church.[47] Miller adapted a process theology[48] as his basis for Christian education and his book was highly influential in the field of religious instruction. He considered it his most influential work. In this book he was seeking to answer the question posed by the Harrison-Elliott debate. He argued that theology is basic to religious education and the unfolding drama of redemption is its central theme. For Miller, theology is in the background, faith and grace in the foreground. Miller's focus on theology opened the gateway for a variation of theological expressions in religious education, including process theology and liberation theology.[49]

The influence of neoorthodox theology was short-lived in America when theological interest shifted to issues of Death-of-God theologies, the rise of analytical philosophy, and process theology.[50] This theological shift provided the foundation for an array of theological influences in Christian education that would follow in the 1950s and 1970s. It is during this period that the profession of Christian education and educators increased through the key voices of C. Ellis Nelson, Randolph Crump Miller, Sara Little, and John Westerhoff III. Their contribution to Christian Education is evident in current research and practices.

Purpose of Education

Harold Burgess provides three primary aims of this period of Christian education. *First, theology is central to Christian Education.* In contrast to the classical liberal view of "humans as central to the educational process," the center of the revelatory approach was God. The aim of education was to give due recognition to cultural change while continuing in the spirit of the biblical tradition.[51] Randolph Crump Miller indicated that the "aims of Christian education must be grounded in a theology which recognizes God as the center and goal of its educational process."[52]

Second, revelation plays an important role in the process of generating aims.[53] Revelation, though, should be distinguished from the concept in which revelation is perceived as a more-or-less static given. Instead, revelation refers to the ongoing human experience within the life of the church.

Third, the church's educational task is to introduce each new generation into the life and ministry of the faith community.[54] John Westerhoff III indicates that "to be a Christian is to be in fellowship with the historic community of faith called the Church . . . and share that experience through their corporate activity in the world."[55] The primary distinction between the neoorthodox approach and the classical-liberal approach is the emphasis on the church as the primary context for Christian education. James Smart affirms this viewpoint by stating that the purposes of religious education from the Christian perspective cannot be understood apart from a clear understanding of the church, which came into being as a consequence of God's breaking into our world in Jesus Christ.[56] Smart's affirmation was supported by Miller, Westerhoff, Nelson, and others. They had adapted the sociocultural focus of the classical-liberal educators, but placed a greater emphasis on the role of theology, revelation, Bible, and church as the primary focus of religious education. These shifts provided a stark contrast to the liberal view of religious education that emphasized experience and social reconstruction as its primary purposes.

Educational Content and Process

Because the primary content of religious education is focused on revelation, content is exclusive, ambiguous, and hard to define. Revelation might be defined as "God actively disclosing to man his power and glory, his nature and character, his will, ways, and plans—in short, himself in order that mankind may know him."[57] It is at the center of the curriculum that the learner encounters the living God, it is where God is revealed. This means that the curriculum must at the same time be God-centered and experience-centered.[58] Content is not disconnected from the historical Christian message nor meaningless in terms of present experience, but they correspond. Such correspondence of subject matter, content, and present experience is a critical element.

Since this approach is concerned with teaching the historical aspects of the Church as well as helping the learner grow in his relationship with God, the role of community is very important. It is through community that persons are shaped and formed as they interact with other persons. Thus, the content of education takes place as the learner interacts with other persons. This is especially emphasized as the learner is being formed in the context of the faith community. These religious educators place a strong emphasis on faith communities as another content in religious education.

Also, given that both experience and the faith community form the primary content of religious education, there is unanimous agreement among Protestants that the primary subject matter in the educational process is the faith tradition. The faith tradition includes the Bible, Christian theology, Church history, and stories of the church today.[59] The faith tradition does not deny the individual interests, differences, and needs of the learner, but places the historical dimensions of faith at the center of the educational process. From the faith tradition the Bible is considered the most important source of the subject matter in Christian education. This doesn't mean that the best religious education is done by direct transmission of biblical content; rather, the central point of teaching the Bible is that God may speak through it to learners as they are being taught. The Word of God becomes the avenue of divine revelation to the student. Therefore, as the teacher communicates the truth of the Bible he/she does so with the expectation that God will make the Word come alive with the power of the Holy Spirit.

The role of the teacher in the educational process is very important as they model the Christian faith for the learner. Here are some characteristics of the teacher in the learning process:

- The teacher will seek to incarnate the Holy Spirit rather than merely convey the subject matter.
- The teacher trusts the role of the Holy Spirit and the learner in the educational process.
- The teacher believes that revelation occurs in the teaching-learning process.
- The teacher develops a relationship with the learner in order to create an environment of trust as the learner searches for the realities of the Christian faith.
- The spiritual, intellectual, and personal development of the teacher is critical to the teaching-learning process.

Since the teacher plays such an important role in the educational process, it is very important for him/her to be competent in biblical understanding, the Christian faith, and active in service, fellowship, and worship. These qualities along with a genuine love for the learner provide key aspects of a competent teacher.

Summary

Neoorthodox theology or the "new" orthodoxy provided a needed corrective to liberal theology. In the same way that liberal theology influenced liberal religious education, the renewed emphasis on the Bible and divine revelation influenced a return of theology as central to Christian education. This theological reorientation was not as concerned about teaching theology as it was about helping people foster a right relationship with God through the Church. It was through the revelatory activity of the teaching process that lives were changed. This new emphasis impacts much of Christian education throughout the following decades, and opens the gateway for a variety of theological influences including process theology, feminine theology, liberal theology, and as is discussed in chapter 15.

Voices

The following are representative voices of the religious educators that represent religious education during this period. The commonality of these religious educators is that they view theology as normative for religious education. However, they differ on their theological approach including neoorthodoxy, process, liberation, and feminine theologies.

Mary Boys (1947–). Boys is Associate Professor at Boston College's Institute for Religious Education. She describes herself as a "liberal, ecumenical Roman Catholic." She is both a biblical scholar and a religious educator (14.5). She is concerned with how the Bible is to be interpreted and then passed on to the community of faith. A reoccurring theme is that the ability to interpret doesn't necessarily translate into the ability to teach for transformation. She is concerned that biblical scholarship is not being incorporated into religious education methodology. She feels that the two fields have lost touch with each other. For her, the primary purpose of Christian education is to educate toward intellectual conversion. Her most recent book, *Educating in Faith*, includes a new proposal for knowing, and the need to hear feminists, the need to integrate the social sciences into religious education, and the need for societal transformation. She also argues for her primary concern of integration of biblical scholarship with religious education.[60]

Iris V. Cully (1914–). Her work has influenced Christian education from the 1950s to the present. She was a professor of religious education at Lexington Theological Seminary and at Yale Divinity School. Her first book, *The Dynamics of Christian Education* (1958), argued the need for the student to participate in the biblical story that would lead to an appropriation or rejection of its implications. This emphasis has led her to employ a variety of teaching methods and to include reflection on experience. She is also concerned that the church impact society.

Maria Harris (1934–). Her experience includes teaching at Andover Newton Theological School, Fordham University, New York University, and Boston College. She has worked within and alongside the Catholic Church. Her book, *Fashion Me a People* (1989), presents curriculum as much more than a design or the printed material used by church educators. "Curriculum" for Harris, is the entire life of the church. She reacts against schooling as the primary concern of curriculum. The curriculum of the church is centered around *koinonia, leiturgia, kerygma, diakonia,* and *didache.* For Harris, education takes place through these aspects of the Church. She emphasizes the responsibility of the whole community to educate the whole community. The result of such education should be to empower the church to enter the world beyond the church.[61]

Sara Little (1919–). Little joined the faculty of the Presbyterian School of Christian Education in 1951 where she taught until 1976. Little is a widely respected Christian educator and scholar who made a significant contribution to the field of Christian education. Her most influential work was *The Role of the Bible in Contemporary Christian Education* (1961). In it she wrote that Christian education cannot function independently of educational theory and philosophy, and it must function as an integrative discipline. She emphasizes that truth must be understood in the context of community and relationships. Therefore, social process and reflection on experience are important factors. She believes that the curriculum should be biblically centered, and when a person studies the Gospels, he experiences its meaning within the worshiping community. For Little, religious instruction is a component of Christian education that enables the student to become part of the faith community.[62] Her more recent work *To Set One's Heart: Belief and Teaching in the Church* (1963) continues the development of the role of religious instruction in faith communities.

Randolph Crump Miller (1910–2002). From 1936 to 1952 Miller taught at Church Divinity School of the Pacific, Berkeley,

California. In 1952 he joined Yale Divinity School as Professor of Christian Education and assumed the Horace Bushnell Chair of Christian Nurture in 1953. He continued in this position until his retirement in 1982, at age 72, after a preaching and teaching career that spanned more than 40 years. His greatest influence was in his insistence that theology is the basis for religious education and that process theology is preferred. He was influenced by process thought and theology from Alfred North Whitehead. Over the course of his career, Miller wrote eighteen books and published many articles. His books include *What We Can Believe*, *Biblical Theology and Christian Education*, *Christian Nurture and the Church*, *Your Child's Religion: A Practical Guide for Parents*, *The American Spirit in Theology*, *This We Can Believe*, and several others.[63] His 1950 book, *The Clue to Christian Education*, was highly influential in the field of religious instruction. In this book he was seeking to answer the question posed by the Harrison-Elliott debate. He argued that "theology is basic to religious education and the unfolding drama of redemption is its central theme."[64] For Miller, theology is in the background, with faith and grace in the foreground.

Gabriel Moran (1935–). He teaches at New York University. His previous experience included teaching 9th-12th grade boys at a Catholic school. For Moran, religious education must take place outside a particular religious tradition. As such it must be taught in educational settings—the public school being the best place. This view is based on two presuppositions: 1) true education is inherently religious and therefore religious education belongs to the educational world, and 2) the public school is the best arena for overcoming the limits of one's primary religious affiliations. The setting for religious education must be broadly educational rather than narrowly theological in nature. He believes that religious education should provide a broad context within which to place one's own tradition and beliefs. In this way one can develop a broader understanding of God.[65]

C. Ellis Nelson (1916–). Nelson joined the faculty of Union Theological Seminary, New York, in 1957. He became the chair of the Department of Religious Education for many years and served as President of Louisville Presbyterian Seminary, Louisville, Kentucky. His most influential works were *How Faith Begins* (1967) and *How*

Faith Matures (1989). In *How Faith Begins*, Nelson argues that faith formation takes place within the context of communities and that the process of socialization needs to be more intentional and more effective. His theory of socialization provides the primary basis for his approach to Christian education.

Lewis Joseph Sherrill (1892–1957). Sherrill was Professor of Religious Education at Louisville Presbyterian Seminary from 1925–1959, and Dean from 1930–1950. He then became Professor of Practical Theology at Union Theological Seminary from 1950–1957. Also he served as President of the American Association of Theological Schools (later ATS) from 1938–1940. His most recognized work on the history of Christian education was *The Rise of Christian Education* (1944). He rejected the experimental and developmental theories in favor of psychoanalytic theories for his views on the religious nature of the person. He was influenced by both Randolph Miller and D. Campbell Wyckoff. He further believed that the "new philosophy of Christian education" must develop from within the Judeo-Christian tradition not from secular society or education. He felt the unique nature of Christian education derived from the unique nature of the Christian community and faith.[66] He spoke of "confrontation" and "encounter" in education. Confrontation meant that God as infinite Personal Being confronted a finite personal being. What is revealed in the encounter (revelation as God's self disclosure) is not information about God but God Himself. He called his theology a "Theology of Wholth" (the wholeness of the person and the holiness of God). Wholeness is the result of positive relationships between oneself and God and others. God is never known apart from relationships with others.[67]

James Smart (1906–1985). Smart pastored several Presbyterian churches in Canada. His most notable books were *The Rebirth of Ministry, The Teaching Ministry of the Church* (1954), and *The Strange Silence of the Bible in the Church*. He served as Professor of Biblical Interpretation at Union Theological Seminary and was editor-in-chief of the *Faith and Life* curriculum of the Presbyterian Church of the U.S.A. from 1944–1950. In keeping with Barthian thinking he rejected the popular liberal theology of optimism that permeated Europe and North America. When the two world wars crippled this optimism, he joined Emil Brunner and Reinhold Niebuhr in denouncing the once popular mood. He supported H. Shelton Smith's attack against the existential approach of the liberals, but he did retain a relatively high regard for liberal religious educators.

In his book, *Rebirth of the Ministry*, he did not view himself as an educator but saw that task as belonging to Sunday school staff and professional religious educators. He began to work more with children and teenagers and in so doing found himself a part of the educational task—an unusual role for the pastor at this time. In his book, *The Teaching Ministry of the Church* he described the typical person's encounter with the Bible as fragmented at best. They would receive "bits" of Bible through the various programs they were involved in. They would never deal with the larger themes and concepts of the Scriptures. As his convictions developed, he expressed the need to involve lay people in the teaching ministry of the church and to equip them in all aspects of the church's ministry so that the Scriptures could be returned to the church.[68]

Paul Herman Vieth (1895–1978). He was the Horace Bushnell Professor of Christian Nurture at Yale Divinity School from 1931–1963. He was active with the International Council of Religious Education and his book *Objectives of Christian Education* served as the guideline for that organization and its successor, the Division of Christian Education of the National Council of Churches. Sara Little described him as "the symbol of a field in transition."[69] He was virtually unique in emphasizing the need for objectives in religious education. For him, two things drove Christian Education: the nature of the student and the objectives. He wanted to make Christian Education understandable and practical for the local congregation.

In his writings he defined Christian Education as a process by which persons are confronted with and controlled by the gospel. He believed that good teaching grew out of insight into the nature of the learner, and a major theme of his writings is the growing to maturity of persons through the educational ministry of the church. He also advocated the integration of Christian Education with the total ministry of the church—whose overall goal was discipleship. His most influential book is considered to be *The Church and Christian Education*—which dealt with issues of concern in education in the mid-1940s.[70]

John Westerhoff III (1933–). Westerhoff is an ordained Episcopal priest and was Professor of Theology and Christian Nurture at Duke University Divinity School for 20 years. During this time he also taught and lectured in colleges, universities, and Protestant, Roman Catholic, and Anglican schools of theology throughout the U.S. and around the world. He feels that his identity is not as a scholar or a practitioner in the field of Christian education but as a parish priest engaged in the formation of clergy. As early as 1987 he admitted, "I have not yet constructed a careful, reasoned, systematic framework for religious education."[71] His major impact has been his emphasis on the role of community in faith formation. He has objected to the schooling model, preferring a socialization model because it includes the hidden curriculum and community life as well as the overt curriculum of the educator. Dissatisfied with the term "church education" he has employed the term "catechesis." Catechesis refers to the whole process of "Christian becoming." In his model he focuses more on relationships than educational systems.

He has published over 500 articles and thirty-four books. *Will Our Children Have Faith?* is a classic in the field of religious education. His latest books are *The Spiritual Life: The Foundation for Preaching* and *Teaching and Sensing Beauty* with John Eusden of Williams College. Presently at St. Luke's Episcopal Church in Atlanta, he is theologian-in-residence and Director of the Institute for Pastoral Studies founded to stimulate, encourage, and support the church's mission and ministry by providing parish-based education, consultation, research, and resources for laity and clergy in pastoral studies.[72]

D. [Dewitte] Campbell Wyckoff (1918–). He is probably among a very few who are considered the shapers of Christian education in the 20th century. He served as Professor of Christian Education at Princeton Theological Seminary for over four decades. His chief concern has been curriculum, method, and administration. One of his most influential books was *The Task of Christian Education* (1954). In this book he outlined his thesis that Christian education is a task to be accomplished—an enterprise that had three primary concerns. 1) The task is the formation of Christian character and the forming of a Christian society. 2) Nurture is a critical dynamic in this task. Nurture involves four activities: giving instruction, imparting a life of integrity, training in social awareness, and training in God awareness. In order to nurture effectively we need to integrate sociology, psychology, philosophy, and theology. 3) The "gospel" is important to Wyckoff and is the basic guide for Christian Education. He distinguishes between Christian Education and Bible education. Christian Education involves learning from experience. The Bible alone is inadequate. He continues to have undiminished enthusiasm for the preservation of the Sunday school as the primary agency of instruction.[73]

Wyckoff's theology is difficult to assess, but he was influenced by neoorthodox theology. He was a driving force behind the Cooperative Curriculum Project of the 1950s which formed the basis for much of curriculum development. He feels that his most satisfying book was *How to Evaluate Your Christian Education Program*, which was a very practical "how-to" book. His concern for the "task," his own gifts as an administrator, and his practice of pulling together people and enterprises, reveals his passion for Christian Education.[74]

What Can We Learn from the "Early Days of Religious Education"?

- What theology you espouse influences the purposes of Christian Education.

- Liberal religious education focuses on experience and social interaction as central to religious education.

- Liberal religious education was influenced by liberal theology and progressive education.

- Neoorthodox theology provided a corrective to classical liberal theology, but did not completely return to an orthodox view of Christianity.

- Karl Barth's emphasis on the Bible and revelation helped move theology back to the center of the church and ultimately influenced the role of theology in Christian education.

- 1939 was the turning point in moving from liberal religious education to a theological view of religious education.

- Christian education became the label used to speak about religious education that proposed a more theologically oriented religious education.

- The influence of theology in Christian education was not just to teach theology but to make theological truth relevant in bringing learners into a right relationship with God and mankind.
- The educational task of Christian education is to introduce a new generation into the life and ministry of the Church.
- The theological approach to Christian education replaced the liberal religious education view of redemption through the social gospel with an emphasis on God, the Church, conversion, and revelation.

Study Helps

Reflection Questions

1. In what ways is the liberal approach to Christian education evident in Christian Education today?
2. What are the primary differences between religious education and Christian education?
3. What is the relationship between theology and Christian education?
4. In what ways did neoorthodox theology influence the purpose of religious education?
5. What was the focus of the debate between Harrison Elliott and H. Sheldon Smith?
6. What was the most significant theological shift in religious education during the first half of the twentieth century?
7. In what ways has the purpose of religious education changed since the beginning of the twentieth century?
8. What are the primary differences between the liberal approach to religious education and the reorientation of theology in Christian education?
9. What are the benefits and weaknesses of each approach to Christian education?

Technical Terms

Christian Education In the early decades of the twentieth century the term referred to Church-related higher education. After 1939, the term became the label for writing and speaking about religious education for those who proposed a more theologically oriented religious education.[75]

Evangelical A term used to identify those who view the proclamation of the gospel as central to the primary mission of the church.

Liberal Religious Education It is a practical expression of liberal theology. The classroom in the local church is where the kingdom of God begins because there are children who are physically and intellectually changing; many may be most effectively exposed to the possibilities of changing the world for a better tomorrow.[76]

Liberal Theology or Classical-Liberal Theology It stressed divine fatherhood and human brotherhood rather than the transcendence and majesty of God, portraying God as immanent in the world and permeating every part of human life. It seeks to relate the message of salvation to society, to economic life, and social institutions as well as to individuals.[77]

Neoorthodoxy Literally meaning a "new" orthodoxy. It is a theological movement whose identity is in rejecting "liberal" theology of the late nineteenth and early twentieth centuries. It does not discard the historical-critical approach to the Bible or reject the application of Christian faith to social and political issues. However, it places a greater emphasis on the authority of the Bible and divine revelation.

Progressive Education Associated with the philosophy of John Dewey, whose work focused on the process by which learners are engaged in directing their own growth and development in relation to subject matter competency. Progressive education focuses on the whole learner, emphasizing problem solving, decision making, and self-expression in all its forms. It is in contrast to an educational approach that focused primarily on the accumulation of factual knowledge.[78]

Process Theology A theological alternative to orthodox theology that conceives God as related to creatures and being affected by creaturely (human) response. God's experience changes as God learns new information, while God's essence remains the same.[79]

Religious Education	In the early decade of the twentieth century the term referred to Sunday school and related organizations. After 1939, the term became the label for writing and speaking about religious education for those who espoused liberal theologies and progressive education.
Religious Education Association *(REA)*	Founded in 1908 because of dissatisfaction with the Sunday school and revivalistic piety, the REA focused on academic and parish educators to professionalize the field of religious education. It embraced liberal theology and many of the features of progressive education.[80]
Theology	Any coherently organized body of doctrine concerning the nature of God and His relationship with humans and the universe.[81]

Recommended Bibliography

Benson, Warren, and Kenneth Gangel. *Christian Education: Its History and Philosophy*. Chicago: Moody Press: 1983.

Burgess, Harold W. *Models of Religious Education*. Wheaton: Victor Books, 1996.

Coe, George Albert. *The Psychology of Religion*. Chicago: The University of Chicago Press, 1916.

Cram, Ronald H. *Understanding Trends in Protestant Education in the Twentieth Century*. Lanham, MD: University Press of America, 1998.

Cully, Iris V., and Kendig Brubaker Cully, eds. *Harper's Encyclopedia of Religious Education*. San Francisco: Harper and Row, 1990.

Elias, John A. *History of Christian Education: Protestant, Catholic, and Orthodox Perspective*. Malabar, FL: Krieger Publishing, 2002.

Elliott, Harrison S. *Can Religious Education Be Christian?* New York: MacMillan, 1940.

Kathan, Boardman W. "Pioneers of Religious Education in the 20th Century." *Religious Education*. (Sept–Oct. 1978). Special Edition.

Reed, James E., and Ronnie Prevost. *A History of Christian Education*. Nashville: Broadman and Holman, 1993.

Schmidt, Stephen. "The Uses of History and Religious Education." 345-372. *Religious Education* 80:3 (1985).

Sherrill, Lewis J. *The Rise of Christian Education*. New York: Macmillan, 1944.

_____. "Theological Foundations of Christian Education." *Union Seminary Quarterly Review*. Special Issue (January 1951): 3–12.

Smith, Shelton. *Faith and Nurture*. New York: Charles Scribner's Sons, 1941.

Wyckoff, D. Campbell. *The Task of Christian Education*. Philadelphia: Westminster, 1959.

_____. "Theology and Education in the Twentieth Century." *Christian Education Journal* 15:3 (1995): 13.

Notes

[1] D. Campbell Wyckoff, "Theology and Education in the Twentieth Century," *Christian Education Journal*, 25,3 (1995): 24.

[2] Kenneth O. Gangel, in **NAPCE Newsletter**, Spring, 1994.

[3] Wyckoff, "Theology," 13.

[4] John A. Elias, *History of Christian Education: Protestant, Catholic, and Orthodox Perspective* (Malabar, FL: Krieger, 2002), 168.

[5] Wyckoff, "Theology," 13.

[6] Harold W. Burgess, *Models of Religious Education* (Wheaton, IL: Victor Books, 2001, 85. Burgess provides the primary models of religious education used in this chapter.

[7] George Albert Coe, *A Social Theory of Religious Education* (New York: Scribners, 1917), 336.

[8] Wilfred Evans Powell, *Educating for Life with God* (New York: Abingdon Press, 1934), 231.

[9] The first edition of Barth's *Epistle to the Romans* was published in 1918. It was extensively rewritten in 1921. The English translation appeared in 1933.

[10] Burgess, *Models*, 79.

[11] Elias, *History*, 167.

[12] Ibid.

[13] Ibid.

[14] Burgess, *Models*, 80.

[15] Ibid., 82.

[16] Horace Bushnell, *Christian Nurture*, The William Bradford Collection, series ed. by Barbara Zikmund (Cleveland, OH: The Pilgrim's Press, 1994 reprint; 1847), 4.

[17] In the development of the Religious Education Association, George Albert Coe argued that religious education should be "religious" as its primary focus as com-

pared to general education. Coe won this argument over Dewey. Thus, Dewey drifted from the Religious Education Association, but it was his emphasis on progressive education that was evident in the early years of the movement.

[18] Burgess, *Models*, 85.

[19] Ibid., 95.

[20] Elias, *History*, 169.

[21] Ibid., 168-170.

[22] Coe, *Social Theory*, 8; adapted from Burgess, *Models*, 168-170.

[23] Burgess, *Models*, 99.

[24] Coe, *Social Theory*, 23-24.

[25] Burgess, *Models*, 102-103.

[26] Jack L. Seymour, "George Herbert Betts," in *Harper's Encyclopedia of Religious Education*, ed. by Iris V. Cully and Kendig Brubaker Cully (San Francisco: Harper and Row, 1990), 59-60.

[27] Ibid., 60.

[28] Burgess, *Models*, 88.

[29] James E Reed and Ronnie Prevost, *A History of Christian Education* (Nashville: Broadman and Holman, 1993), 334.

[30] Ibid., 339.

[31] Ernest J. Chave, *A Functional Approach to Religious Education* (Chicago: University of Chicago Press, 1947), 2-3.

[32] Reed and Prevost, *History*, 334.

[33] Ibid.

[34] Ibid., 341-342.

[35] Elias, *History*, 169.

[36] C.R. Foster, "Hugh Hartshorne," in *Harper's Encyclopedia of Religious Education*, ed. by Iris V. Cully and Kendig Brubaker Cully (San Francisco: Harper and Row, 1990), 287.

[37] Reed and Prevost, *History*, 341.

[38] Kevin Lawson, ed., *Theology and Christian Education in the 20th Century: An Annotated Bibliography* (Talbot School of Theology, CD version, 2002), 30-31.

[39] Ibid.

[40] Warren Benson and Kenneth Gangel, *Christian Education: Its History and Philosophy* (Chicago: Moody Press, 1983), 316.

[41] Burgess, *Models*, 112.

[42] Kendig Brubaker Cully, "A Later Look at Harrison Sacket Elliott," in *Pioneers of Religious Education in the 20th Century: A Festschrift for Herman E. Wornom*, ed. by Kathy W. Broadman, *Religious Education*, 73 (Sept.-Oct. 1978), S-57.

[43] Elias, *History*, 172.

[44] Cully, "Later Look," S-58.

[45] Paul H. Vieth, *The Church and Christian Education* (St. Louis: Bethany Press, 1947), 145-147.

[46] Randolph C. Miller, *The Clue to Religious Education* (New York: Scribners, 1950), 15.

[47] Elias, *History*, 174.

[48] Process Theology is broadly defined as, "A theological alternative to orthodox theology that conceives God as related to creatures and being affected by creaturely (human) response. God's experience changes as God learns new information, while God's essence remains the same."

[49] See Randolph C. Miller's *The Clue to Religious Education* for a complete discussion on the role of theology and Christian education. For Miller, theology was the instrument in bringing learners into a right relationship with God through the Church.

[50] Cully, "Later Look," S-59.

[51] Burgess, *Models*, 122.

[52] Miller, *Clue*, 54.

[53] Burgess, *Models*, 122.

[54] Ibid., 122-123.

[55] John Westerhoff III, *Values for Tomorrow's Children: An Alternative Future for Education in the Church* (Philadelphia: Pilgrim's Press, 1970), 9-10.

[56] James Smart, *The Teaching Ministry of the Church* (Philadelphia: Westminster, 1974), 88.

[57] J.D. Douglas, ed., *New Bible Dictionary, Second Edition* (Wheaton, IL: Tyndale House, 1984), 1024.

[58] Burgess, *Models*, 129.

[59] Ibid., 131.

[60] Linda Cannel, "Summaries of Historical Periods," class handout (Trinity Evangelical Divinity School, 2000), 53-57.

[61] Ibid., 54-55.

[62] Ibid., 53.

[63] Rosinah Kelebogang and Martha Lund Smalley, eds., "Guide to the Randolph Crump Miller Papers," Yale University Library, Divinity Library Special Collections, 2002; http://webtext.library.yale.edu/xml2html/divinity.173.con.html.

[64] Ibid., materials adapted from Kelebogang and Smalley.

[65] Cannel, "Summaries," 57.

[66] Ibid., 57.

[67] Ibid.

[68] Ibid., 58.

[69] Randolph Crump Miller, "Paul Vieth," in *Harper's Encyclopedia of Religious Education*, ed. by Iris V. Cully and Kendig Brubaker Cully (San Francisco: Harper and Row, 1990), 681.

[70] Linda Cannel, "Summaries," 58.

[71] Ibid., 53.

[72] http://www.stlukesatlanta.org/staff.html.

[73] Cannel, "Summaries," 53.

[74] Ibid.

[75] Elias, *History*, 172.

[76] Wayne R. Rood, "Liberalism," in *Harper's Encyclopedia of Religious Education*, ed. by Iris V. Cully and Kendig Brubaker Cully (San Francisco: Harper and Row, 1990), 378-379.

[77] Ibid., 379.

[78] L.E. Bowman, "Progressive Education," in *Harper's Encyclopedia of Religious Education*, ed. by Iris V. Cully and Kendig Brubaker Cully (San Francisco: Harper and Row, 1990), 514-515.

[79] Definition provided by Dr. Tom Oord, Professor of Theology, Northwest Nazarene University.

[80] Elias, *History*, 167.

[81] Peter A. Angeles, *Dictionary of Philosophy* (New York: Harper & Row, 1981), 292.

Chapter 15

The Rise of Evangelical Christian Education 1951–2000

Mark A. Maddix

Overview of Period

The first four decades of the twentieth century were dominated by liberal religious education. Liberal theology and progressive educational theories gave rise to a perspective on religious education that was certainly out of harmony with evangelical thinking, committed as it was to the communication of a divinely ordained message.[1] The renewal of the theological approaches of neoorthodoxy in the '30s and '40s provided a needed corrective for liberal religious education, but did not completely move religious education back to an evangelical emphasis. Evangelical Christian education was reawakened in America by the end of the twentieth century when evangelical and revivalist approaches to Protestant religious education became dominant.[2] Along with the rise of evangelical Christian education came a wide variety of other approaches to Christian education that significantly impacted the field of Christian education.

The first half of this chapter focuses on evangelical Christian education and its leading contributors, while the last half of this chapter focuses on a variety of other influences that shaped Christian education during the last half of the twentieth century.

Evangelicalism

In order to understand evangelical Christian education it is very important to understand how to define "Evangelicalism." What are the primary tenets and beliefs of the evangelical movement? Evangelicalism is a distinct movement that is very difficult to define, primarily because it encompasses a broad range of meaning and understanding. Many of the Christian educators during this period view themselves in the broad framework of evangelicalism. Thus, a wide variety of denominations identify themselves under the label of "Evangelical." George Marsden, in his book, *Understanding Fundamentalism and Evangelicalism* (1991), provides the following definition of evangelicalism:

> "Evangelicalism" does not refer simply to a broad grouping of Christians who believe the same doctrines, but its meaning includes a self-conscious interdenominational movement, with leaders, publications, and institutions with which people from many subgroups identify.
> —George M. Marsden
> (*Understanding Fundamentalism and Evangelicalism*, 5).

> Evangelicalism today includes any Christians traditional enough to affirm the basic beliefs of the old nineteenth century evangelical consensus. The essential evangelical beliefs include (1) the reformation doctrine of the final authority of the Bible, (2) the real historical character of God's saving work recorded in Scripture, (3) salvation to eternal life based on the redemptive work of Christ, (4) the importance of evangelism and missions, and (5) the importance of a spiritual transformed life.[3]

Also, Marsden indicates that evangelicalism does not refer simply to a broad grouping of Christians who believe the same doctrines, but its meaning includes a self-conscious interdenominational movement, with leaders, publications, and institutions with which people from many subgroups identify.[4] For the purposes of this chapter, evangelicalism is designating a point of view that emphasizes the authority of Scriptures, endorsing doctrinal formations common to orthodox Christianity, and placing particular stress upon the importance of personal salvation through Jesus Christ.

Evangelical Christian Education

The rise of evangelical Christian education began during the 1930s and 1940s. In 1931, Clarence H. Benson, developed the Evangelical Teacher Training Association (ETTA). The ETTA's curriculum exhibited a primary emphasis on the Bible as the key to a revitalized program of church education. The ETTA became very influential as a source of renewal for the Sunday school movement.[5]

In 1942 the National Association of Evangelicals (NAE) was established to maintain the orthodox doctrines of historic Protestantism (🕭 15.1). The NAE provides the center of theological and education identity for evangelical Protestant thinkers. The NAE is a Protestant interdenominational movement to promote interchurch fellowship and cooperation on an evangelical theological basis. Throughout the 1940s evangelicals had a strong desire to renew the Sunday school by establishing the National Sunday School Association through the NAE's Church School Commission in 1946.[6]

> The National Association of Evangelicals, formed in 1942, is a Protestant interdenominational movement to promote interchurch fellowship and cooperation on an evangelical theological basis.

In 1946, the NAE authorized a "Study of Christian Education" chaired by Frank E. Gaebelein. The report, *Christian Education in a Democracy*, was released by Gaebelein in 1951. Gaebelein's work served to establish the theological foundation for evangelical Christian education. The foundation is the "fully inspired Bible" for which liberalism attempted to substitute "a fallible book."[7] For Gaebelein, the Bible provided the basis for "the fundamental doctrines of the Gospel, such as personal union with Christ, the Trinity, the fallen condition of man, Christ's atonement for sin, salvation by faith, not by works, and regeneration by the Holy Spirit."[8]

Gaebelein clarifies the distinction between evangelicalism and neoorthodoxy and modernism by stating,

> Neo-orthodoxy, despite its emphasis on man's sin and his need for redemption, denies the full inspiration of the Bible; modernism, with its tendency toward a naturalistic interpretation of Christianity and its repudiation of inspiration, is less concerned with sin and the need for redemption than with the innate perfectibility of man and the building of a new order by human efforts.[9]

Gaebelein's proclamation placed a clear distinction between the place of evangelical Christian education and the influence of neoorthodox theology on Christian education. Evangelical Christian education provided a needed corrective to the theological reorientation to Christian education, as described in chapter 14, by asserting the following educational viewpoints:

- The Bible is normative for Christian education.
- Communication of the gospel is central to the purpose of Christian education.
- The teacher is supernaturally assisted by the Holy Spirit
- Acceptance of the gospel is necessary for salvation.[10]

Also, Harold Burgess in his book *Models of Religious Education* (2001), provides the following criteria for Evangelical Christian education:

- Theological views derived from data thought to be received by authoritative revelation are normative for theory and practice. The Bible is the source of authoritative revelation for Protestants.
- The aim and content are fundamentally concerned with transmission of a unique message derived from the facts of revelation.
- The primary teaching task is to fully and faithfully transmit the message to learners.
- Learners will then live out the implications of the message with respect to Christian living and eternal destiny.[11]

Both Gaebelein's educational viewpoint and Burgess's criteria provide a basis for the separation of evangelical Christian education from both liberal religious education and the influence of neoorthodox theology.

Another development that came out of the National Sunday School Association (NSSA) was a commission focusing on National Directors of Christian education. The Commission met yearly in conjunction with the NSSA Convention. Although Commission members represented Christian higher education institutions, much of the work was directed toward improving Christian education in local churches. As the Research Commission grew, it became more concentrated on the needs of higher education, and as a result the Research Commission members expressed their desire for a name change in 1970.

In 1971, the Research Commission changed its name to the North American Professors of Christian Education (NAPCE).

In 1971, the Research Commission changed its name to the North American Professors of Christian Education (NAPCE). NAPCE's primary function was to provide fellowship and dialogue for teachers of Christian education and related disciplines who serve in evangelical Bible colleges, liberal arts colleges, and theological seminaries (🔗 15.2).[12] It was not until 1980 that NAPCE became separate from the NAE. NAPCE continues to provide a place for teachers of Christian education to present current research, and has continued to grow with 275 members.

In order for Evangelical Christian educators to continue to expand both professionally and theoretically, issues are regularly addressed in the *Christian Education Journal*, published by Trinity Evangelical Divinity School, Deerfield, Illinois. The journal is something of an evangelical counterpart to *Religious Education*, an interfaith journal that focuses on research in the field of religious education. *Christian Education Journal* is "designed to promote growth and advancement in the field of Christian education by stimulating scholarly study in Bible and related fields; providing a forum for the expression of facts, ideas, and opinions on Christian education topics; promoting the understanding and application of research."[13]

Summary

While evangelicalism was admittedly defensive of liberalism at the turn of the century, since World War II it has made a remarkable comeback. Through the evangelical voices of evangelistic crusades of Billy Graham; the founding of *Christianity Today* magazine; the emergence of distinctively evangelical seminaries (Fuller Theological Seminary, Asbury Theological Seminary, Gordon-Conwell Seminary, Trinity Evangelical Seminary, and Talbot School of Theology); the growth of the National Association of Evangelicals (NAE) to over 27 million members, including 43,000 churches, and 50 denominations; evangelicalism has regained intellectual status and moral credibility.[14]

By the end of the twentieth century evangelical and revivalist approaches to Protestant religious education had a remarkable growth.[15] The strength of evangelical Christian education is seen not only in increased membership, but also in the establishment of Christian schools, Bible colleges, and theological seminaries. Concern with Christian education had been a major preoccupation in evangelical Protestantism during the last half of the twentieth century.[16]

Purpose of Education

Evangelical Christian education places a greater investment in specific theological foundations compared to other approaches to Christian education. These theological foundations include the centrality of God's written revelation as revealed in the Bible, the necessity of regeneration, and the continual work of the Holy Spirit. Thus, the primary purpose of Christian education is to transmit a divinely given message as revealed in the Scriptures. Gaebelein declares, "that while the goals of Christian education concern man and society, the creative source of these goals is not within man and society. Rather it is implicit in a philosophy which is derived neither from a sociological context nor from the pragmatic method but from revealed truth."[17] Therefore, the purposes of Christian education can only be grounded in divine purposes.[18] The goal and aim for teaching is to convey the Christian message. Christian education is the communication of biblical or supernatural truths to the student. If faith comes by hearing, then students hearing these truths taught and preached will live by these truths.[19]

Transmissive Aims: Transmission of the Christian message comprises a key element for evangelical Christian education. Teachers are concerned with communicating God's written revelation to the students.

Supernatural Aims: Evangelical Christian education often distinguishes itself from secular education because it provides students with a direct, experiential encounter with God's truth. Thus, the teaching process includes dimensions that are supernatural and are transcendent.

Christian Living: Even though evangelical Christian education is concerned with imparting the truth of the Scriptures, the primary goal of Christian education is the character development of the student. The character and quality of the learner's life is the larger end toward which knowledge and understanding is contributory. Therefore, teachers are concerned with teaching content, but more concerned that students live out their Christian faith. The goal of Christian education is not only gaining knowledge of the Bible, but includes living the Christian life.[20] Since the concern is for students to live the Christian life and to embody its truths, Christian educators are most concerned about the individual learner. As Burgess states, this hasn't always been the case, "Sunday school teachers have sometimes labored under the impression that if they teach the facts of the Bible, the Holy Spirit will accomplish the necessary work of bringing about the desired goals in the lives of individual learners."[21]

Therefore, in order for the divinely given message to be properly communicated, the teacher must understand both God's specific and general revelation. God's specific revelation is the Bible, and God's general revelation is creation. Humanity's inquiry into the Bible is a means to understand God's purposes, and humanity's inquiry of creation is a means to understand how God has made the universe and

> Since all of Scripture is true, but not all truth is contained in Scripture, Christian educators must study both specific and general revelation to understand God's creation and to design ministry in accordance with how God has designed his world (Perry Downs, 15).

humans. Thus, the study of the sciences provides a greater understanding into the nature of human persons and human life. Perry Downs provides the following explanation for this process:

> Christian education must be guided by a worldview that values both general and specific revelation. Clearly theological issues, such as the nature of spiritual maturity, must be considered from a theological base. But issues regarding normal human functions, such as how people learn, should be addressed from a scientific base. Naturally, none of these issues is purely theological or purely scientific; therefore an integrative approach must be maintained.[22]

Because all of Scripture is true, but not all truth is contained in Scripture, Christian educators must study both specific and general revelation to understand God's creation and to design ministry in accordance with how God has designed humanity.[23]

The Role of Conversion: Gaebelein indicates that the acceptance of Jesus Christ through a conversion experience is an essential task of Christian education and is the foundation for Christian living. Gaebelein states, "The pupil must be guided toward a crisis in his education that involves repentance, his/her not withholding acceptance of Christ as his/her personal Lord and Savior, his/her obedience, and his/her infilling by the Holy Spirit."[24] Also, Robert Pazmiño argues that the emphasis on evangelism and conversion can be complemented by an emphasis on catechesis and nurture, "Catechesis is instruction that fosters the integration of Christian truth with life. Nurture is the interpersonal sharing among Christians characterized by love and spiritual nourishment that result in the education of the Christian church."[25]

Christian Maturity: Even though conversion plays an important role in the purpose of Christian education, some argue that the primary purpose of evangelical Christian education is Christian maturity.[26] Christian education is concerned with the transformation of the human person into the image and likeness of Christ Jesus. It is through the educational process that lives are being shaped and formed. For example, Lawrence O. Richards in his book, *Theology of Christian Education* (1975), emphasizes the role of the body of Christ as the place where lives are shaped and transformed. Through worship, fellowship, evangelism, and community life, lives are changed. He states, "We must recognize the teacher as a leader especially equipped by God to take the lead in bringing others to Christ's likeness, not as the classroom expert."[27]

Educational Content & Process

The primary source of content is the authoritative message to be given to learners by teachers who are a witness of the divinely given message. The Bible is the major source of content, and Christ is its central theme.[28] As Sara Little states, "Revelation is equated with the Words of the Bible, then the Church can turn to the Bible as an objective authority, and the task of Christian education is to offer biblical instruction."[29] Thus, the Bible is normative for both Christian faith and practice.

> "The primary source of content is the authoritative message to be given to learners by teachers who are a witness to it. The Bible is the major source of content, and Christ is its central theme."
> —Harold Burgess, 168.

Since the Bible is the primary content of Christian education, then it is also the primary subject matter. Evangelicals draw subject matter directly from the Bible, and they deduce the authority of the message from it as well. Thus, evangelicals argue for the term *Christian education* because of what they consider to be its distinct content and subject matter.[30] The Bible is the only authoritative source and it should be at the center of the educational process. However, one of the dangers of placing such a strong emphasis on the Bible as guiding the educational process is that it can lead to a dead orthodoxy, a literalism emphasizing biblical propositions divorced from life.[31] Also, it can result in an educational practice that imposes truths on persons without enabling them to think seriously about these truths. This kind of teaching leads to indoctrination and doesn't provide opportunities for the learner to internalize truth.

Christ is the central theme in Christian education. The centrality of Jesus Christ is taken to be the distinguishing element in the Christian faith. Christ is considered to be the theme, the underlying principle— the heart of the content of education, which enables learners to live as Christians. Gaebelein states that Christ is absolutely central to the educational process, "Its center is a Person, and in a wholly unique sense every Christian is organically united to his Lord. To be a Christian is nothing less than to be 'in Christ' through personal rebirth into the family of the redeemed through faith in the finished work of the Savior."[32] An experience with Christ as personal Lord and Savior will produce a regenerated person and lay the foundation for a Christian life by enabling the learner to conform to God's will and grow toward Christian maturity. Effective Christian education is measured not by the content that is learned, but by the student's acceptance of Jesus Christ as personal Savior and their growth in their relationship with Him.

Role of the Teacher: Since evangelical Christian educators are concerned with communicating the Bible as the primary content and subject of Christian education, they place great stock in the role of the teacher in the educational process. The teachers are the agents that transmit the Christian message, thus they must be selected with great care. Teachers must be models of Christian faith that exemplify a strong Christian witness. Thus, if they are to nurture others in the faith it is imperative that they have a vibrant faith as well. Teachers must be persons of integrity and moral character. They must "practice what they preach" and must be a witness to the message that is proclaimed. Some even argue that the teacher should be "called" to the educational process since he/she is conveying a divinely given message.[33]

The Learner/Student: The role of the learner in evangelical Christian education is deeply rooted in biblical and theological foun-

The learner is viewed as created in the image of God, with the capacity to know and to learn, thus it is important that the Christian educator understand the distinct psychological differences of the learner in order for them to grasp the Christian faith.

dations including both supernatural and natural elements. The supernatural element is that the learner is viewed as being created in the image of God. Learners are spiritual beings, but sinful and in need of redemption. It is through the educational process, as the learner encounters the living Christ, that the image of God is being renewed and restored. Also, the natural or human aspects of being created in the image of God means that the learner has the capacity to know and to learn, thus it is important that the Christian educator understand the distinct psychological differences of the learner in order for him/her to grasp the Christian faith.

Educational Context

Traditionally the primary context for Christian education is the Sunday school. The Sunday school has persisted for more than two hundred years and is the major teaching arm of evangelical churches. Its primary function is to communicate a divinely given message, and to pass on the Christian faith.[34] Also, the Sunday school is a place for evangelism as well as for community development. It continues to be an agency that develops disciples, deepens faith, builds character, and provides awareness of the role of the Church in the world. Sunday school is the longest lasting vital religious movement in American Protestant history.[35]

However, in recent years Sunday school has declined and evangelical congregations have developed a variety of other ministries to meet their educational needs. The development of Vacation Bible School, small groups, Christian camping, retreats, and conferences are alternatives to the traditional Sunday school.

Since many parents can no longer depend on the church to provide adequate Christian education, and because Christian education is not being taught in public schools, evangelicals have looked to other educational alternatives for their children, hence, the emergence of Christian colleges and universities, Bible colleges and seminaries, Christian schools, and home schooling.[36] These educational institutions provide a context for the integration of learning in light of the Christian faith. Therefore, all subject matter and educational experience is to be seen as contributing to the working out of God's creative purposes and the redemption of humanity in Jesus Christ.[37]

The growth of both Christian colleges and the Christian school movement are most evident the last half of the twentieth century. One Christian school organization, the Association of Christian Schools International (ACSI), has over 5,000 member schools from approximately 100 countries with an enrollment of over 1 million students (15.3).[38] ACSI's vision statement states, "Christian school students worldwide will acquire wisdom, knowledge, and a biblical world view as expressed by a lifestyle of character, leadership, service, stewardship, and worship."[39] The Christian school is an extension of the home and the church and therefore partakes in the general goal of making the individual like Christ.[40]

Summary

The emergence and growth of evangelicalism in the last half of the twentieth century had a significant influence on the development of evangelical Christian education. The explosion of Christian colleges and universities, parachurch organizations, professional organizations, and evangelistic efforts provided the context for Christian education to emerge. The distinctive quality of evangelical Christian education, which separates it from liberal religious education and neoorthodox influences reflected in the previous chapter, emphasizes the authority of Bible as central to both the content and process of Christian education. Thus, the primary purpose of Christian education is to transmit a divinely given message as revealed in the Scriptures.

Voices

The emergence of evangelical Christian education in the last half of the twentieth century was accomplished by some very significant voices. These voices proclaimed the heart of evangelical Christian education through their research, writings, and the investment of their lives in others. Below is a representative list of some of the most influential voices in evangelical Christian education.

Clarence Herbert Benson (1887–1954). Benson was very influential in shaping Christian education in the early days of its development. He founded the Evangelical Teacher Training Association (ETTA) in 1931. The organization used his textbook, *Introduction to Child and Sunday School Administration* for training teachers in Bible colleges and seminaries. Benson began teaching and directing the Christian education department at Moody Bible Institute, Chicago, Illinois, in 1924. In 1934, he cofounded Scripture Press to publish his Bible graded series of Sunday school lessons. Benson's writing grew out of the need for textbooks for college classes and lay development which included *The Christian Teacher* and *A Popular History of Christian Education.*[41]

Warren S. Benson (1929–2002). Benson was professor of Christian education at Dallas Theological Seminary for 12 years and professor of Christian education at Trinity Evangelical Seminary for more than 25 years until his retirement in 1998 (15.4). Benson served as president of the North American Professors of Christian Education (NAPCE) from 1986–88, and president of the Professional Association of Christian Educators (PACE). Benson is best known for his leadership in the field of Christian education. He wrote many articles, book reviews, and several books including: *The Complete Book of Youth Ministry* (1987) coauthored with Mark Senter; *Youth Education in the Church* (1986) with Roy Zuck; and *Christian Education: Its History and Philosophy* (1983) with Kenneth O. Gangel. In 2002, NAPCE renamed the Distinguished Christian Educators Award to the Warren S. Benson Distinguished Educators Award in honor of Benson's contribution to the field of Christian education. Benson received this award in 1994.

Charles Burton Eavey (1889–1974). Eavey was professor of Christian education at Wheaton College, Wheaton, Illinois. He is best known for his book, *History of Christian Education* (1964) which became the standard evangelical textbook in colleges and seminaries for many years.[42] His book *Principles of Teaching for Christian Teachers* (1968) was reprinted twenty times and provided many useful constructs derived from the social sciences.[43]

Finley Edge (1916–2002). Edge received his Th.D. from Southern Baptist Seminary, Louisville, Kentucky, in 1945, where he studied under Gaines S. Dobbins. After receiving his doctorate, Edge taught religious education at Southern until his retirement in 1984. Edge's major contributions to Christian education related to the theme of his dissertation, *Religious Education and the Problem of Institutionalism.*[44] He related the development of Christian education to the cycle of institutionalization and was concerned that just as institutions proceed through cycles, so does Christian education. He warned the Southern Baptists to avoid these pitfalls of institutionalism that would rob them of their historical distinctive. He called for a creative, self-evaluating, experience-based system of religious education.[45] Edge continued this theme by calling on Christian education to be involved in church renewal through training and equipping laity as ministers. This concern is most evident in his books, *The Greening of the Church* (1971); *The Doctrine of the Laity* (1985); and his most influential book, *Teaching for Results* (1956), which is still in print. Edge argued in these books that clergy should act as equippers and enablers, emphasizing the call and vocation of laypersons to exercise their gifts within the church.[46]

Frank E. Gaebelein (1899–1983). Gaebelein may well be the most important spokesperson for evangelical Christian education in the latter half of the twentieth century. His major work, *Christian Education in a Democracy* (1956) provided the primary basis of his theological views. He was deeply concerned that the Bible, the inspired Word of God, be the foundation for Christian education. The unfolding of truth through the Scriptures was an important part of his belief system. Also, the heart of Christian education is the communication of biblical truths by teachers who are able to lead learners to an understanding and wholehearted acceptance of these truths.[47]

Gaebelein served as associate editor for *Christianity Today*; General Editor of the *Expositor's Bible Commentary Series*; and was the founding principal of Stony Brook School, Long Island, New York. Through these efforts Gaebelein was concerned about the integration of faith and learning. The Bible was the essential component of a liberal arts education. This is expressed in his most popular book, *The Pattern of God's Truth* (1968), originally published as *Christian Education in a Democracy* (1951). In this work he popularized the phrase, "All truth is God's truth." An education that departs from God and His Word will be always searching for truth and never finding it.[48]

Kenneth O. Gangel (1935–). Gangel has served in a variety of leadership positions including Vice President for academic affairs at

Calvary Bible College; Professor of Christian Education at Trinity Evangelical Divinity School, Deerfield, Illinois; and department chair of Christian Education at Dallas Theological Seminary (❧ 15.5). During the 1970s, Gangel rose to prominence as an articulate and theologically consistent shaper of the evangelical perspective.[49] His major contributions to the field of Christian education have been in the areas of history and philosophy of Christian education. His book, *Christian Education: Its History and Philosophy* (1983), coauthored with Warren Benson, provides a strong theological, philosophical, and historical foundation for evangelical Christian education. Other contributions include Gangel's attention to the importance of Church leadership and administration in Christian education. His books, *Leadership for Christian Education* (1970), *Building Leaders for the Church* (1981), and *The Church Education Handbook* (1985) addressed the issues of developing proper programs in Christian education, and the lack of leadership in local churches.

Donald M. Joy (1928–). Joy was Professor of Human Development and Family Studies at Asbury Theological Seminary in Wilmore, Kentucky, for more than three decades. Joy's primary contribution to Christian education was his emphasis on moral development and the family (❧ 15.6). In *Moral Development Foundations: Judeo-Christian Alternatives to Piaget/Kohlberg* (1983), Joy provides a critique of modern approaches to human development and establishes alternatives from a Christian perspective. Joy's scholarship stretched beyond evangelical circles to include a broader ecumenical influence. He was able to wrestle with issues of evangelical faith along with findings from the social sciences. Joy is well known for his speaking and writing on issues of human development, family, relationships, human sexuality, and parenting. His most significant books include: *Bonding: Relationships in the Image of God* (1985); *Lovers: What Ever Happened to Eden?* (1987); *Risk-Proofing Your Family* (1995); *Re-Bonding: Preventing and Restoring Damaged Relationships* (1997); and *Empowering Your Kids to Be Adults* (2001). In 1999, Joy was acknowledged for his contribution to the field of Christian education by receiving the Distinguished Christian Educator award from NAPCE.

Lois LeBar (1907–). LeBar is considered among the major contributors to the renewal of evangelical Christian education. Her long tenure as Professor of Christian education at Wheaton College in Wheaton, Illinois, from 1946 to 1975 provided a powerful platform to influence the evangelical Sunday school movement.[50] Prior to this she taught at Moody Bible Institute. While at Moody in the 1930s there was no consensus among evangelicals as to the philosophical basis for Christian education. LeBar, who had been an elementary school teacher, believed that teaching methods should derive from the Bible not from secular theory. She assigned her students passages in the Scriptures to search for principles. Her subsequent writings derived from this work. She believes that learning is an inner, active, continuous, disciplined process. Christian education is not rote memorization of facts but a leading of students to discover God's ways of working in Scripture.[51] The Bible is not the end of education, but the means of changing life. Within this framework of truth the Spirit works creatively with the human teachers to meet the particular needs of students where they are. Her teaching theory was Christ centered and emphasized inner growth.[52] LeBar's most influential and enduring book, *Education That Is Christian* (1958), is still available in print.[53]

Robert Pazmiño (1948–). Pazmiño received his doctorate in Education from the Teacher's College of Columbia University and Union Theological Seminary in New York. He joined the faculty at Andover-Newton Theological School, New Centre, Massachusetts, as professor of Christian education in 1986. As an ordained Baptist minister, his research focuses on diversity in Christian education, with particular attention given to multiculturalism. He views himself as an "ecumenical evangelical" who writes from the perspective of a bicultural Hispanic North American.[54] His book, *Foundational Issues in Christian Education* (1988), is a widely used textbook in Christian education that affirms the authority of the Bible as the groundwork for a version of Christian education that is responsive to the Christian heritage, to changing cultures, and to proven educational theories.[55] His books include: *Principles and Practices of Christian Education* (1992); *By What Authority Do We Teach?* (1994); *Basics of Teaching for Christians* (1998); and his most recent work, *God Our Teacher: Theological Basics in Christian Education* (2001).

Lawrence (Larry) O. Richards (1931–). Larry Richards has been a creative and wide-ranging contributor to Christian education for nearly three decades.[56] Richards has taught Christian education at Wheaton College; was editor of Nursery Curriculum for Scripture Press; associate pastor at Wheaton Bible Church, Wheaton, Illinois; and founder of Renewal Research Associates, which developed the innovative *Sunday School Plus* materials. Richard's primary contribution to the field of Christian education is expressed in his book, *A Theology of Christian Education* (1975), which was republished in 1988 as *Christian Education: Seeking to Become Like Jesus Christ*. In his book, Richards is critical of formal education in congregations and advocates nonformal approaches to Christian education. He challenges churches to open up their traditional programs to new patterns of community, group life, leadership, social concerns, and the home as the primary place of Christian nurture. He accuses evangelicals of seeing the Word as information only.[57] He argues that the goal is to be responsive to the One who speaks in the Word. Faith should effect a change in people. His writings were influenced by social learning theory and adolescent psychology. He encourages a socialization model of Christian education and sees the Christian educator as the designer of church life.[58] Richards has written extensively in the field of Christian education. His books include: *Children's Ministry* (1988), *Youth Ministry* (1991), *It Couldn't Just Happen: Fascinating Facts about God's World* (1994), and *Creative Bible Teaching* (1998).

Ted W. Ward (1930–). Ted was born in Punxsutawney, Pennsylvania, and reared in Avon Park, Florida (15.7). Ted is a graduate of Wheaton College (1951) and holds a Doctor of Education degree from the University of Florida (1956). After teaching from 1951–1956 as an Assistant Professor at the University of Florida, he accepted a teaching position at Michigan State University in Education and Curriculum Research in 1956. He spent the next 30 years teaching in a wide variety of areas including moral development, teacher training, curriculum instruction, and research in education. Ted's influence is best seen through the development of his doctoral students who serve in universities, seminaries, and Christian colleges. Ted is an educator of educators. Ted is well known in the Evangelical community for his work in education in Third World countries. Over a 100 missions professors and executives, and Christian education leaders did doctoral work with him. His contributions in Third World education include nonformal education and involvement in the production of the *World Dictionary of Mission Related Educational Institutions* (1968). He was very influential in the early years of the Theological Education by Extension movement from 1967–1976. In 1995, Ted continued his last year of teaching at Michigan State University and began teaching at Trinity Evangelical Seminary as Professor of Christian Education and Mission and Dean of International Studies, Mission, and Education. He was named Aldeen Professor of Missions Education, and International Studies. At Trinity, Ted continued to impact future missionary and church leaders by developing research doctorates in Education and Intercultural Studies. He officially retired in 1994, but continued an active teaching role until 1999.

Spanning more than fifty years, Ted Ward has served the field of professional education as teacher, administrator, innovator, researcher, educator of educators, and consultant to institutions and government ministries of education. He has been published widely and his writings contributed extensively to formal and nonformal education. Ted's major recognitions have included Dag Hammer-skjöld, *Citation for Service in Developing Nations*, Uppsala, Sweden (1975); *Faculty and Alumni Award for Service*, College of Education, Michigan State University (1986); Establishment of *The Ted W. Ward Consultation on Education and Intercultural Studies*, Trinity Evangelical Divinity School (1995); *Lifetime Service Award*, NAPCE (1996). Ted Ward's life and career continues to be grounded in a passion for service and justice and in the development of people.[59]

Other Approaches to Christian Education from 1951–2000

Even though evangelical Christian education dominated much of the twentieth century, there was a broad range of theological influences and approaches influencing religious education. As the dominance of theological neoorthodoxy ended in the 1960s, a wide range of theological influences became prominent. With the emergence of diverse theological views came a variety of approaches to religious education. Sara Little describes this period of religious education as a time of critical reflection in Protestant religious education, a time in which "there is no one clue, no dominate theory . . . but a spectrum of theories and divergent interests."[60] Jack Seymour and Donald Miller provide five primary metaphors to describe a variety of theological approaches in the field of Christian education in their book, *Theological Approaches to Christian Education* (1990). These five metaphors include: religious instruction, community of faith, development, liberation, and interpretation. These metaphors provide an example of the diverse approaches to religious education.[61]

The last part of this chapter highlights a variety of diverse approaches and their influence on religious education. These approaches are not inclusive to the field of religious education, but are very influential in shaping Christian education in the last half of the twentieth century. They include the following approaches: James Fowler's faith development theory; James Michael Lee's Social-Science Approach; Liberation approaches developed from Paulo Freire's critical pedagogy; and Thomas Groome's "shared praxis" approach to Christian education.[62]

Faith Development Theory

James Wiley Fowler received his Ph.D. from Harvard University in 1971 (🔍 15.8). After his graduation, he taught applied theology and directed a research project on faith and moral development at Harvard Divinity School. In 1976, he became professor of theology and human development at Boston College and in 1977 became professor and director of the Center of Faith Development at the Candler School of Theology of Emory University in Atlanta, Georgia.[63]

Fowler's most influential book, *Stages of Faith* (1982), provides a faith development theory that included sequential and ordered movement of individuals through clearly defined stages that become increasingly complex. Fowler's theory suggests that a

> James Fowler's faith development theory suggests that persons move through predictable stages in order to reach maturity in faith.

person moves toward the goal of full maturation through his interaction with the environment. Fowler builds his scheme on Jean Piaget's theory of cognitive development and Lawrence Kohlberg's theory of moral development. These developmental theories provide predictable stages that persons can move through at different points in their development.

Fowler's faith development theory provides an ordered process of growth in individuals from a mythical and literal form of faith in childhood to an acceptance of church doctrine in adolescence to the development of personal and mature faith in adult-hood.[64] Fowler proposed that faith development be understood in seven stages: (1) Undifferentiated Faith (Infancy); (2) Intuitive-Projective Faith; (3) Mythical-Literal Faith (early childhood); (4) Synthetic-Conventional Faith (adolescent); (5) Individuative-Reflective Faith (Young Adulthood); (6) Conjunctive Faith (mid-life and beyond); and (7) Universalizing Faith.[65] Fowler's view of faith was influenced by the theologies of Paul Tillich and Richard Niebuhr. Faith was viewed as a universal factor in human experience that transcends religion and dogma. A person's faith and growth in faith can be outlined in developmental stages just as cognitive, moral, and psychosocial stages are identified.

Fowler argued that faith development is a lifelong process and religious education should continue throughout life. He suggested that if people reflected on their faith development, it could be a valu-able learning process. Fowler admonished religious educators not to go beyond the learner but to work within the limits of an individual's faith development. As Elias states, "Since faith development is close-ly related to other aspects of human development, education in other domains can aid in growth in faith."[66] Finally, faith development the-ory makes clear that transitions in faith often involve disruption, pain, confusion, and a sense of loss.[67]

Faith development theory has not gone without criticism in the field of religious education. Critics have indicated that the theo-ry is culturally biased, gender specific, and doesn't address regres-sion of faith or repudiation of faith.[68] And to many practitioners and observers the concept of developmental theory doesn't do justice to the Christian concept of conversion. Even amidst such criticism, the theory has a prominent place in the field of Christian education.

Social-Science Approach

The social-science approach to religious education is developed in a systematic way in the writings of James Michael Lee, a Roman Catholic religious educator. Lee's social-science approach focused pri-marily on the teaching-learning act, or religious instruction. He decid-ed to elaborate on the theory and practice of the art of religion teach-ing from a scientific framework. He intended to help teachers and learners to be successful in the teaching-learning act of religious instruction. He developed a macrotheory to deal adequately with a wide range of religious instruction theory and practice. The macrotheory of religious instruction was offered in a massive three-volume trilogy: *The Shape of Religious Instruction* (1971), *The Flow of Religious Instruction* (1973), and *The Content of Religious Instruction* (1984).

Lee's macrotheory of religious instruction provided a scientific approach to religious instruction and rejects the notion that theology can provide an adequate theory for religious instruction.[69] In his rejection of theology, religious education is not subject to theology. Rather, religious instruction is a separate and independent field.[70] Lee is arguing that religious learning isn't any different from any other form of learning, so religious instruction uses the same theories, laws, concepts, and procedures which apply to all general laws of instruction.

Harold Burgess, a student of James Michael Lee, provides a summary of Lee's theory:

> The social science model is properly set apart from the theological models of religious education in that it considers the findings of the social sciences as normative for instructional decisions. This viewpoint enables the body of empirically validated facts and laws pertaining to the teaching-learning act to play a central role in religious instructional decisions. The model assumes that a learner's religious behavior is learned in essentially the same way as any other human behavior. Accordingly, a heavy responsibility falls upon the teacher, as a professional, to be in command of relevant religious and educational variables.[71]

Lee's social-science approach to religious education is limited in its approach to religious instruction. Because it denies any subjective aspects of religious instruction such as revelation, the role of the Holy Spirit, and the student-teacher relationship it has not been well accepted by many Christian educators. Because his theory places the focus on the role of the teacher to provide relevant educational variables, some religious educators believe that his approach leads to a form of behavioralism.[72] Others reject his theory because of his denial of theology as normative for religious instruction.[73] For them, Lee is rejecting the heart of religious instruction. Regardless of the criticism, Lee's social-science theory of religious instruction is a major contribution to the field of religious education.

Liberation Approaches

Another key influence on religious education in the last half of the twentieth century was the writings of Brazilian educational philosopher, Paulo Freire (❀ 15.9). Freire was born in Recife, Brazil, to a middle-class family. Due to the Great Depression Freire's family became very poor. Freire was educated at the University of Recife where he received his Ph.D. in 1959. He was influenced by Karl Marx's writings on alienation as well as his own experiences as a hungry child and working with the poor.[74] Freire concluded that education should awaken oppressed persons to their plight and help them find ways to free themselves.

Freire's liberation theology expressed a deep concern for social injustice and social liberation. His classic book, *Pedagogy of the Oppressed* (1973) criticized what he called the "banking" method of education in which the teacher was set above the student as professor of knowledge the student needed but did not have. Freire was concerned that student and teacher function as both student and teacher. He viewed education as a means of power and influence on others and believed that everyone should have the right to learn. Religious educators follow Freire's concern for social justice by developing explicit social and political approaches in religious education. Such religious educators as Allan Moore, William Kennedy, and Daniel Schipani have identified and used liberation approaches in their views of religious education. In some ways, these religious educators are going back to a liberal religious education because of their emphasis on experience.[75]

The liberationist approach to religious education aligns and couples the social experiences of learners and social analysis of oppressive structures to liberation theology and appropriate learning strategies.[76] As Elias states,

> In doing this, religious educators desire to raise the learners' consciousness of social injustices and to motivate them to participate in the struggle for injustice and social transformation. For example, Allan Moore[77] has proposed a liberating education appropriate for churches in North America. He grounds this education in a reflection on the actual experiences of oppression that people have endured. For him this education entails a critical reflection on praxis that is sensi-

tive to forms of human injustice, discrimination, sexism, and racism. Thus, a Christian vision of a just society should be the basis of any reflection on social situations.[78]

The liberationist approach to religious education has received much of the same kind of criticism as liberal religious education described in chapter 14. The primary criticism is that it blurs the distinction between education and political action.[79] Others criticize it for emphasizing social reconstruction rather than personal conversion.

Shared Praxis Approach

Thomas Groome was born and raised in Ireland to a Roman Catholic family (✪ 15.10). He received his Ph.D. from the Teacher's College of Columbia University and Union Theological Seminary in New York in 1976. He taught theology and religious education at Catholic University of America in 1975 and took his present position as professor of theology and religious education at Boston College in 1976. Groome's educational philosophy was influenced by Jürgen Habermas and Paulo Freire. He rejected their prevailing educational philosophies as giving too little place to the student's lived experience. He deemed the socialization approach of Westerhoff inadequate, because it held within it the interest of maintaining the status quo. And, Groome regarded the social science approach of James Michael Lee as controlling and manipulative.[80] After rejecting these other approaches to religious education, he developed his own approach to religious education called, the "shared praxis" approach.

Groome's most significant contribution to Christian education has been his "shared praxis" approach to Christian education as defined in his book, *Christian Religious Education: Sharing Our Story and Vision* (1980). He defines his "shared praxis" approach as a "group of Christians sharing in dialogue their critical reflection on present action in light of the Christian story and its vision toward the end of lived Christian faith."[81] For Groome, "story" means Scripture and tradition; "vision" is God's vision for creation; and "the kingdom of God" is the realization of God's reign characterized by justice and liberation. Groome's pedagogy is based on a process view of revelation. God continues to reveal himself to us in our present. Therefore, we must be "in touch" with both past and present revelation. Groome's shared praxis is a form of experiential education influenced by the Hebrew call to "know" as well as Groome's understanding of the nature of faith, faith development (he relies on Fowler at this point), and the need of persons for freedom and empowerment. Here he relies on Paulo Freire.[82] Groome describes shared praxis in terms of molding six components (present action, critical reflection, dialogue, the "story," the "vision," and present dialectical hermeneutics) into five movements:

- *Naming Present Action*—in which participants describe what they do corporately and individually as the faith community in reaction to the lesson content.

- *The Participant's Story and Visions*—in which the participants begin to critically reflect on what led to the "present action" and what was expected to come of it.

- *The Christian Community Story and Vision*—in which Groome would rely on Scripture, tradition, and history communicated through a variety of possible media and urge the participants toward growth and change or maturity in Christian faith.

- *Dialectical Hermeneutic between the Story and Participant's Story*—in which participants can discover how their stories compare to, contrast with, rise out of, and are part of the Story of the Christian faith community.

- *Dialectical Hermeneutic between the Vision and the Participant's Vision*—participants are challenged to discover ways in which their hopes and future actions can be a part of or *are* a part of the hope and future actions of the Christian faith community and will, indeed, be a part of the birthing of that community.[83]

Like all new theories of Christian education, Groome's theory has received a variety of criticism. However, his work has inspired a great deal of interest and has developed a significant theory of Christian education that cannot go without investigation and dialogue. As stated by Reed and Prevost, "perhaps Groome's most lasting contribution to Christian education will be in the pattern he sets for developing his own approach to Christian education."[84]

What Can We Learn from Christian Education Since 1950?

- Evangelicalism refers not only to Christians believing the same doctrine, but its meaning includes a self-conscious interdenominational movement, with leaders, publications, and institutions with which people from many subgroups identify.

- Evangelical Christian education emerged in the 1930s with the establishment of the Evangelical Teacher Training Association (ETTA).

- The National Association of Evangelicals (NAE) was established to maintain the doctrines of historic Protestantism.

- Frank Gaebelein provided a theological foundation for evangelical Christian education that separated it from neoorthodoxy influences.

- The primary teaching task of evangelical Christian education is to transmit a divinely given message to learners.

- Conversion and Christian maturity are two primary purposes of evangelical Christian education.

- The Bible is the major source of content, and Christ is the central theme in evangelical Christian education.

- The historic educational context for evangelical Christian education is the Sunday school.

- Christian colleges and universities, Bible colleges, theological seminaries, and Christian schools provide a context for integration of learning in light of the Christian faith.

- James Fowler's faith development theory suggests that persons move through stages in order to reach maturity in faith.

- James Michael Lee developed the social-science approach to religious instruction and rejected theology as wholly adequate for religious education.

- Liberation approaches to religious education desire to raise the learner's consciousness of social injustices to motivate the learner to participate in social transformation.

- Thomas Groome developed the theory of a "shared-praxis" approach to religious education.

Study Helps

Reflection Questions

1. What are the strengths and weaknesses of Evangelicalism as a movement?

2. In what ways is evangelical Christian education different from liberal religious education described in chapter 14?

3. What makes evangelical theology different from neoorthodox theology?

4. Why did evangelical Christian education emerge in the last half of the twentieth century?

5. What are the primary purposes of evangelical Christian education?

6. What is the role of the teacher in evangelical Christian education?

7. What are the strengths and weaknesses of James Fowler's faith development theory as it relates to Christian education?

8. In what ways is James Michael Lee's social-science approach critiqued?

9. What can evangelical Christian education learn from Paul Freire's emphasis on social injustice and social transformation?

10. What are the implications of Thomas Groome's "shared-praxis" approach to Christian education?

Technical Terms

Christian Religious Education	It is a term used to identify the process whereby Christian learning occurs. Broadly speaking, it is the adoption and deepening of Christian beliefs, attitudes, values, and dispositions to experience and act in a Christian way. The term is used to identify both evangelism and Christian nurture within the context of religious education.[85]
Dialectical Hermeneutic	Dialect is used in religious education to refer to the type of hermeneutics (interpretations) that exists between "the faith handed down" and present lived experience. A dialectical hermeneutic means that learners are to come to see for themselves how the tradition affirms, questions, and calls one beyond present faith practice, even as the tradition is itself reinterpreted in light of contemporary experience.[86]

Evangelical Christian Education

A term used to describe Christian education within the context of Evangelicalism. The purpose is to communicate the divinely ordained message as revealed in the Bible as normative for faith and practice.

Evangelicalism

Designates a distinct movement that emphasizes the authority of Scriptures and the proclamation of the gospel. Evangelicals typically endorse doctrinal formations common to orthodox Christianity, placing particular stress upon the importance of personal salvation through Jesus Christ.

Liberal Religious Education

It is a practical expression of liberal theology. The classroom in the local church is where the kingdom of God begins, because children who are physically and intellectually changing may be most effectively exposed to the possibilities of changing the world for a better tomorrow.[87]

Liberation Theology

It stressed divine fatherhood and human brotherhood rather than transcendence and majesty of God, portraying God as immanent in the world and permeating every part of human life. It seeks to relate the message of salvation to society, to economic life, and social institutions as well as to individuals.[88] Liberation Theology is concerned with liberating the impoverished and oppressed.

Protestantism

The name given to all Christian denominations, sects, or groups, rising out of the Reformation. Protestant churches generally agree that the principle of authority should be Scriptures rather than the Church or the pope.[89]

Shared Praxis Approach

Christian religious education by shared praxis can be described as a group of Christians sharing in dialogue their critical reflection on present action in light of the Christian story and its Vision toward the end of lived Christian Life.[90]

Social-Science Approach

The social science model, developed by James Michael Lee, considers the findings of the social sciences as normative for instruction. This viewpoint enables the body of empirically validated facts and laws pertaining to the teaching-learning act to play a central role in religious instructional decisions.

Recommended Bibliography

Anthony, Michael. *Introduction to Christian Education*. Grand Rapids: Baker, 2001.

_____, ed. *The Evangelical Dictionary of Christian Education*. Grand Rapids: Baker, 2001.

Burgess, Harold W. *Models of Religious Education*. Nappanee, IN: Evangel, 2001.

Downs, Perry G. *Teaching for Spiritual Growth*. Grand Rapids: Zondervan, 1994.

Eavey, Charles B. *History of Christian Education*. Chicago: Moody Press, 1964.

Elias, John A. *History of Christian Education: Protestant, Catholic, and Orthodox Perspective*. Malabar, FL: Krieger, 2002.

Fowler, James W. *Stages of Faith: The Psychology of Human Development and the Quest for Meaning*. San Francisco: Harper and Row, 1981.

Freire, Paulo. *Pedagogy of the Oppressed*. New York: Seabury, 1973.

Gangel, Kenneth O., and Warren S. Benson. *Christian Education: Its History and Philosophy*. Chicago: Moody Press, 1983.

Groome, Thomas. *Christian Religious Education: Sharing our Story and Vision*. San Francisco: Harper & Collins, 1980.

Kathan, Boardman W. "Pioneers of Religious Education in the 20th Century." *Religious Education* (Sept.-Oct. 1978) Special Edition.

LeBar, Lois. *Education That Is Christian*. Wheaton: Victor Books, 1989.

Little, Sara. *To Set One's Heart: Belief and Teaching in the Church*. Atlanta: John Knox Press, 1983.

Mayr, Marlene. *Modern Masters of Religious Education*. Birmingham, AL: Religious Education Press, 1983.

Pazmiño, Robert W. *Foundational Issues in Christian Education: An Introduction to Evangelical Perspective*. Grand Rapids: Baker, 1999.

Reed, James E., and Ronnie Prevost. *A History of Christian Education*. Nashville: Broadman and Holman, 1993.

Seymour, Jack L., and Donald E. Miller. *Theological Approaches to Christian Education*. Nashville: Abingdon Press, 1990.

Thompson, Norma H., ed. *Religious Education and Theology*. Birmingham, AL: Religious Education Press, 1982.

Notes

[1] Harold W. Burgess, *Models of Religious Education* (Wheaton, IL: Victor Books, 2001), 149.

[2] John A. Elias, *History of Christian Education: Protestant, Catholic, and Orthodox Perspective* (Malabar, FL: Krieger, 2002), 181–182.

[3] George M. Marsden, *Understanding Fundamentalism and Evangelicalism* (Grand Rapids: Eerdmans, 1991), 5.

[4] Ibid.

[5] Burgess, *Models,* 149.

[6] Ibid.

[7] D. Campbell Wyckoff, "Theology and Education in the Twentieth Century," *Christian Education Journal* 25,3 (1995): 19.

[8] Frank E. Gaebelein, *Christian Education in a Democracy* (New York: Oxford University Press, 1951), 15–16.

[9] Ibid.

[10] Burgess, *Models,* 150.

[11] Ibid., 152.

[12] See NAPCE web site at **www.napce.org**, "An Historical Perspective on NAPCE" by Eileen Starr.

[13] The purpose statement is given on the copyright page of each issue of the journal.

[14] Gabriel Fackre, "Evangelicalism," in *Harper's Encyclopedia of Religious Education,* ed. by Iris V. Cully and Kendig Brubaker Cully (San Francisco: Harper and Row, 1990), 235. Also, see National Association of Evangelical web site at **www.nae.net**.

[15] Elias, *History,* 181–182.

[16] Ibid., 182.

[17] Gaebelein, *Christian Education,* 259.

[18] Burgess, *Models,* 162

[19] Elias, *History,* 182.

[20] Burgess, *Models,* 164.

[21] Ibid., 165.

[22] Perry G. Downs, *Teaching for Spiritual Growth* (Grand Rapids: Zondervan, 1994), 15.

[23] Ibid.

[24] Gaebelein, *Christian Education,* 229.

[25] Robert W. Pazmiño, *Foundational Issues in Christian Education* (Grand Rapids: Baker, 1997), 57.

[26] The author argues that this is the primary purpose of Christian education, even though conversion has a significant place in the aims of Christian education. The author provides the following definition, "Christian Education is the ministry of

bringing the believer to maturity in Jesus Christ." See Perry G. Downs, *Teaching for Spiritual Growth: An Introduction to Christian Education* (Grand Rapids: Zondervan, 1999), 16-17.

[27] Lawrence O. Richards, *A Theology of Christian Education* (Grand Rapids: Zondervan, 1975), 312-315.

[28] Burgess, *Models*, 168.

[29] Sara Little, *To Set One's Heart: Belief and Teaching in the Church* (Atlanta: John Knox Press, 1983), 24-25.

[30] Burgess, *Models*, 168.

[31] Pazmiño, *Foundational*, 57.

[32] Gaebelein, *Christian Education*, 25.

[33] This view is supported by Gaebelein.

[34] Doris Cox Borchert, "Sunday School," in *Harper's Encyclopedia of Religious Education*, ed. by Iris V. Cully and Kendig Brubaker Cully (San Francisco: Harper and Row, 1990), 623-624.

[35] Ibid., 624,

[36] Wyckoff, "Theology," 20.

[37] Ibid.

[38] See Association of Christian School International (ACSI) web site at **www.acsi.org**.

[39] See **www.acsi.org**, Vision statement.

[40] Warren Benson and Kenneth Gangel, *Christian Education: Its History and Philosophy* (Chicago: Moody Press, 1983), 356-357.

[41] Lin Johnson, "Clarence Herbert Benson," in *The Evangelical Dictionary of Christian Education*, ed. by Michael Anthony (Grand Rapids: Baker, 2001), 70-71.

[42] Burgess, *Models*, 155.

[43] Ibid.

[44] James E Reed and Ronnie Prevost, *A History of Christian Education* (Nashville: Broadman and Holman, 1993), 350.

[45] Ibid., 350-351.

[46] Ibid., 351.

[47] Burgess, *Models*, 154.

[48] Linda Cannel, "Summaries of Historical Periods," Class Handout (Trinity Evangelical Divinity School, 2000), 58.

[49] Burgess, *Models*, 156.

[50] Ibid., 154.

[51] Cannel, "Summaries," 52.

[52] Ibid.

[53] Lois LeBar, *Education That Is Christian* (Wheaton, IL: Victor Books, 1995).

[54] Burgess, *Models*, 159.

[55] Ibid.

[56] Ibid., 157.

[57] Cannel, "Summaries," 56.

[58] Ibid.

[59] Biographical information taken from "An Outline of Ted W. Ward Life and Career" at http://www.wardconsultation.org/Ted%20pages/Ted2.htm.

[60] Sara Little, "Theology and Education," in *Harper's Encyclopedia of Religious Education*, ed. by Iris V. Cully and Kendig Brubaker Cully (San Francisco: Harper and Row, 1990), 652.

[61] Seymour and Miller's 1990 text is an update of the original text, *Contemporary Approaches to Christian Education* (Nashville: Abingdon, 1982).

[62] John Elias proposes the following categories: Faith Community or Socialization Approaches; Faith Development Theory; Liberation Approaches.

[63] Reed and Prevost, *History*, 359.

[64] Elias, *History*, 178-179.

[65] James W. Fowler, *Stages of Faith: The Psychology of Human Development and the Quest for Meaning* (San Francisco: Harper and Row, 1981), 113ff.

[66] Elias, *History*, 179.

[67] Ibid.

[68] Ibid.

[69] See James Michael Lee, "The Authentic Source of Religious Instruction," in *Religious Education and Theology*, ed. by Norma H. Thompson (Birmingham, AL: Religious Education Press, 1982), 100-197. In this article Lee attacks religious educators who hold theology as normative for religious theory and practice.

[70] Burgess, *Models*, 189.

[71] Ibid., 221.

[72] Didier J. Piveteau and James T. Dillon, "Two Scholarly Views on Religious Education: Lee and Westerhoff," *Lemen Vitae* 32,1 (1997): 22.

[73] Lee, "Authentic," 100-197.

[74] Reed and Prevost, *History*, 354-355.

[75] Elias, *History*, 180.

[76] Ibid., 180-181.

[77] Allan Moore, "Liberation and the Future of Christian Education," in *Contemporary Approaches: Christian Education*, ed. by Jack Seymour and Donald Miller (Nashville: Abingdon Press, 1982).

[78] Elias, *History*, 180.

[79] Ibid., 181.

[80] Cannel, "Summaries," 56-57.

[81] Thomas H. Groome, *Christian Religious Education: Sharing Our Story and Vision* (San Francisco: Harper and Row, 1980), 25.

[82] Reed and Prevost, *History*, 361.

[83] Groome, *Christian*, 207-223. List taken from Reed and Prevost, *History*, 361.

[84] Reed and Prevost, *History*, 361.

[85] For a complete discussion on the term "Christian Religious Education" see Jeff Astley, *The Philosophy of Christian Religious Education* (Birmingham, AL: Religious Education Press, 1994), 9-12.

[86] Thomas H. Groome, "Dialectic(s)," in *Harper's Encyclopedia of Religious Education*, ed. by Iris V. Cully and Kendig Brubaker Cully (San Francisco: Harper and Row, 1990), 188.

[87] Wayne R. Rood, "Liberalism," in *Harper's Encyclopedia of Religious Education*, ed. by Iris V. Cully and Kendig Brubaker Cully (San Francisco: Harper and Row, 1990), 378-379.

[88] Ibid., 379.

[89] William L. Reese, *Dictionary of Philosophy and Religion* (Amherst, NY: Humanity Books, 1999), 614.

[90] Groome, "Dialectic(s)," 184.

Chapter 16
Christian Education in Our Millennium

Jonathan H. Kim

Chapter Overview

The new millennium has begun. The world has entered an era of change that is unprecedented in the history of humankind. Already, the force of the millennium is causing a widespread dislodgment of long-established traditions, beliefs, ideologies, and institutions. What is amazing is how enormous and rapid these changes are. What used to take years now happens in a matter of hours. What was once considered valuable becomes seemingly worthless in a blink of an eye. Long-held traditions are forgotten overnight. Century old institutions which once stood with pride and dignity suddenly collapse and disappear. Changes are taking place at an ever increasing pace.

With the arrival of the new millennium came unprecedented challenges to the church and ministry. Although Christian educators are seeking for ways to improve educational ministry and proposing a number of ways to address and respond to the challenges, such initiatives are still too unformed. Added to the complexity are the serious and pervasive effects of postmodernism, globalism, and technological advancement which the church is still trying to assess. Conducting a comprehensive review and analysis of the millennial issues affecting the church and its educational ministry is timely, necessary, and valuable.

Given the complexity and magnitude of the challenges posed by the new millennium, this chapter offers a descriptive analysis of the issues affecting the purpose, context, content, process (or method-ology), and voices (or who teaches under what authorities) of Christian education. The chapter is not meant to introduce a new philosophy of Christian education, rather to offer a limited progno-sis of the future of Christian education.

Purpose of Education

As has become increasingly clear, the third millennium has brought many unanticipated challenges to the overall purpose (or direction) of Christian education. While the challenges were inevitable, developing a clear vision to improve educational ministry in the new millennium entails much consideration and labor. To do this requires effort to think outside of the traditional box and critically reexamine millennial issues affecting the purpose (or direction) of current min-istry so that creative and innovative ideas can arise. Such an effort will add more value to the overall ministry of Christian education.

A key to success in 21st-century Christian education lies in the church's ability to provide a truth-based vision for the future. As long as the direction of Christian education is guided by the truth, there will be continual progress and improvement. Educators must culti-vate students with principles grounded in the timeless truth and pro-viding necessary skills to appropriate knowledge intelligibly and crit-ically. In order to do this, educators have to re-authenticate the truth-value of the Scriptures, and help students comprehend the Bible as the metatruth (or the highest truth). This begins with developing a personal passion for the eternal Logos, namely Christ Jesus, who is the source of all truths and through whom all other truths are judged and validated. Such education will help both teachers and students achieve the integrated, holistic selves of intelligibility and spirituality taught in the Bible. Providing a truth-based vision that is philosoph-ically and methodologically pertinent in the culture of the new mil-lennium is the first step toward successful Christian education.

Educational Content

If we could name one of the millennial forces that represents the ideological shift in the world, it is pluralism. The force of plural-ism combined with millennial fever is ubiquitously challenging the long-established, epistemological foundation of Christian education.

For us, pluralism poses a unique challenge to what should be taught in Christian education since it allows the expression of all ideas and beliefs without authenticating their validity and reliability. In determining the principal content of a new millennial curriculum, reflecting on the epistemological basis of Christian education is necessary since teaching by definition represents the task of transmitting the content of truth. This requires resolving the complex debate regarding the relation between Christian education and the social sciences.

For decades, the debate on the relation between the social sciences and theology has persisted, and produced an integrated perspective on Christian education. A variety of themes and issues have been discussed; many suggested ways to outline the content of Christian education. Those with a social-science persuasion approached Christian education as a subset of education, placing it within a realm of sociology or psychology. Their assertion was complementary in nature where the content of instruction was drawn from both secular and sacred sources which indirectly implied the equal stance of theology and the social sciences. The complementary view to some audiences is understood as a legitimate form of integration while others see it as a form of secularization that undermines the authority of the Bible in Christian education. In any case, whether we agree with the proponents of the social sciences or not, the complementarian view continues to inform and shape the way Christian education is carried out today.

On the other hand, those with a theological persuasion contended Christian education was a primary branch of church ministry and emphasized the Scriptures as the primary text to be taught in Christian education. The proponents of this view asserted the transmission of the Scriptures and Christian beliefs as the chief function of Christian education. Often, integrating the content of the social sciences is discouraged, and a major emphasis is placed on teaching the Bible. Such a perspective rests on a traditional view where the sacred text is seen as the precursor to all other texts, hence incorporating other texts is considered a form of secularization. Their goal is to train students to learn and think theologically and biblically. To some, the traditional view is seen as Christians' reaction against the church's over reliance on the social sciences (as is the case with many megachurches), while others see it as a legitimate position that Christians should hold since the principal function of Christian education is the instruction of the Bible.

Whether Christian education is seen as a subset of education or church ministry, the critical issue here is understanding the role of the Scriptures in instruction. If the Scriptures are perceived as the metatruth (or the highest truth), then they should play a central role in religious instruction and be used as a primary basis to judge and validate the authenticity and reliability of other texts used in teaching. Such a process involves the understanding and appropriate use of theology and philosophy involving critical analysis, reflection, and integration. Having this type of teaching will help students develop biblical awareness essential in learning the Scriptures as logically coherent, semantically relevant, and educationally satisfying.

Knowledge and Christian Education

As we continue our reflection on millennial issues regarding the content of Christian education, it is important to remind ourselves of the problems associated with the startling biblical illiteracy of today's believers.[1] Allow me to express my concern on the issue since the success of Christian education depends largely on the intellectual landscape and (biblically informed) knowledge base of believers.

Contemporary people are experiencing the ever-expanding knowledge-base of education, which, in my opinion, was influenced by an increasing societal movement toward higher education and a significant explosion of knowledge in the era of information technology. However, despite this extraordinary movement toward knowledge, there is a tendency among Christians to downplay knowledge as if knowledge and faith are two separate matters in life. While the demand for a deeper and broader knowledge-base is increasing in the world, Christians are becoming intellectually challenged. How do we know this? The readership of the Bible is declining, and, even worse, churches are resisting content-based teaching. In an effort to build a seeker-friendly ministry, churches are compromising their educational standards; less and less emphasis is placed on the content of faith. If the trend continues, the average Christian may have a very limited knowledge of the Bible in a very short time.

What an irony. Shouldn't the church become more sophisticated and expect much knowledge to maintain its intellectual distinctiveness? When the secular community is looking to deepen its knowledge base to increase its propensity to better social welfare, shouldn't Christians seek to deepen their understanding of the Bible and move toward a more dynamic spiritual life? Christian educators' responsibility in the 21st century is crucial. As ministers of the Bible, we must battle the superficiality of faith and reverse the declining readership of the Bible. The answer to this dilemma lies within Christian educators' ability to exegete and communicate the content and meaning of the Scriptures effectively in a culturally relevant way.

Educational Contexts

Perhaps the greatest challenge facing Christian education in the third millennium is responding to the changing culture. As many have already felt the impact of the third millennium, it is profitable to comprehend cultural issues affecting the theory and practice of Christian education. By doing this, we will have an opportunity to improve the overall direction of our ministry. Let's consider two contextual issues that need our attention—multiculturalism and globalism.

Multiculturalism. In the third millennium, what came to distinguish our society from others is multiculturalism. Various cultural ideologies now constitute the American culture.[2] Unlike centuries before, the composition of the American society including that of Christians is becoming very diverse. Several times a day, a person encounters people of different cultures and ethnicities, and even of different religions. This increasing diversity is not only affecting daily living but challenging the long-held assumptions and beliefs of ministry, raising new questions and even causing the church to reevaluate its philosophy of education. No matter how one feels toward multiculturalism, the fact of the matter is that God has created a world of tremendous diversity and the church on earth will always remain, if not become more, multicultural. Therefore, it is the church's responsibility to develop an appropriate response toward multiculturalism and enhance the overall quality of Christian education. The challenge is on translating the content and meaning of Christian education to students who come from diverse cultures.

Before we explore further on the issue, let me explain my perspective on multiculturalism since it has caused much confusion in the Christian community. When secular scholars discuss multiculturalism, it is customary for them to focus on the tolerance of ideology concerning belief, morality, sex, and religion. I am not approaching multiculturalism as secular scholars do; instead I am trying to focus on cultural issues pertinent in ministry if the church is going to penetrate and transform various individuals' lives in our society. I am contending that for the purpose of improving the quality and relevance of Christian education, the general features of our culture need to be studied and understood. We must set out a compelling case for making educational ministry relevant to today's audience. In a society that is becoming increasingly multicultural, developing pertinent educational ministry depends on the recognition of the influence that culture has on teaching. Before teaching is carried out, educators need to first engage in an accurate exposition of the central features of multiculturalism and its influence on people.

In the past, Christian educators never faced such a challenge of responding to a rapidly diversifying society. Although cultural awareness among Christian educators is stronger now than ever, a deeper understanding of the relation between culture and education is still needed. Foremost, the major responsibility rests on Christian educators' ability to understand how the contemporary audience thinks and behaves. Such a process will help educators develop a culturally pertinent theory and practice in the new millennium.

In the new millennium, Christian educators have a unique opportunity to set a new paradigm for contextually pertinent education. Christian educators have to reevaluate their approach to education, which has always been practiced locally under a particular set of beliefs endorsed by a denomination persuasion, and enlarge their vision to revitalize the ministry. While affirming the value and uniqueness of diversity, educators need to transcend beyond denominational or local church borders and move toward multicultural ministry. Our task, as teachers of the future, is to create a rich learning environment that transcends denominations and cultures where people of different races and ethnicities can come together to experience God.

Globalism. To further our reflection on the American society, let me suggest another issue that is reshaping the landscape of Christian education—Globalism. With the arrival of a new millennium came the major shift in cultural contours, reconfiguring social and ministry interactions to a global level. The result has been quite astonishing: nations, businesses, educational institutions, and churches interact in close proximity. People are developing a deeper interest and appreciation of other cultures; although in some places, a separation by locality still persists. Globalization is transforming the nature and function of Christian education, creating an international network and cooperation of churches and leaders.

In the third millennium, various Christian communities are inextricably tied to and dependent on each other to sustain and to increase the effectiveness of ministry. This growing globalization will not only affect the way people live but the way church education is carried out. Learning will not be limited to a local church, pastor, and denomination; instead congregations will learn from various churches, pastors, and scholars from all around the world. Just look at how some churches and congregations are connected via Internet—sermons are downloaded; prayer requests are being shared; valuable manuscripts, lectures, books, articles, and even different versions of the Bible are freely circulated. It is particularly important for Christian educators to recognize the arrival of global ministry and step toward creating a collegial network of ministries.

The success of millennial Christian education can only occur when collaboration takes place among churches. Christian educators need to establish a network of ministry that extends beyond classrooms and church buildings. This includes partnership and support of various local and global sectors of Christian communities, which, in my opinion, will contribute to the success of Christian education in the new millennium.

Educational Process

Having explored the contextual issues regarding Christian education, I will now focus on millennial challenges on teaching and learning process. Never before has the need for the church to study the educational process of its congregation, both within and beyond its ministry boundary, been more imperative than today. Unlike earlier generations, the mosaic-like millennial generation prefers nontraditional ways of learning. The untamed evolution of knowledge and technology are having profound effects on how people learn these days. In this portion of the chapter, I will briefly describe the impact of rapidly changing learning styles and technology on Christian education.

Nontraditional Learning Style. The relation between Christian education and ministry has evolved over the years and continues to do so today. Although there are some exceptions, what continues to emerge in the field of Christian education is a concern for holistic learning. Compared to the past several decades, students now possess radically different desires and ways of learning where knowledge, meaning, and skills are sought after through nonconventional ways of learning. Ground-breaking pedagogy is needed to cope with changing students' needs. The solution lies in Christian educators' ability to effectively study the contemporary audience and offer meaningful teaching that invites and nurtures students with knowledge important in life. For decades, the paradigmatic world of ideas dominated the way Christian educators approached teaching. Such an approach focused on the world of theories and gave little room for contextual issues affecting learning. Thus knowledge was confined to content and remained irrelevant.

The challenge comes as educators explore ways to develop critical pedagogy that offers meaning, reflection, and experience in learning. In a way, Christian educators have to respond to the treacherous forces of pragmatism and rationalism. In my opinion, such an endeavor requires current educators to have the ability to understand the issues affecting students' learning, making their teaching meaningful and relevant without yielding to the pragmatic demands of our culture. However, there might be those who are satisfied with the current condition of Christian education and may even oppose the change. But having explored rather different dimensions and models of Christian education, I like to contend that critical pedagogy which gives more systematic and methodological attention to the process of learning is needed. Many commendable steps have been taken to improve general church curriculum including varied teaching and learning models; however these efforts were frivolous, lacking specific critique and critical analysis of learning styles affecting students. More attention should be given to the overall quality of learning. Part of the problem with the past effort was that changes were made for the sake of change without developing a holistic vision for new pedagogy. The past effort was far from corresponding to the needed changes the church has been waiting for, and may even end up damaging the advancement of Christian education in the long run. The task of teaching has become an exigent task in the third millennium.

Technological Impact on Learning. The technological advancement of the new millennium is creating a wave of challenges to Christian educators. In recent decades, a remarkable development in technology infrastructure has changed almost every segment of American society, ranging from a network of homes and small offices to national and global business communities.[3] Consider this: the impact of the Internet alone has been far greater than other forces that the world has experienced. The rapid advancement of technology has not only changed the world but the church as well. The wave of rapid technological advancement has reconfigured the way that teaching is carried out. Even a decade ago, technology was not as deeply integrated to ministry as it is today. Many churches, if they had decent financial resources, were using overhead projectors to provide quality teaching; but today, the advancement of technology has dramatically improved the church's ability to minister and teach, producing a God-sized impact on ministry. Churches are now using information technology to enhance the quality and effectiveness of teaching. They heavily depend on inter- and intranets, web sites, computer networks, e-mails, and even via-satellite sessions to teach and nurture their congregations. The change also indicates that the expected role of Christian teachers will change dramatically in the near future. Soon pastors and educators who are technologically challenged will have a difficult time attracting audiences to their churches and classes. Although the content and theology of education should not change, the methodology or process involving education should change and be upgraded as technology advances.

The evolution of technology is bringing the vast array of changes to educational ministry. Exploring and creating radically new ways to improve Christian education will need to take place now.

Voices: The Changing Role of Educator

Christian education in the third millennium is very different from any other generations we have seen. Unlike before, scholarly modality of the Christian educator is changing; greater emphasis is now being placed on the educator's ability to transform and nurture students, contrasted from the past century's model of the highly educated, professor-like image. The office of Christian education is thus no longer confined to extraordinary knowledge that a teacher possesses but rather to his or her ability to facilitate meaningful learning. Unlike traditional educators whose main concern was on didactic teaching with the exclusive focus on content delivery, the emerging concern among contemporary educators is on dialogical teaching where students are taught to comprehend, experience, integrate, and apply knowledge. The focus of today's education is on creating a highly active, collaborative, and relevant experience in learning. It is reasonable to conclude that the mode of education is switching from formal to informal and nonformal. Entirely new models of teaching are expected to emerge in the near future.[4]

Never has the need for creative and interactive teaching been as demanding as it is today. Educators will need more sophisticated training to engage in timely pertinent teaching ministries. Beyond principal and ideological realms of Christian education, the church needs to introduce innovative and creative ways to equip its future workers.

Conclusion and Implication

Millennial challenges confronting Christian education are the opportunities for progress. As we look toward a new era, it is profitable to pause and critically reflect on the challenges that Christian education faces. Having opportunities to reflect will produce a comprehensive overview of the present and provide an appropriate direction for the future. To do this is to identify and explore issues affecting the church and to have a candid and unwavering critique of the existing theory and practice of education.

As culture moves deeper into the 21st century, raising new awareness and appropriate response will bring a strategic solution to the future of Christian education. Although millennial issues confronting Christian education may seem overwhelming, these challenges must be met with a reasonable attitude of optimism particularly as Christian educators seek to serve local and global faith communities. Grounded in biblical truth, Christian educators need God-sized courage to pioneer innovative ways to transform the third millennium culture.

What Did We Learn From This Chapter?

- Millennial challenges confronting Christian education are the opportunities for progress.

- We live in a transient period where the force of postmodernism is bringing unprecedented challenges to the church. The church's desire to be bibliocentric is challenged by the postmodern audience's dismissal of absolute truth.

- Perhaps the most critical issue affecting Christian education in the 21st century is the biblical illiteracy of believers.

- The epistemological stance of postmodern educators is very different from that of Christian educators; instead of defining truth based on its authenticity, validity, and reliability, the postmodernists would define truth solely based on its relevancy.

- The direction of millennial Christian education should be determined by metacultural principles grounded in the Scriptures.

- What continue to shape the context of Christian education in the 21st century are multiculturalism and globalism.

- Generally speaking, contemporary Christians are losing (or have lost) their interest and appreciation of biblical truth.

- The decline of biblical significance in Christian education calls for a nonconforming way of doing education. To do this, the Bible in its full revelation has to control the theory and practice of education, and theology needs to function as the point of reference in determining the principal content of instruction.

Study Helps

Reflection Questions

1. What sociocultural, philosophical, and theological challenges are facing Christian education in the third millennium?

2. How should Christian institutions and churches respond to millennial challenges regarding teaching and learning?

3. What role should Christian educators play in leading the church through the third millennium?

4. How does knowledge about various cultural groups help Christian educators teach and work more effectively in our society?

5. List crucial goals for Christian education in the third millennium. How can these goals be reached?

6. Can you identify the major societal and religious issues that influence the theory and direction of Christian education?

7. How have the perspectives of Christian education changed within a decade or so?

Technical Terms

Didactics The word "didactics" is a derivative of the Greek word, *didaktikos*, which means "to teach or to educate." The term came to denote *the art of skillful teaching* in education.

Epistemology The branch of philosophy that studies the theory (i.e., origin, nature, method) of knowledge. The word "epistemology" comes from two Greek words, *episteme* (knowledge) and *logos* (theory).

Formal education The mode of education that focuses on the transmission of knowledge through innate or internal forces. Its main concern is on the didactic teaching of knowledge (e.g., indoctrination).

Informal education The mode of education that focuses on the transmission of knowledge through influences (or socialization process) rather than by innate or internal forces. Its main educative concern is life-transformation.

Nonformal education The mode of education that is intentional and systematic. Usually a student's need or situation determines the content and process of education. Its main educative concern is on transmission of skills.

Pedagogy	*Pedagogy* comes from the Greek word, *paidagogia* (originally from *paidagogos* which refers to the slave-tutor, *Paedagogus* (Lat.), who worked as an advisor and guide to his young master). *Pedagogy* refers to the art of teaching, especially to a theory and principle of teaching children.

Recommended Bibliography

Duderstadt, James J. *A University for the 21st Century*. Ann Arbor, MI: The University of Michigan Press, 2000.

Lee, James Michael, ed. *Forging a Better Religious Education in the Third Millennium*. Birmingham, AL: Religious Education Press, 2000.

Losco, Joseph, and Brian L. Fife, eds. *Higher Education in Transition: The Challenges of the New Millennium*. Westport, CT: Bergin and Garvey, 1999.

Patterson, Glenys. *The University from Ancient Greece to the 20th Century*. Palmerston North, NZ: Dunmore Press, 1997.

Notes

[1] Gary M. Burge, "The Greatest Story Never Read: Recovering Biblical Literacy in the Church," *Christianity Today* (August 9, 1999). (Retrieved November 12, 2002, from http://www.christianitytoday.com/ct/9t9/9t9045.html).

[2] Norma Cook Everist, "Issues and Ironies of the New Millennium," in *Forging a Better Religious Education in the Third Millennium*, ed. by James Michael Lee (Birmingham, AL: Religious Education Press, 2000), 53-56.

[3] James J. Duderstadt, *A University for the 21st Century* (Ann Arbor, MI: The University of Michigan Press, 2000), 220.

[4] Ibid., 291-318.